NIETZSCHE AND THE ORIGIN OF VIRTUE

ROUTLEDGE NIETZSCHE STUDIES

The intention of this series is to promote and contribute to the reckoning with Nietzsche that has at last begun in earnest in the English-speaking philosophical community. During most of this century he was deemed by most mainstream analytical philosophers to deserve little attention (except perhaps in his dubious purported role as one of the sources of existentialism), and to have nothing of significance to contribute to serious philosophical inquiry. This is no longer the case – owing in part to changes within this community itself which are transforming and broadening the understanding and practice of philosophical endeavor in it. The efforts of a growing number of interpreters of Nietzsche who are at home in this community, as well as drawn to him, have also contributed to the dawning recognition that there is much more of philosophical interest to be found in his writings than was once supposed.

Yet our reckoning with him has only just begun. Many who are now prepared to concede that Nietzsche's thought may indeed be worth taking seriously have no very clear idea of what there is in it that warrants attention and is relevant to contemporary inquiry. The Nietzsche literature is burgeoning; but much of it is of relatively little help to philosophers who are not themselves Nietzsche scholars. Many now have an open mind with respect to Nietzsche, but are unsure of where to look for what might be relevant to their philosophical concerns – and of what to make of it.

Routledge Nietzsche Studies is intended to help meet this need, through the publication of a series of volumes that will at once contribute to the interpretation of Nietzsche's philosophical thought and show how it bears upon issues of contemporary philosophical interest. The series will serve this double purpose by including both monographs and collections of essays. Comments and proposals are both welcome, and should be directed to the Editor of the series.

Richard Schacht, Editor

NIETZSCHE AND THE ORIGIN OF VIRTUE

Lester H. Hunt

London and New York

First published in 1991 by Routledge

First published in paperback in 1993
by Routledge
11 New Fetter Lane, London EC4P 4EE

Simultaneously published in the USA and Canada
by Routledge
29 West 35th Street, New York, NY 10001

Typeset in 10/12pt Baskerville by
Mayhew Typesetting, Bristol, England
Printed and bound in Great Britain by
T J Press (Padstow) Ltd, Padstow, Cornwall

British Library Cataloguing in Publication Data
Hunt, Lester H.
Nietzsche and the origin of virtue. – New edn (Routledge
Nietzsche studies)
1. German philosophy. Nietzsche, Friedrich, 1844-1900
I. Title   II. Series
179.9

Library of Congress Cataloging in Publication Data
Hunt, Lester H.
Nietzsche and the origin of virtue/Lester H. Hunt.
p. cm. – (Routledge Nietzsche studies)
1. Nietzsche, Friedrich Wilhelm, 1844-1900 – Ethics.
2. Nietzsche, Friedrich Wilhelm, 1844-1900 – Political and
social views. 3. Ethics, Modern – 19th century. 4. Political
science – Philosophy.
I. Title.   II. Series
B3319.E9H85   1991   90-32305
170´.92–dc20

ISBN 0-415-09580-8

For Deborah and Nathaniel

CONTENTS

EDITOR'S FOREWORD

For a very long time, most English-speaking philosophers had no use for Nietzsche at all, except perhaps as a convenient scapegoat and whipping-boy. In recent years, however, he has been discovered to have a good many more interesting uses – sometimes, to be sure, simply as a formidable foe or foil, but also, increasingly, as a thinker providing considerable resources and inspiration for a wide variety of philosophical initiatives. Partisans of one sort of philosophical use of him are often unhappy about uses others make of him; but their differences are both understandable and fruitful. Scholarly purists, whose primary concern is that the most rigorous traditional standards of scholarship be adhered to, may be heard to take objection when any such use at all is made of him by those purporting also to interpret him. Nietzsche's own sympathies, however, would undoubtedly lie with the former rather than with the latter, with whom he had little patience. Indeed, he undoubtedly would have been delighted and gratified to know that, a century after the sad and early end of his productive life, his thought would be of such great and growing interest, and would be finding so many different uses and responses.

As Nietzsche himself was at pains to point out, philosophers are not all of a single kind, cut from the same cloth; and philosophical situations likewise are not always and everywhere the same. In philosophy, as in life, there are times when things need to be shaken up, and also times when they need to be settled down. Among philosophers, as among the rest of humanity, moreover, temperaments vary, and some tasks are found to be more congenial than others. As in the case of culture, the flourishing of which mattered so greatly to Nietzsche, this is all to the good.

Nietzsche's thought is exceptional, if not utterly unique, in that

ix

it lends itself readily to appropriation and fruitful use in connection with both sorts of need, and by philosophers of markedly differing temperaments, drawn to the most diverse tasks. This is perhaps because he himself was of many minds, many voices, many tasks, and many engagements. Interpretations that reduce his thought to any one of them do not do justice to him – but complete justice cannot be done to him by any single interpretation, as he himself observes in other contexts. The best that philosophically minded interpreters can do is acknowledge this, and then get on with trying in their own ways to discern what Nietzsche is up to and what is to be made of it, seen through the eyes and from the perspectives and with the intellectual conscience and philosophical interests that they individually bring to it – counting upon others to join in and do likewise, in a continuing conversation, both collectively and mutually enlightening.

Few debates are more pointless than debates about what Nietzsche's primary task or fundamental insight or basic method was, or about whether he was mainly concerned to dynamite or dissect, to construct or deconstruct, to criticize or create, to analyze or advocate – or whether the hammer he used was a sledge or a sculptor's mallet or a sounding instrument. (The only more ridiculous dispute I have witnessed was a heated one between two German historians of philosophy, who both agreed that Nietzsche was a great philosopher and both subscribed to the thesis that every great philosopher thinks a single great thought, but who disagreed violently over what his single great thought was.) Nietzsche proclaims many philosophical tasks, employs many methods, announces many insights, and undertakes to do all of the things mentioned above on various occasions. He is by turns cautious and incautious, responsible and irresponsible, logical and illogical, fair and unfair, reasonable and unreasonable, wise and foolish, critical of prejudice and in thrall to it.

Small wonder, then, that "Nietzsches" abound. One can get him very wrong indeed (and that has happened often enough); but one can also get him partly and interestingly right in a great many different ways. One can find him almost any kind of philosophical (or anti-philosophical) friend – or foe – one looks for. The past century of Nietzsche interpretation is replete with portraits of the most diverse sorts; and their number and variety continue to grow. One could hardly find a better example of something he made much of: creativity begetting further creativity.

There is no right general answer to the question: What are we to make of Nietzsche? What one makes of him will depend very much upon what one's own philosophical disposition, interests, and agenda may happen to be – even though his texts do at least partially constrain one whatever they may be. Some readers and interpreters have grown tired of traditional ways of making sense in philosophy, or are hostile to them, and so seize sympathetically upon that in Nietzsche that lends itself to repudiation of the tradition. Others, defensive of these same ways of making sense of things, may likewise make "nonsense" of him, but with the opposite intent. Others still, dissatisfied but not entirely disaffected with these ways of sense-making, look to him as one who explores the possibility that they might be *aufgehoben*. And others seek to make sense of *him* through *them*, as a thinker who can be understood in relation to them despite the radicalness and distinctiveness of the turns and twists he gives them.

Lester Hunt's concern in this book is to make sense rather than nonsense of Nietzsche – and more than that, to use the sense he makes of him to good philosophical effect, and to suggest how his thought might be modified in certain respects to make further sense, where Nietzsche would appear to be at odds with himself. In doing so, Hunt is guided by his feel for what Nietzsche is driving at and trying to say; by his intuition of what would be truest to the spirit of Nietzsche's mature thinking when Hunt attempts to resolve the tensions between various strands of Nietzsche's thought; and by his own philosophical sensibility when he suggests criticisms or modifications of Nietzsche's views that would render them more plausible.

All of this will make Hunt's treatment of Nietzsche more congenial to some readers than to others. It is an analytically minded contribution to the growing body of philosophical literature in which attempts are made to take Nietzsche seriously as a philosopher and to reckon with him. Hunt's way with Nietzsche may be only one possible way of understanding and dealing with him; but it is a way that enables important interpretive and philosophical questions about Nietzsche's thought to be posed and addressed.

Hunt's book is a thoughtful philosophical meditation on Nietzsche's views on a number of topics related to ethics, character, and the ethics of character, addressed primarily to like-minded readers who are interested in these topics and open to the idea that Nietzsche may have some things of interest to say about them. It is attentive to changes in Nietzsche's thinking as he worked his way into them, and to tensions among different lines of thought relating to them that Nietzsche explored and pursued. Hunt seeks to cut through the surface difficulties that may easily confuse or distract Nietzsche's readers, and to work out these lines of thought in a manner that enables one both to grasp their main points and reasoning and to confront the significant points of difficulty in them. His fundamental concern is to show the relevance of aspects of Nietzsche's thought to issues of contemporary philosophical interest, and to suggest that and how the consideration of these issues may benefit by taking account of Nietzsche's unconventional reflections on them.

Hunt regards Nietzsche as "a source of insight in ethical and political matters," and in many other related matters along with them; but he does not content himself merely to explicate them. He further performs the service of attempting to discern and set out the arguments or cases for them that are often more latent than explicit in Nietzsche's texts. It is often complained of Nietzsche that he offers provocative and interesting ideas but nothing like arguments for them, leaving one with no way of knowing what to make of them. Hunt recognizes that there is a problem here; but he believes that one sells Nietzsche short if one leaps to the conclusion that he has no arguments where none are clearly and explicitly given. The accounts Hunt gives of the arguments he discerns may be disputed, and the arguments as he presents them may not be of the sort to which many are accustomed. It will be well for the understanding of Nietzsche, however, when the advancing and disputing of such accounts becomes a more common feature of the literature. It also will be well for philosophy when an appreciation of the kind of case-making argumentation in question becomes more widespread.

Throughout his discussion Hunt remains patient, sensible, and deliberate in working out what he takes Nietzsche to have in mind, and in discussing how it might be adjusted at certain points of difficulty. His experiments of reconstruction and revision are well worth undertaking, both interpretively and philosophically. They are, furthermore, very much in the spirit of the Nietzsche who was not content to be a mere scholar and philosophical laborer, but rather ventured persistently and boldly to make philosophical use of what he found in his predecessors even as he interpreted and assessed both their thinking and the questions they considered.

Hunt ventures to ascribe some specific views to Nietzsche which many other interpreters (the present writer included) will question. For example, he presents "Nietzsche's final views on the way society should be ordered" as involving the advocacy of a "three-caste system," with Nietzsche's "new philosophers" on top. He is quite convincing, however, on many of the more general points he is concerned to make – as when he argues that one cannot begin properly to understand and appreciate Nietzsche's views on "ethical and political matters" unless one recognizes that Nietzsche is concerned to effect a fundamental change in our entire way of thinking about ethics and politics. Too often Nietzsche's views on these matters are treated in the harsh manner of Procrustes, and are either contorted to fit conventional ideas of ethics and politics or dismissed because they fail to fit them. Hunt is far more perceptive in his treatment of Nietzsche here, and shows how greater justice to him can be done.

The same is true of his accounts of Nietzsche's handling of the central notions of the book – "virtue" and "character." They likewise can only be properly understood and appreciated if it is recognized that Nietzsche not only appropriates them but also subjects them to a fundamental reconsideration and reinterpretation. Other recent writers have taken note of the importance of these notions in Nietzsche's thought; but Hunt is a good deal more sensitive than most to what he does with them, and devotes closer attention to the distinctive features of his revision of them.

Hunt further observes that Nietzsche's thinking with respect to both character and virtue requires to be understood in relation to what he calls Nietzsche's "experimentalism," his "vitalism," and his "relativism"; and he undertakes to explore these relations, with due attention to the distinctive versions of each of these "-isms" to which Nietzsche subscribes. More needs to be said about each of them than Hunt says; but he does well to recognize the need to take account of them in dealing with Nietzsche's views on character and virtue (and so on ethics and politics), and has much of interest to say in this connection.

Perhaps the most intriguing suggestion Hunt makes is that there is to be found in some of Nietzsche's writings the outlines of a "Nietzschean liberalism," that not only differs from conventional forms of liberalism but also is at odds with at least some of Nietzsche's own later views. One of the virtues of the book is its attention to such tensions within Nietzsche's thought. Another of these tensions – and the one that Hunt is most concerned to bring out

– is that between Nietzsche's thinking in what Hunt calls his "immoralist" and his "legislating" moods or "modes."

This tension, Hunt argues, gives rise to seemingly conflicting conceptions of character and virtue, with importantly differing ethical and political implications. Whether or not one sides with Hunt in the way in which he would prefer to see this tension and these conflicts and differences resolved, one must confront this issue; and it is Hunt's greatest contribution in this book to have raised it so clearly. Addressing it – as others now also must – should do more than advance the cause of achieving a better understanding and assessment of Nietzsche's thought with respect to character, virtue, ethics, and politics. For in the course of doing so, the ongoing and increasingly lively philosophical debate about these matters themselves should be advanced as well.

Richard Schacht
University of Illinois at Urbana-Champaign

PREFACE AND ACKNOWLEDGEMENTS

I think the best way to indicate the point of view from which this book was written would be to tell something, very briefly, of its history and pre-history.

When I first bought a copy of *The Portable Nietzsche* in a suburban bookstore in 1964, I had no idea that most Americans who were professionally qualified to hold an opinion on the subject thought at the time that Nietzsche was at best a very marginal philosopher. I doubt that I even knew that there are fads and fashions in philosophy as in everything else. This particular fashion would not have impressed me much because, within days after I first began to read him, and for my first few years in college, I was more or less immersed in what I took to be Nietzsche's view of the world. While other students, elsewhere on campus, were arguing about whether they could have solidarity with the orthodox Trotskyites, my friends and I were sitting up nights arguing about whether the *Übermensch* would ever vote or get married. It is easy to make such concerns sound foolish (as I think I just did), but I am sure that most of the effects Nietzsche had on us were beneficial. Mainly, we derived from him, by a sort of psychic contagion, a *love* of integrity (if not integrity itself – there is a limit to what one can get from an author) and that touch of arrogance without which a consistent dedication to goals over the long haul seems to be impossible.

Nietzsche's writings were a source of insight and encouragement. They were certainly not, as Henry Miller would say, mere "literature." One attitude I picked up from Nietzsche became more important than any other as I studied philosophy in the years that followed. From him I got the impression that the most interesting questions of ethics cannot be answered by formulating rules that tell us what we must do. He convinced me that these questions can only be answered by somehow giving an account of the life of the individual as a whole: they are about character, a subject which includes the thoughts and passions of living human beings, and not merely their behavior. This impression of mine was later deepened and fixed when I first read Aristotle. Unfortunately, such questions were seldom being discussed in the professional journals at the time, as far as I could tell. Indeed, most of the things I found interesting were not considered "current" or "hot" issues among the people around me. This untimeliness, for which Nietzsche must take much of the blame, caused some problems for me. The most serious problem had to do with the fact that, as far as I knew at the time, contemporary philosophers were using their impressive analytical tools to solve problems that did not feel very important to me. I had a hard time seeing how the things that did matter to me the most could be written about with a degree of clarity and rigor that contemporary philosophers – and I myself, for that matter – would find respectable. It was obvious, though, that the great philosophers of the past had, in a variety of antique methods and styles, treated the issues that were important to me and had done so at great length. Having no other easy way out, I took the (for me) somewhat cowardly expedient of studying almost nothing but the history of philosophy while I was a student. If I could not figure out how to talk about what seemed important, at least I could talk about what various other people thought about such things.

When I first began to discuss these matters on my own behalf, it was with a good deal of help from Nietzsche. At one point in my career as a graduate student, I was expected to submit a paper to my department which, if it passed, would qualify me for a candidacy for the Ph.D. I had recently written a seminar paper which was a commentary on the chapter called "On the Gift-giving Virtue" in *Thus Spoke Zarathustra*, and it occurred to me that I could defend what I took Nietzsche was saying there, using the methods of the ordinary-language philosophy which was then fashionable among the people around me, if I rather arbitrarily interpreted what he was saying as an account of the virtue that we ordinarily call generosity. I rewrote the old paper as a piece of first-person philosophy, moving the reference to Nietzsche into footnotes.[1] The result seemed successful enough to me to justify trying to write a dissertation in which I would produce a theory of the virtues and of traits of character in general and, eventually, that is what I did.

In these researches I soon found myself wandering out of the Nietzschean fold. I developed a position which was more influenced by Aristotle – and even by Kant (something I would have found horrifying a few years earlier) – than by Nietzsche. Mainly, I found myself laying much more stress on the value of the intellect and acting on principle than Nietzsche does. After working on these ideas and others that are closely related to them for some years, I began (for reasons I need not go into here) to entertain the possibility of explaining the basic principles of justice as a sort of order which tends to arise spontaneously among free individuals who interact within certain very minimal constraints: perhaps a certain valuable part of morality can be understood as a product of freedom. I remembered that Nietzsche is generally very skeptical of the sorts of order which arise spontaneously among people, particularly in the moral realm. It seemed a good idea to go back to Nietzsche and see if he had anything to say which could dissuade me from doing what I was thinking of doing. At the same time, I thought I should try to sort out, in a general sort of way, the ethical ideas of my former master, to see if I was justified in my denial of him. I wanted to see how much of him I should deny and how much I should accept after all. You see the result of this attempt in the pages that follow.

I have come out of this general sorting out with the following conclusions. It is clear to me that there are certain Nietzschean ideas which I am, at any rate, committed to denying. These include his devaluation of the intellect, his attempt to formulate an ethic which is *entirely* based on a conception of character, and his denial (at least in certain moods) of the value of spontaneous order. But there are other ideas of his – including his relativism, his experimentalism, and his emphasis on the role the passions play in virtue – which seem to me to be valuable and important. In fact they bring to light aspects of the truth which are insufficiently acknowledged in my own earlier work. Further, I have also found that the ideas in the latter group tend to logically undermine those in the former one. While some of Nietzsche's ideas seem ultimately unacceptable to me, I think some interesting explanations of why they are unacceptable can be found in Nietzsche's own writings. I have come out of my re-evaluation of Nietzsche encouraged but also chastened and (I hope) enlightened.

Implicit in the story I have just told are some caveats and disclaimers which probably have to be made explicit. First, this book is mainly an attempt to take Nietzsche seriously as a contributor to the ethics of character. The point of view taken here is not primarily antiquarian. It is meant for readers who want to use Nietzsche as a source of insight in ethical and political matters. For this reason, I suspect that there are features of this book which might seem odd to someone whose interest in Nietzsche is mainly scholarly. The approach to Nietzsche that seems to be currently in vogue in the Nietzsche literature – especially among French and French-influenced scholars – is to focus on his metaphysics (or his rejection of metaphysics, depending on one's interpretation) and his epistemology (or whatever one should call his "perspectivism" and related themes); his ethics is often treated as an application or illustration of these themes, and his politics is typically not treated at all.[2] Here, of course, my focus is entirely on ethical and political matters. Other themes are brought in only when they really seem necessary for an understanding of my central concerns. I suspect that some would say that a discussion of Nietzsche's ethics which is not accompanied by a sustained and detailed discussion of other supposedly more fundamental themes will seriously distort his ethical views. The only reply I can give them is to offer my own project as an experiment in which that hypothesis is tested. I think the experiment shows the hypothesis to be false. Nietzsche's ethical and political philosophy turns out to be, at any rate, more autonomous than this hypothesis implies.

The peculiar focus of this book requires me to deviate from standard practice in another way. It is typical of writers on Nietzsche nowadays to pay but scant attention to his earliest writings – to the whole first decade of his literary output, in fact.[3] This is not at all what I propose to do. Whether this practice makes any sense at all depends on which Nietzschean themes one is dealing with. If the subject is epistemology, it is one which seems to have interested Nietzsche most at the end of his career. It is at least conceivable that all the really interesting texts are from his last few years. If one ignores his earliest remarks on the subject – which do tend to be rather crude – one might perhaps not be missing much. But the situation is entirely different if the subject is ethical or political. In the *Untimely Meditations* he is already taking great pains to understand issues of this kind and producing original results. If we leave these writings out of our account, we are missing too much that is interesting and worth thinking about. Further, we are apt to misunderstand or underemphasize some important aspects of Nietzsche's thinking on ethical and political matters. The *Meditation* on Schopenhauer contains his only sustained and explicit critique of spontaneous order. Important parts of is later work simply assume the conclusion he reaches there, as if he has treated the subject once and for all. If we miss what he has said there, we are liable systematically to miss his point later on.

More generally, I think there is an obvious sort of value in knowing where Nietzsche's thinking begins, despite the well-known fact that he undergoes a strong and continuous intellectual development and eventually abandons his early views on some important subjects. For instance, where he does change his mind it might be very illuminating to find out why he felt compelled to do so. The greater the change is, the stronger the intellectual force which must have brought it about and, consequently, the more important it will be to know that it *was* a change.

There is one last caveat which is perhaps obvious from what I have already said. This book is not by any means an introduction to Nietzsche or his ethics. Those who try to use it as such are liable merely to find it confusing. I have to assume that the reader is familiar with some of Nietzsche's works and has done some reading in the secondary literature. To those who do need an introduction, I can recommend Morgan's *What Nietzsche Means*, which is still serviceable despite the fact that it was written half a century ago.[4]

I would like to thank all the people who gave me their advice or encouragement while I was working on this book. The members of the Philosophy Department at the University of Wisconsin, Madison, listened to and discussed drafts of chapters. Special thanks in this regard are due to Claudia Card, Terry Penner, and Ivan Soll. Robert Solomon read a draft of Chapter 3 and made a suggestion which I proved to be wise enough to follow. Raymond Sybul graciously agreed to check many of my translations from Nietzsche's German. I also had many discussions of Nietzsche with two graduate students at Wisconsin – Kenneth Westphal and Steven Weiss – and I hope the benefits of these discussions are visible here. I owe a special debt to Richard Schacht for his help and encouragement when my Nietzsche project was nearing completion. It should go without saying that none of these people necessarily agree with what I have to say about Nietzsche. They made an honest effort to convince me of my errors and are off the hook. This is an appropriate place to acknowledge a general sort of debt to a professor of mine, the Heidegger scholar William B. Macomber. I have recently realized all over again what an impact he had on my approach to Nietzsche and my conception of teaching as well. If he had not fallen a victim to the tenure massacres of the middle 1970s he would have influenced a whole generation of scholars and teachers by now.

In addition, I must thank the Graduate Schools of the University of Wisconsin and the University of Minnesota, and especially the Institute for Humane Studies and the Earhart Foundation, for grants which enabled me to spend several summers working on Nietzsche free from all distractions.[5] I should also thank the Social Philosophy and Policy Center at Bowling Green State University, where I enjoyed ten months of strenuous leisure during which, while I was mainly occupied with other projects, this book was being prepared for the press. I am grateful to the editor of the *History of Philosophy Quarterly* for permission to reproduce material from an earlier draft of Chapter 3, which appeared in his journal. I am especially grateful to Deborah Katy Hunt for preparing the index.

The author and publishers would like to thank the following for permission to include in this volume Nietzsche translations from the sources indicated: Cambridge University Press for *Untimely Meditations*, trans. R.J. Hollingdale; Random House Inc. for *Basic Writings of Nietzsche*, trans. and ed. Walter Kaufmann, © 1966, 1967, 1968 Random House Inc., for *The Will to Power*, trans. Walter Kaufmann and R.J. Hollingdale, ed. Walter Kaufmann, © 1967 Walter Kaufmann, and for *The Gay Science*, trans. Walter Kaufmann, © 1974 Random House Inc.; Viking Penguin for *The Portable Nietzsche* (*Homer's Contest, Thus Spoke Zarathustra, Twilight of the Idols, The Antichrist*), trans. Walter Kaufmann.

June 1990
University of Wisconsin, Madison

NOTES ON TRANSLATIONS,
CITATIONS, AND
ABBREVIATIONS

I began writing this book over seven years ago. At that time, there were no recent and philosophically sophisticated translations of some of Nietzsche's earliest works. Consequently, the translations I use for the *Untimely Meditations* and for *Human, All-Too-Human* and its supplementary volumes are often my own, even when I have listed another translation below. For various reasons, I sometimes use my own translations when quoting other works by Nietzsche as well, but for the most part I use the translations listed below.

The works by Nietzsche from which I will be quoting are listed below in the order in which they were apparently written. Unless otherwise noted, the number given after the German title is the year in which the book was published.

The Birth of Tragedy (*Die Geburt der Tragödie*, 1872: GT). Translated by Walter Kaufmann (New York: Vintage Books, 1966).

"Homer's Contest" (*Homers Wettkampf*, written in 1872, published posthumously: H). Translated in part by Walter Kaufmann in *The Portable Nietzsche* (New York: Viking Press, 1954). For the other parts, I have used my own translations.

Second Untimely Meditation: On the Uses and Disadvantages of History for Life (*Unzeitgemässe Betrachtungen, Zweites Stück: Vom Nutzen und Nachteil der Historie für das Leben*, 1874: U II). Translated by R.J. Hollingdale (Cambridge: Cambridge University Press, 1983).

Third Untimely Meditation: Schopenhauer as Educator (*Unzeitgemässe Betrachtungen, Drittes Stück: Schopenhauer als Erzieher*, 1874: U III). Translated by R.J. Hollingdale (Cambridge: Cambridge University Press, 1983).

Human, All-Too-Human (*Menschliches, Allzumenschliches*, 1878: MAM).
I have used my own translations.

Mixed Opinions and Maxims (*Vermischte Meinungen und Sprüche*, 1879:
VMS). Published by Nietzsche as an "appendix" to *Human, All-
Too-Human*. I have used my own translations. It was translated
by R.J. Hollingdale together with VMS and WS as *Human, All
Too Human: A Book for Free Spirits* (Cambridge: Cambridge
University Press, 1986).

The Wanderer and His Shadow (*Der Wanderer und sein Schatten*, 1880:
WS). Published by Nietzsche as the "second and last sequel" to
Human, All-Too-Human. I have used my own translations.

Daybreak (*Die Morgenröte*, 1881: M). Translated by R.J. Hollingdale
(Cambridge: Cambridge University Press, 1982).

The Gay Science (*Die Fröhliche Wissenschaft*, 1882: FW). Translated by
Walter Kaufmann (New York: Vintage Books, 1974).

Thus Spoke Zarathustra (*Also Sprach Zarathustra*, 1885: Z). Translated
by Walter Kaufmann in *The Portable Nietzsche* (New York: Viking
Press, 1954).

Beyond Good and Evil (*Jenseits von Gut und Böse*, 1886: JGB). Translated by Walter Kaufmann (New York: Vintage Books, 1966).

The Gay Science, second edition (1887). Aphorisms 343–83 (available
in the Walter Kaufmann translation cited above) appeared for
the first time in this edition.

On the Genealogy of Morals (*Zur Genealogie der Moral*, 1887: GM).
Translated by Walter Kaufmann and R.J. Hollingdale (New
York: Vintage Books, 1966).

The Case of Wagner (*Der Fall Wagner*, 1888: W). Translated by
Walter Kaufmann (New York: Vintage Books, 1966).

Twilight of the Idols (*Götzen-Dämmerung*, 1889, completed by Nietzsche in 1888: G). Translated by Walter Kaufmann in *The Portable
Nietzsche* (New York: Viking Press, 1954).

The Antichrist (*Der Antichrist*, 1895, completed by Nietzsche in 1888:
A). Translated by Walter Kaufmann in *The Portable Nietzsche*
(New York: Viking Press, 1954).

Ecce Homo (*Ecce Homo*, 1908, completed by Nietzsche in 1888: EH).
Translated by Walter Kaufmann (New York: Vintage Books,
1968).

The Will to Power (*Der Wille zur Macht*, 1911, a compilation of
unpublished notes from the 1880s: WM). Translated by Walter
Kaufmann and R.J. Hollingdale (New York: Vintage Books,
1968).

I cite Nietzsche's works by using the abbreviations listed on pages xxi–xxii followed by numbers indicating chapter, section, or aphorism numbers: e.g. (Z I 22 iii). Prefaces are represented with a "P": e.g. (GT P 3). A long stretch of the third part of *Ecce Homo* is divided into unnumbered sections, each of which discusses a different earlier work by Nietzsche. I cite these sections by identifying the titles of the works discussed in them: e.g. (EH III JGB 1). When a series of quotations from the same section or aphorism runs over more than one sentence of my text, I give the relevant source after the last quotation in the series and, if any paragraphs end within the series, at the ends of the last quotations in each of those paragraphs. I refer to other parts of my own book by indicating the chapter in arabic numerals, followed by a comma, followed by the relevant page numbers of the section: e.g. (Chapter 4, pp. 66–8).

1

INTRODUCTION: READING NIETZSCHE

One must be an inventor to read well.
　　　　　　　　Emerson, "The American Scholar"

NIETZSCHE'S ARGUMENT

Reading Nietzsche presents a great and obvious difficulty for one who has been reared in any of the many traditions which for over two thousand years have insisted that philosophy must live up to high standards of logical rigor. His books contain rather few passages in which he appears to be offering arguments for the opinions he expresses in them. The books from his hand that are most often taken seriously in the Anglo-American philosophical community are *Beyond Good and Evil* and *On the Genealogy of Morals*, probably because it is in those two books that he most often comes close to arguing for what he says. People who admire those books above all his others must find it discouraging to know that their author regarded them as far less important than his *Thus Spoke Zarathustra*, a book that not only appears to contain virtually no arguments at all, but is not even written in prose. He says that in *Zarathustra* he accomplishes "the Yes-saying part" of his task while the books he wrote later – including *Beyond Good and Evil* and the *Genealogy* – represent the "No-saying, *No-doing* part" (EH III JGB 1). That is, if we wish to know what Nietzsche was *for* we must go to *Zarathustra*; his other late works indicate mainly what he was *against*. It is understandable if one recoils at the thought of doing this. About *Zarathustra*, even more than the other works of his last period, one is sometimes tempted to repeat what he himself later says of his own first book: that it is "without the will to logical cleanliness, very convinced and therefore disdainful of proof, mistrustful even of the *propriety* of proof" (GT P 3).

For many of us, the first issue that must be settled in an attempt to understand Nietzsche is whether, in order to read his

1

books and take them seriously as philosophy, one must discard one's conception of what philosophy is. My approach to Nietzsche is based on the assumption that it is not necessary to abandon one's conception of what the activity of philosophy is, though it is entirely necessary that one alter one's view of what a philosophical *book* must be like.

He believes that his books cannot be read in the same way that the works of other philosophers are read:

> To understand the most abbreviated language ever spoken by a philosopher . . . one must follow the *opposite* procedure of that generally required by philosophical literature. Usually, one must *condense*, or upset one's digestion; I have to be diluted . . . else one upsets one's digestion.
>
> Silence is as much of an instinct with me as garrulity is with our dear philosophers. I am *brief*; my readers themselves must become long and comprehensive in order to bring up and together all that I have thought, and thought deep down.[1]

Zarathustra uses this idea of selective silence to define Nietzsche's most characteristic literary form, the aphorism:

> Whoever writes in blood and aphorisms does not want to be read but to be learned by heart. In the mountains the shortest way is from peak to peak: but for that one must have long legs. Aphorisms should be peaks – and those to whom they are addressed, tall and lofty.
>
> (Z I 7)

Nietzsche obviously regarded all of his mature works as aphoristic in this sense. He is telling us that, in order to read his aphorisms, we must fill in the lowly valleys between his exalted peaks, we must supply what he omits.

Naturally, this prescription will be much easier to follow if we have some general notion of what sorts of things he tends to omit. In the past, some writers have feared, and with good reason, that they would suffer persecution if they revealed their true beliefs to the public, and accordingly they omitted their most offensive doctrines from their writings. This was notoriously not Nietzsche's practice. In that case, what sorts of things *does* he leave out? There is apparently one place where he answers this question in a general way, and that is the passage in which he has Zarathustra declare:

I am not one of those whom one may ask about their why. Is my experience but of yesterday? It was long ago that I experienced the reasons for my opinions. Would I not have to be a barrel of memory if I wanted to carry my reasons around with me?

(Z II 17)

That is, we must expect him to omit, perhaps among other things, the arguments that support what he says. Interestingly, he acknowledges that *he* must have reasons for the things he believes: he seems to think of the reasons that underlie them as being what causes him to believe them (see MAM 526). But recalling them and setting them forth requires a special effort which the reader apparently has no right to expect of him. Nonetheless, Zarathustra is certainly not giving his audience a license to take what he says on faith, for he says soon afterward: "Faith does not make me blessed . . . especially not faith in me." He adds that they should suspect, rather, that much of what he says is a lie (Z II 17). Elsewhere, he warns his disciples: "You revere me: but what if your reverence tumbles one day? Beware lest a statue slay you" (Z I 22 iii).

Thus Nietzsche sees his readers as living under the same obligation that he accepts in his own case to believe things only when there is reason for doing so. He is consistent enough to apply this idea, so to speak, against himself. We are to test what he says by seeing whether we can work out good reasons for them. This explains his paradoxical belief that only those who disagree with him have learned what he has to teach. When Zarathustra takes leave of his disciples at the end of Part I, he tells them "One repays a teacher badly if one remains nothing but a pupil. . . . Now I bid you lose me and find yourselves; and only when you have all denied me will I return to you" (Z I 22 iii).[2] What he teaches, first of all, is the activity of subjecting beliefs to a certain test, and as long as we merely agree with him it is obvious that we have not done this to his beliefs.

Suppose that a philosopher really intends, primarily, to somehow impel his or her readers to work things out for themselves. How should one try to do this? The traditional procedure would be to announce that the reader ought to think for him- or herself and then give impressive proofs of various doctrines, some of which show why this is so, and others of which show how the reader must

3

go about thinking independently. But here there would be a sort of tension between the author's immediate objective and the ultimate goal it is meant to serve. For whoever seeks to prove something intends to provide premises which are such that logically acute readers, once they understand them, will be trapped with the conclusion, with no escape other than violating the integrity of one's own intellect. Authors who give reasons for what they believe always tend to do this to some extent or other. To give reasons is to try to influence people, and to try to influence people is to try to exert one's power over their minds. The philosophers' traditional practice of giving proofs is, in this regard, a particularly strong form of giving reasons. Philosophers generally make the machinery of intellectual coercion as intimidating as possible and place it in the psychological foreground of their books. They make it overwhelmingly salient that their immediate objective is to control their readers' thoughts, to get the reader to accept the author's thoughts as their own. If one accepts this particular arrangement between the author and reader as appropriate and a matter of course, one is thereby encouraged to think of reading as a process in which one is filled with enlightenment by someone else, and thus one is also encouraged to think of enlightenment as something that comes from outside oneself. Thus the traditional literary method of philosophers is a troublesome one if one's ultimate goal is to get one's readers to work things out for themselves. It tends to foster illusions that get in the way of this goal.

I submit that it is at least in part in order to avoid producing such illusions that Nietzsche writes as he does. Before one has read very far into his works, one realizes that, although arguments are seldom given in the text, many are latent within it and must be sought and found rather than passively received. Each idea is logically connected with others in such a way that these others constitute evidence for it, and form an argument which leads to the idea as its conclusion. To find the premises which lead to a given idea, we often find that we have to go to books other than the one in which the idea appears, and not seldom we find that we cannot find enough premises to make a complete argument. In that case, we must have enough imagination to think of what premises *would* complete the argument, consistent with the other things the author says. As is always the case in reconstructing an author's arguments, the missing premises we supply must be, not merely consistent with the rest of what the author says, but as plausible as we can make them, since the more plausible they are, the more likely it is that they represent what the author had in mind.

This is something we *must* do in order to understand his books at all. Without engaging in this sort of activity, his writings are nothing more than the collection of witticisms, paradoxes, and oracular declarations which some readers take them to be. But once we have begun to do this, we find that we have rehearsed one of the most important activities of the philosopher, one that is particularly difficult to teach and learn because it relies heavily on one's own creativity. This is the activity in which the philosopher casts about for arguments for a new idea in order to see whether it is defensible and, consequently, acceptable.

In attributing arguments to Nietzsche, we try to make them as good as we can, and we are thus constantly aware of the very real possibility that we will not be able to make them good at all. Perhaps the needed missing premises will be inconsistent with something the author says, or perhaps we can find none that are both logically appropriate and plausible. In that case, we know that we will not be able to accept what he says, unless we can find better arguments ourselves. The process by which we come to understand Nietzsche includes, as a part of it, one in which we subject him to a test. Thus it may also represent the beginning of a process which results in our denying him and going beyond him. If we assume a conception of philosophy according to which the most important thing it teaches is the autonomous use of one's own reason, we should think of Nietzsche as one of the most philosophical authors.[3]

WRITING ON NIETZSCHE

My conception of how we ought to read Nietzsche, as I have described it, obviously commits me to some notion of how a scholarly book about Nietzsche ought to be written. Naturally, it is the one I will try to follow here. Much of what I will say will have no direct and immediate purpose other than getting Nietzsche right. But the things I will say to this end will include rather more philosophical reasoning than is usual in interpreting a philosophical author. I will be fairly free – some will no doubt say generous – in supplying Nietzsche with premises needed to make his arguments work. I will pause from time to time to show that the ideas I attribute to him are plausible ones, at least in the context of what he does explicitly say. One should not suppose that this means that

I agree with these ideas. It is simply a necessary part of getting at what his ideas are and how they hang together.

As I have said, the process of understanding Nietzsche as I have described it is continuous with the process of subjecting what he says to criticism. We understand him by trying to make his ideas work, and this activity includes the permanent possibility of being unable to make them work. In light of this, it is remarkable that most studies of Nietzsche contain very little critical comment. Their authors calmly quote him viciously criticizing nearly everything that ordinary, right-thinking people believe, and they seldom either agree or disagree.[4]

To me, this sort of inertness seems inappropriate to the subject-matter at hand. Still, it is not very difficult to understand. Nietzsche attacks the contents of ordinary human consciousness at so many levels that it seems one would have to build a system of one's own – or at least some fully developed theories – in order to reply to what he says. And doing so is not usually appropriate to a work of philosophical scholarship. Usually, the scholar has to assume that the reader is interested in understanding Nietzsche rather than mastering the scholar's own philosophy. One needs a way to avoid both of the dangers involved here: remaining inert on the one hand and impertinently holding forth on one's own views on the other.

The strategy I will use in what follows will be to make my main critical remarks on Nietzsche from inside his point of view. As I expound his views, certain themes in his writings will become much more plausible than they were at first. Interesting and powerful arguments in favor of them will emerge from the text. As these arguments develop, however, they will make certain other of his themes increasingly difficult to accept. We will see a strong logical tension between different parts of his philosophy. My point will certainly not be to smugly convict Nietzsche of contradicting himself. It will be to show that certain of his ideas can function as arguments against certain others. When we have worked through his ethical and political views, they – or, rather, our own efforts in working through them – will enlighten us about which of these ideas are acceptable and which are not.

2

IMMORALISM

THE PROBLEM OF NIETZSCHE'S IMMORALISM

Nietzsche claims to be an "immoralist" – indeed, he claims to be "the first immoralist" and adds: "that makes me the *annihilator par excellence*" (EH IV 2). Undoubtedly, this means that in some way or other he is a critic of morality, but beyond this small area of certainty the exact nature of his immoralism is quite problematic. The word *suggests* a particularly extreme sort of doctrine. Indeed, he predicts that immoralist ideas will become influential precisely because the "spell that fights on our behalf . . . is the *magic of the extreme*, the seduction that everything extreme exercises: we immoralists – we are the most extreme" (WM 749). There are important passages in which he explicitly describes his way of thinking as an alternative to the moral way of thinking as such (e.g, JGB 32 and WM 299).

Yet there are other times when he gives a quite different impression of what his immoralism amounts to. In the only passage in which he defines "immoralism," he says that "fundamentally" it "involves two negations." One of them is his opposition to "a type of man that has so far been considered supreme: the good, the benevolent, the beneficent." This apparently means that he is opposed to the idea that being a good person is the same thing as trying to have beneficial effects on other people.[1] The other negation is his opposition to "a type of morality that has become prevalent and predominant as morality itself – the morality of decadence or, more concretely, *Christian* morality" (EH IV 4).

If this is all his immoralism amounts to, however, it makes his claim that immoralists are "the most extreme" a mysterious one, and it also makes his belief that he was the first immoralist very difficult to account for. Both these "negations" can plausibly be

7

attributed to a number of people before Nietzsche, including Hume, Thoreau, and Goethe.

The mystery is merely intensified by the fact that he says a number of things which at least seem to support the idea that the scope of his attack on morality is restricted and does not extend to the limits of morality as such. In the chapter, "Morality as Anti-nature" in *Twilight of the Idols* he attacks morality "insofar as it *condemns* for its own sake, and *not* out of regard for the concerns . . . of life" (G V 6), which clearly means that, at least at that point, he is not attacking morality as such, but only morality that condemns in a certain way. In the same chapter, he makes disparaging remarks about "almost every morality which has so far been taught" (G V 4) and about morality "as it has so far been understood" (G V 5), and he explicitly contrasts these moralities with "naturalism in morality – that is, every health morality" (G V 4). Elsewhere in the same book he says "the whole improve-ment-morality, including the Christian, was a misunderstanding" (G II 11), which suggests that there is a morality that is not part of "improvement morality" and is not being said, at least at this moment, to be a misunderstanding. Finally, as is well known, his comments on what he calls "noble morality" are uniformly favorable (e.g., GM I 10; A 24).

There is probably no way to make all of Nietzsche's remarks on the scope of his immoralism entirely consistent. There is likely to be at least one instance in which he is simply not choosing his words as carefully as he usually does. In this chapter I will argue, though, that *most* of the apparent inconsistencies can be eliminated by a close look at what he actually says about morality. What emerges when we have done this is a position that is indeed both original and extreme.

SOME DISTINCTIONS

There is a fairly simple consideration that helps in removing some of these apparent inconsistencies. Nietzsche does recognize a distinction between what he variously calls "antinatural" or "denaturalized" morality – moralities which show no "regard for the concerns . . . of life" – on the one hand, and naturalistic moralities which *do* show this sort of regard (WM 298 and 299). As we shall see later, he has special reasons, ones that are particularly important to him, for opposing moralities of the latter sort. The fact that he singles them out for condemnation on various occasions does not mean that he lacks other reasons – perhaps less important ones – for opposing morality as such.

This, however, does not explain how he can speak favorably of some moralities while at other times he seems to oppose morality as such. Here we have two tendencies in Nietzsche's rhetoric which seem flatly contradictory. It is certainly tempting to say that he is always speaking sloppily when he evinces one of these tendencies and to only take the other one seriously, as Walter Kaufmann does when he says that Nietzsche "seems to condemn . . . morality altogether and lacks the patience to make clear that his criticism is directed only against certain types" of morality.[2] Actually, I believe we can take both these motifs seriously without denying Nietzsche's familiarity with the requirements of logic. One can be consistent in admiring some moralities while condemning morality as such.

This is possible because of a distinction between uses of "morality" (*Moral*, *Sittlichkeit*) which is implicit in Nietzsche's writings and in ordinary language as well. It is rather similar to a familiar distinction between uses of "god." At one point, Nietzsche remarks that, for someone who believes in God, it is impossible to doubt that "God could not be evil and could not do anything harmful" (WM 290). This is a more or less plausible statement as it stands, but it becomes obviously false if one takes "God" out of it and replaces it with "gods." The gods of the Greeks did not a few things which are evil and harmful. There is a use of "god" that is distinguished by being capitalized and, more importantly, by the fact that it does not have a plural form. It refers to the gods of monotheism, to gods who have imperialistic ambitions and wish to be the only god. They also are generally very moral beings. The use that admits of a plural refers to these beings and others besides, who are not like this at all.

Similarly, there is a use of "morality" that admits of a plural, and when it appears in the singular always requires an article (as in "a morality of self-sacrifice" and "the morality of mores"). In this sense, a morality is a code by which one lives; one which, moreover, enables one to distinguish between good and bad or right and wrong in human conduct and ways of life. One can say "Speculators who trade on inside information think there is nothing wrong with what they do – they have a morality of their own" or "Oscar Wilde believed in a morality of aestheticism." It was in this spirit that Professor Higgins said Eliza's father was "the most original moralist in all of England." As these examples indicate, "morality" in this use of the word may have little to do with "morality" in another usage, one which is only found in the singular and without an article. Wilde's code specified that life should only be judged on aesthetic – that is, *non-moral* – grounds. In the singular sense, morality is one kind of morality in the sense that admits of a plural. In an attempt to avoid ambiguity as gracefully as possible, I will distinguish this so to speak monotheistic sense of "morality" by capitalizing it, together with its cognate adverb and adjective, in what follows (except when it appears in quotation marks).

When we apply the adjective, "moral," to persons and reasons for acting, we are always associating them with Morality in the capitalized sense of the word. If the fact that there is a difference between moralities and Morality is not obvious, consider what is and is not being said about a *person* who is said to be "moral." By the definition I have given, the identity of the traits one regards as virtues are part of the morality one tries to live by, so that virtue is quite generally a moral concept. But if someone were to tell me "John is a very moral person" and then explain that what they meant was that John is a very courageous person, I would wonder what they were trying to say. The explanation – in the absence of further explanation – seems irrelevant to the thing being explained. Courage does not make a person "moral." However, if they were to explain that what they meant was that John never lies, always pays his debts, and treats everyone fairly and with respect I would think that, whether true or not, this was entirely in order as an explanation.

Of course, I have not said what Morality means and, in particular, I have not said what it means in Nietzsche's writings. I will try to show what it means for Nietzsche – which, of course, in the present context is the main issue –by a rather roundabout method. I will go through various remarks in which he appears to be attacking something that could be called "morality" and see what is the object of his attack in each case. In each case he will be saying that one thing or another is impossible or does not exist or should not be part of one's ideal. When we add together these various impossible or non-existent or non-ideal things, we will have a conception of Morality that will be plausible and, in fact, very familiar. It will be what moral philosophers today generally mean when they discuss "morality."

RESPONSIBILITY

One of the most important passages in Nietzsche's writings for understanding his critique of morality is section 32 of *Beyond Good and Evil*. There he discusses three stages of human history that are distinguished by three different ways of evaluating human conduct and ways of life. They are "the *pre-moral* period of mankind," the "period that one may call *moral* in the narrower sense," and a period that may now be beginning, which "should be designated negatively, to begin with, as *extra-moral*." In this section, all his disparaging remarks are directed at what he calls the "moral in the narrower sense" – a locution in which he is clearly employing a distinction between senses of "moral" and selecting one of them as representing the target of his attack.

During the pre-moral period, which in its pure form coincides roughly with the pre-historic part of human development, "the value or disvalue of an action was derived from its consequences." An act was seen as good if its results turn out to be good, and bad if the results turn out to be bad. The value of the results is the cause of the value of the act, and a cause that works backwards, temporally, in "rather the way a distinction or disgrace still reaches back today from a child to its parents, in China." Very gradually, during "the last ten thousand years or so . . . in a few large regions of the earth" the pre-moral phase has given way to the moral, which involves a complete "reversal of perspective" from the preceding period. He speculates that the transition was "the unconscious aftereffect of the rule of aristocratic values and the belief in 'descent,'" for the moral period was ruled by the idea that the value of an action was produced by the value of its origin. More particularly, "the origin of an action was interpreted in the most definite sense as origin in an *intention*; one came to agree that the value of an action lay in the value of the intention." To think this, one had to think that the intention is "the whole origin and prehistory of an action" (JGB 32).

We can only understand Nietzsche's defense of the extra-moral point of view in this passage if we understand the reason why it is necessary for Morality to identify the intention behind an act as the whole origin of the act. This, in turn, requires that we understand what the aristocratic "belief in 'descent'" is and how it applies to judgements about actions. In a culture with strongly aristocratic values, the most important distinction between the value of persons

11

is between those who are noble and those who are not. If one is noble, that is simply because one's parents were noble, which in turn was because *their* parents were noble, and so forth. The belief in descent is apparently one's acceptance of a principle that the value of an act or other human fact (such as a person, a thought, and so forth) is produced by and identical with the value of its source. It is important to notice that if the source is also a human fact in this sense, then the value of the source will derive from the value of *its* source in the same way. Consider, as an example, the way in which we ordinarily view acts in which one acquires property rights. If the act whereby I attempt to acquire the rights to a house constitutes a legitimate acquisition of the rights to a house, this is because it was preceded by another act that has the same sort of legitimacy. If I succeeded in acquiring rights to my house by buying it from you, you must have had the very same rights yourself, and if you bought the house, you must have acquired it from someone else who had such rights in the first place. If they acquired the house by fraud, then I cannot acquire rights to it in this way. The relationship whereby a human fact derives its value from its source is a transitive one.

It is also important to realize that the principle of the belief in descent is used as a method of *discovering* the value of an act. Its value is presumed to be unknown until the value of the source is known. Thus, if our belief in descent is the only such method we have, and if act *a* derives from source *b* and *b* derives from *c*, and so on, back to *n*, the original source of the value of *a*, we do not know the value of *a* until and unless we know the value of *n*.

Nietzsche sees that this raises some very serious problems. He says in a late note that the "entire theory of responsibility rests on the naive psychology that the only cause [of an action] is will." If I am to be responsible for the goodness or badness of my actions, then it is not enough if my conscious intention is one efficacious link in a chain of causes leading to the action. The principle of the belief in descent shows why this is so. The idea that the value of something derives from its source implies that the value of my intention may derive from something which is anterior to it, something which is not an act of my will at all. In that case, even though my intention is *among* the factors which produce my act, the value of the act will not be in my control. It will instead be in the control of the mysterious something which is anterior to my intention. Thus, the idea of responsibility presupposes an extreme version of the doctrine of free will. As he says in the same note, if "the value of man is posited as a *moral* value," then "there must be a principle in man, a 'free will' as *causa prima*" (WM 288). The will must have the status that it seems *n* must have, it must be an event that produces others but is not itself produced by anything.

At this point, there is a response that is open to the defenders of Morality. They can point out that what the belief in descent requires is that the value of the intention derives from the *value* of its source. If the antecedents of an intention are not the sort of thing that can be good or bad, noble or ignoble, then an intention can be the source of the value of what follows from it, while its own value derives from no other source. This can be true even though the intention itself does derive from some other source, and is thus not a first cause. But Nietzsche denies precisely the assumption that is being made here: that the antecedents of intention do not have the relevant sorts of value. In his description of the extra-moral point of view, he claims that the intention derives from other factors in such a way that it must be viewed as "merely a sign and symptom" which "betrays something and *conceals* even more." What it both betrays and conceals is what might be called the agent's deep character, the many thoughts, feelings, and motives that are neither conscious nor intentional. And he takes it as obvious that such things can be noble or ignoble. For this reason, "today at least we immoralists have the suspicion that the decisive value of an action lies precisely in what is *unintentional* in it" (JGB 32). This idea – what the immoralists suspect is true – is what Nietzsche calls the extra-moral point of view.

In a way, the extra-moral is continuous with the Moral; it represents, "in a certain sense . . . the self-overcoming of morality" – that is, it is produced by the same basic principle, applied more consistently and in the light of a deeper psychology. The Moral point of view was "precipitate and perhaps provisional – something on the order of astrology and alchemy" (JGB 32, see also M 103). It leads to the extra-moral point of view in something like the same way that primitive pseudo-sciences led to astronomy and chemistry. The continuity between the extra-moral and the Moral consists, partly, in the fact that both are ways of evaluating human conduct and ways of life. This thread of continuity suggests a problem for someone who wishes to take the position that Nietzsche takes. The Moral point of view rests on the intuition that one cannot judge the worth of human beings without the notion of responsibility; that, as he puts it, an "irresponsible" being would have "no business before the moral tribunal" (WM 288). In his favored perspective, the concept of responsibility, in his sense of the word, has entirely disappeared. Is it possible to judge the worth of persons from such a point of view, without covertly employing the rejected idea?

To understand Nietzsche's likely answer to this question, one must look a bit closer at the reason why, as he sees it, the Moral point of view requires the concept of responsibility. Consider, again, the fact that the principle of the belief in descent implies that the value of an act is not known until the original source of its value is known. Our knowledge of the ancestry of an act usually does not go back very far. If Nietzsche is right, the relevant antecedents of an act are a chain which disappears into the murk of the unconscious, where we are seldom able to follow it. This would imply that, as he says in a late note – probably exaggerating his views somewhat – we "do not know nearly enough to be able to measure the value of our actions" (WM 294). It follows, at least, that understanding the value of an action would be a relatively rare occurrence. By the time we could succeed in using the methods of depth psychology to dig out the ultimate noble or base antecedents of one piece of behavior, the agent will have performed many others, so that the value of most behavior will not in the strict sense be known to us. (See also WM 291.) In the Moral view of life this problem is solved by placing the original source of the value of the action in the agent's consciousness. This means that there is one person on earth, at least, who has access to knowledge of the value of the act – namely, the agent. The rest of us can hope to know the same thing by whatever means we use to find out what is in someone else's mind. For instance, if we can trust the agent to tell the truth, we might try asking him or her.

Morality cannot function at all unless this problem is solved, because of the peculiar importance that individual acts have in the Moral point of view. The Moral tribunal is one in which the primary subject matter of judgement is acts. Acts are judged to be right or wrong, guilty or innocent and, on the basis of this judgement, the agent who does the act is judged to be a guilty or innocent person.[3] If the first sort of judgement cannot be made, neither of them can. Thus, the Moral judge must be able to know the value of actions.

14

In the extra-moral perspective, actions do not have this sort of importance. We can judge that people's character is marked by what Nietzsche calls "slave morality" by noting that many of their actions and gestures fall into patterns that indicate that certain attitudes lie behind much of what they feel and think. We can make this inference without thinking that we know which of their thoughts and feelings proceed from these attitudes, or which of their actions proceed from these thoughts and feelings. It is not a matter of catching them doing something slavish and inferring a slave mentality from the slavish act. But once we have made the inference that certain individuals are characterized by slave morality, their mentality seems to color most of what they do. We may not think we know which of their actions are slavishly motivated but, at least if we agree with Nietzsche's evaluation of the slave mentality, we think we know something about their worth as persons. As we will see in Chapters 5 and 7, judgements about the worth of persons are the ones Nietzsche believes are ethically important. Since we can hope to make judgements of this sort without first knowing the value of particular actions, the reason for which we have found Morality to stand in need of the concept of responsibility is lacking in the extra-moral point of view.

"OUGHT"

Some of Nietzsche's harshest negative comments on Morality have to do with the fact that its judgments, as he understands them, are expressed as "oughts." In the *Twilight of the Idols*, we find him making the following declaration:

> Let us finally consider how naive it is altogether to say: "Man *ought* to be such and such!" Reality shows us an enchanting wealth of types . . . and some wretched prig of a moralist comments: "No! Man ought to be different."

One reason he often gives for this harsh view of thinking in "oughts" is not really an ethical one. As he goes on to say in the same paragraph, "The single human being is a piece of *fatum* from the front and from the rear, one law more, one necessity more for all that is yet to come and to be." This suggests that what he is advancing here is a platitudinous form of hard determinism, that he is saying that it is naive to think that things ought to be otherwise because, in fact, they cannot be otherwise. But he goes on to say, in the next sentence: "To say to him, 'Change yourself!' is to demand that everything be changed, even retroactively" (G V 6). That is, what concerns him here is not so much the necessity of things as their connectedness.

He is clearly making at least two assumptions here: first, that facts depend on one another in such a way that, if one were different, all the others would be different in some way or other; and, second, that the judgement that a certain state of affairs ought to obtain entails the further judgement that everything else which in that case *would* also have to be so *ought* also to be so. The roots of the first of these assumptions – certainly the less immediately plausible of the two – lie deep in the ontology (or whatever one should call it) he developed during the last years of his career and probably cannot be fully understood without wandering rather far out of the range of topics to which I have limited myself.[4] Fortunately, he gives another reason for rejecting "oughts" which is more directly ethical in nature and does not require that I desert my chosen subject-matter. It is closely connected with his criticism of responsibility.

The reason I have in mind is hinted at in *The Gay Science* when he declares that "sitting in moral judgment should offend our taste" and contrasts "moral judgement" with a different way of conceiving of the ideal: "We, however, *want to become those we are*" (FW 335). It is hinted at again when, in a late note apparently written in connection with the *Twilight*, that all statements of the form "man ought to be thus and thus" should be "spoken with a grain of irony" because "in spite of all, one will become only that which one is (in spite of all: that means education, instruction, milieu, chance, and accident)." Here he is speaking of becoming what one is, not as an ideal, but as an ineluctable fact. Among the several questions that suggest themselves here is: How does the idea that one becomes what one is stand in the way of judging people by means of moral "oughts"? He gives a clue to the answer to this question when he says, in the same note, that "virtue and vice are not causes but only consequences," and adds by way of explanation: "One becomes a decent man because one *is* a decent man: i.e., because one was born a capitalist of good instincts and prosperous circumstances" (WM 334).

He is saying that the actions that are called virtuous and vicious are consequences of deeper facts about the agent, which suggests that the principles lurking in the background here are the same ones he used in attacking the Moral use of the idea of descent. This is borne out by another note from the same period in which he gives the following explanation of his belief that "the realm of so-called moral improvement" is one of "universal cheating and deception":

> We do not believe that a man will become another if he is not that other already; i.e., if he is not, as is often the case, a multiplicity of persons, at least the embryos of persons. In this case, one can bring a different role into the foreground and draw "the former man" back.

Of course, he admits that, if we do this, we may have radically altered the behavior of the persons, but in that case:

> The aspect is changed, not the essence – That someone ceases to perform certain actions is a mere *fatum brutum* that permits the most various interpretations. It is not always the case that the habit of a certain act is broken, the ultimate reason for it is removed.

As in his critique of responsibility, he takes the agent's deep character to be what determines the ethical meaning of the agent's behavior (WM 394).

The same idea supports his critique of the Moral "ought" in more or less the following way. The point of an "ought" judgement is that, through it, something is to be changed for the better in an ethically relevant way. There are only two sorts of subject-matter which such a judgement can be about: the agent's deep character and the things which arise from it. The latter includes the agent's actions and, as we saw before, the various goings-on in the agent's consciousness. But the agent's deep character is virtually impossible to change (let alone to change for the better) and if the other things are changed while it remains the same, they are not improved in an ethically relevant way. Their *worth* is a function of the character from which they spring. In fact, Morality does direct its imperatives at the agent's behavior, but this means that "it stays everywhere on the surface, at signs, gestures, words to which it gives an arbitrary meaning" (WM 394). This is the nature of its "universal cheating and deception."

Nietzsche admits that we do have reason to be concerned with the agent's behavior purely as such. But what reason we do have constitutes merely "an *economic*" – as opposed to ethical – "justification of virtue" (WM 888). Because of the unwelcome social consequences of certain forms of behavior, society sometimes has reason to lock some people away where they have no opportunity to do those things (WM 394), but to the extent that we thereby change the individual's patterns of behavior we merely "make him as useful as possible and . . . approximate him, as far as possible, to an infallible machine" (WM 888; see also G IX 29). That is, we engineer the individual's external behavior without touching its living source. For obvious reasons, this does not count as "improving" the person.

Thus, the factual claim that people generally do not become other than they are stands in the way of the Moral "ought" because the fundamental self to which it refers is the source of the worth of persons and actions. This enables this claim to function as a standard by which ethical ideals can be evaluated. By this standard, Nietzsche believes, Moral "oughts" do not do very well.

OPPOSITE VALUES

Nietzsche has another important objection to thinking in terms of oughts which is distinct from, though closely related to, the ones I have just discussed. In fact it is to some extent implicit in some of the passages I have already quoted. He believes that when we make "ought" judgements we take a certain rather narrow view of the world. At the moment we make such a judgement, we attend to two different states of affairs, one of which is actual and the other of which is non-existent. One of them is thought of as having positive value (as the one that ought to exist) while the other one, at that moment, is regarded simply as something of negative value (it ought not to exist). Typically, the state of affairs which is seen as having positive value is the one that does not exist, while the actual one is accorded merely negative value. Thus he speaks of the moralist as saying of human beings as they are: "*No!* Man ought to be different" (G V 6; emphasis added).[5]

Because they typically involve saying "No!" to the facts as they actually are, Nietzsche regards "ought" judgements as particularly dangerous ones. By nature, they are well suited to playing a crucial role in pathological fantasies in which one gets even with painful facts by utterly denying their value. But, quite aside from pathological motives, such judgements are dangerous for a reason that is more or less a matter of logic alone. Because of the connectedness of things, negating the value of one thing requires one to negate the value of the next thing, and this is a process which can go very far: "indeed there have been consistent moralists who wanted man to be different, that is, virtuous . . .: to that end, they *negated* the world" (G V 6). Here Nietzsche is regarding "ought" judgements as typical of a broad range of habits of thought which he calls "the faith in opposite values" (JGB 2). "Opposite values" include all those pairs of evaluative concepts one of which is positive and the other of which is purely negative. They include not only "ought" and "ought not" but right and wrong, good and evil, and the pair of opposites which he believes is the model and source for all the others: true and false (WM 552c; see also JGB 34). Nietzsche rejects each of these distinctions because in each case he rejects its negative pole: "we immoralists . . . do not easily negate; we make it a point of honor to be *affirmers*" (G V 6). To apply one of these negative concepts to a human action is, in some way or other, to think of the act as reprehensible, and because of the connectedness of things, a "reprehensible action means: a reprehended world" (WM 293).

To some extent, then, Nietzsche's rejection of opposite values rests on his thesis that all things are in a certain way very strongly dependent on one another.[6] But this is not the only sort of argument he has for opposing these distinctions. He also has arguments in favor of other sets of evaluative concepts which are logically incompatible with them. One cannot believe in an "essential opposition of 'true' and 'false'" if one believes that there are only "degrees of apparentness and, as it were, lighter and darker shadows and shades of appearance – different 'values,' to use the language of painters" (JGB 34). A number of the remarks in the *Nachlass* of the 1880s constitute an argument that cognitions must be ranked in this way, and thus these remarks must also be counted as an argument against the opposition between true and false. As we shall see in Chapter 7, he also has arguments to the effect that persons and ways of life can only be ranked along a continuum of degrees of a certain sort of goodness. An argument in favor of thinking in terms of *Rangordnung*, as he likes to call it, is an argument against thinking in terms of "ought" and "ought not," right and wrong, and good and evil.

DISINTERESTEDNESS AND UNIVERSALITY

In an unpublished note from the 1880s, Nietzsche writes: "What is the criterion of a moral action? (1) its disinterestedness, (2) its universal validity, etc.'' (WM 261). As the reader might be able to guess, he does not believe that any action has either of these characteristics. His objections to the idea of universal validity are partly ethical and partly psychological in nature. As he says in a late note, one should not claim that one's ideal is ''*the* ideal: for one therewith takes from it its privileged character. One should have it in order to distinguish oneself, not in order to level oneself.'' To claim that one's ideal is for everyone is to lower it. He is clearly assuming a view of the ideal according to which any characteristics that people could possibly have in common would be ethically second-rate at best. As we shall see in Chapters 5 and 7, his theory of virtue does have precisely this implication. Further, he objects to the psychological thesis that people sometimes actually do things because they believe that these things are right for everyone to do. His objection is that this would be to act disinterestedly and, in this sense of the word, no one acts ''disinterestedly.'' He says in the same note that those who say that they are fighting for their rights because they are the rights of everybody do so because it is ''under the banner of 'For others' that they can most prudently forward their own little private separatism''; by claiming to represent the rights of all ''they 'transfigure' themselves in the eyes of those who believe in disinterestedness and heroism'' (WM 349).

His objections to bringing disinterestedness into one's conception of the ideal go deep into his conception of human action, including his complex views on psychological egoism and psychological hedonism. In this context they can be simplified by thinking of them as a dilemma which he presents to the defenders of the ideal of disinterested action. Clearly, ''disinterestedness'' can mean more than one thing. On the one hand, it could refer to actions which do not aim at the agent's self-interest, actions which are not based on prudence. This is a notion about which Nietzsche has fairly definite views. The self, as he sees it, includes a great many drives each of which, ''in as much as it is active, sacrifices force and other drives'' to satisfy itself. Each must meet some resistance some-where, ''otherwise it would destroy everything through its excessiveness.'' The drives that are parts of the self all have their own separate interests; the only sort of behavior that would serve the interests of the self itself, so to speak, would be that which maximizes the satisfaction of the whole system of drives, on balance. Unegoistic behavior would be that which does not do this. But in this sense, ''the 'unegoistic,' self-sacrificing, imprudent, is nothing special – it is common to all the drives – they do not consider the advantage of the whole ego (because they do not consider at all!)'' (WM 372). In this sense, disinterested behavior is a familiar fact – too familiar to qualify as part of the ideal. Unegoistic behavior is simply that which comes naturally to us, and consequently egoistic behavior represents a genuine achievement (though Nietzsche would not consider it a very lofty one).

On the other hand, disinterestedness might refer to action in which one does not respond to the promptings of any of these drives, in which one is not lured or repelled by the emotional charges with which they invest their various objects: one is moved simply by one's understanding of the rightness – perhaps the universal validity – of what one is doing. Nietzsche denies that understanding ever does move us to act in this way. What we think of as understanding is simply "the form in which we come to feel" several different drives at once, including at least the "desires to laugh, lament, and curse." He claims that each of our drives presents us with a view of the facts, a onesided view in each case, and understanding occurs when the conflict between several different passionate prejudices "results in a mean." Then "one grows calm . . . and there is a kind of justice and a contract; for by virtue of justice and a contract all these instincts can maintain their existence and assert their rights against each other." Action that is based on understanding cannot be disinterested because understanding itself is not disinterested. It merely seems that it is, because "only the last scenes of reconciliation" between one's passions "rise to our consciousness" (FW 333).

There are reasons why our own actions can appear to us to be disinterested, even though they are not. The same is true, more obviously, of the actions of others. Though the agent is aware of responding to things that passionately "interest and attract" him or her, they may be things that the rest of us find "totally 'uninteresting.'" Seeing only the agent's outward behavior, we foolishly begin to wonder "how it is possible to act without interest" (JGB 220).

IMMORALISM

We now have a fairly large collection of criticisms which Nietzsche directs at several different sorts of ideas. Some of these ideas are standards of value, while others are psychological or metaphysical theories. The one thing they all have in common is that in each case he tells us that the notion he is attacking is either part of something he calls "morality" or that it is among the indispensable presuppositions of "morality." One thing, at least, is very obvious: whatever this word means to him, he is using it in these contexts to refer to something which he rejects. Further, the meaning of the word is no longer particularly mysterious. We can understand at least a large part of what "morality" means for him, insofar as it is something he rejects, by drawing together in one place the targets of his various attacks.

Morality is a collection of ideas that evaluate human actions and, on the basis of its evaluation of these acts, also evaluates the agents who do them. Because of the way in which it infers the worth of the agent from the worth of the agent's behavior, it requires the assumption that people are responsible for what they do. Actions are evaluated Morally by judging that something or other "ought" or "ought not" be done. Nietzsche does not deny that other sorts of evaluative judgements might also be included in the Moral approach to problems of value, but he clearly thinks that no system of ideas which fails to make judgements of this form could be a Moral one. Further, to say that something Morally ought to be done does not mean merely that it would be nice, desirable, a good idea, and so forth. It also means that omitting to do it would have negative value. Thus morality uses at least one pair of opposite values, one of which is positive and the other of which is negative. Further, to think that an action has Moral worth is to make a judgement which in some way is deemed to be applicable to everyone. This is the sort of thing one does, for instance, if one judges that a certain action, which ought to be done by a certain person, ought also to be done by anyone in the same circumstances. From this we can infer, though Nietzsche does not say so, that Moral "oughts" can always be either stated as or derived from general rules which apply to everyone. Finally, to think that an action has moral worth is also to think that it is done *because of* its moral worth – which could mean, for instance, that one does it because one understands that there is a legitimate Moral rule that requires it. In this sense (and perhaps in some other senses as well) it is an action which is done disinterestedly.

Taken together, these ideas constitute an elaborate definition of a familiar sense of the word "morality." More specifically, anyone who knows the history of philosophy should immediately recognize that they represent Immanuel Kant's conception of "morality." This fact is particularly striking if one focuses on two ideas which stand out from the others here in that they identify metaphysical and psychological assumptions which are supposed to make the Moral point of view possible. These are the ideas of responsibility and disinterestedness. Nietzsche's explication of the idea of a responsible action as one which is caused by the agent's will, while the will itself has no antecedent cause, is clearly drawn directly from Kant's writings. His conception of disinterestedness is apparently an interpretation of Kant's notion that actions fail to have moral worth to the extent that they are done on the basis of "inclination."[7]

This might be taken to trivialize Nietzsche's immoralism into an attack on Kant. Many philosophers have attacked Kant; what makes Nietzsche different from the others? What makes him different is, in part, the fact that he opposes *every one* of the characteristics of morality which I have just described.[8] This certainly places him in an extreme position, far from the center of moral philosophy. After all, if we subtract the rather strong interpretations he gives to the ideas of responsibility and disinterestedness, Nietzsche's conception of Morality is identical to the one we find in the writings of most ethical philosophers today. It represents their analysis of the sense "morality" has when it does not admit of a plural, the sense I have represented by capitalizing the word throughout most of this chapter. It also, of course, represents something they believe in and defend. What Nietzsche attacks is what these philosophers believe in.

In a perfectly straightforward and familiar sense of the word, Nietzsche rejects "morality." It is consequently not at all misleading of him to call himself an immoralist. It is also at least plausible to say that he was, in this sense, the first immoralist. Probably no one before him had consciously formulated and rejected all – or even most of – the characteristics of Morality which he formulates and rejects.[9] Finally, we can see now that there is no inconsistency in admiring some moralities while attacking Morality as such. Morality, in the capitalized sense, is a very distinctive sort of code, and is clearly only one way to distinguish between good and bad in human conduct and ways of life.[10] There obviously are others, and there may be ones that do not have any of the characteristics Nietzsche attacks. To decide whether he succeeds in formulating such a system of ideas, and one that lacks all the characteristics of morality which he opposes, we will have to look at the positive side of his ethical theory. This is what I will do in Chapters 5–8.

Before moving on to a different subject, I should probably acknowledge that I have omitted, for the time being, any discussion of the most familiar – or notorious – aspect of Nietzsche's immoralism. So far, I have only treated his remarks on what might loosely be called the "formal" aspects of Morality as such. He saves his most passionate criticisms for the *content* of certain Moral judgements. I have in mind the many attacks in his late writings on what he calls, at different times, the "antinatural," "denaturalized," or "ascetic" versions of "Morality." His favorite example of this target of his invective is, of course, Christianity. This more substantive side of Nietzsche's immoralism is another subject which I will have to delay discussing until I have had a chance to examine the positive side of his ethical theory. I will take it up again in Chapter 7 (pp. 115–30).

3

POLITICS AND ANTI-POLITICS

The appearance of character makes the State unnecessary.
The wise man is the State. He needs no army, fort, or navy,
– he loves men too well. . . . He needs . . . no church, for
he is a prophet; no statute book, for he is the law-giver; . . .
no experience, for the life of the creator shoots through him
and looks from his eyes.

Emerson, "Politics"

THE PROBLEM OF NIETZSCHE'S POLITICS

In recent years, a number of scholars have argued that Nietzsche held political views which would require the state to possess enormous powers, powers so great that, if they are right, it would be quite reasonable to describe his views as "totalitarian."[1] The passages in Nietzsche's writings that at least seem to support this sort of interpretation are numerous and, in many cases, very familiar to Nietzsche's readers.

However, Nietzsche makes other statements, many of them less well known, which could easily lead to the opposite sort of interpretation. In an early aphorism, for instance, he describes a particularly individualist kind of stateless society and his ambiguous remarks about it might well be understood as being favorable. Discussing the future of democratic societies after the collapse of religion, he confidently predicts that as the chaos of factional disputes grows worse and worse, people will become more mistrustful of all government, leading, as he puts it in mock-Hegelian language, "to the superseding of the concept of the state, the transcending of the antithesis between private and public." "Step by step, private organizations draw the business of the state into themselves: even the stickiest residue which from the ancient work of the state remains behind (that activity, for instance, which protects one private person from another) is taken care of by private entrepreneurs." He comments that, when this has been

25

accomplished, and "all relapses into the old disease have been over-come," the book of mankind will yield "all sorts of curious stories and perhaps some good ones, too" (MAM 472). Not surprisingly, it has been suggested that Nietzsche was in fact an anarchist, that he believed that we ought to abolish the state altogether.[2] Walter Kaufmann defended the view – which, at least on the surface, seems similar to this one – that Nietzsche's attitudes were deeply "anti-political."[3]

In the face of the widely disparate interpretations of Nietzsche's view of the state, one inevitably wonders what his political beliefs were. In what follows, I will try to show that he, in fact, did not hold any of the standard political ideologies. This becomes reason-ably clear, I think, when one realizes that he was not interested in the same questions to which the standard ideologies are answers. If one hastily assumes, on the contrary, that he was interested in the same questions as we are, we can find evidence that he believed any one of several different, mutually inconsistent ideologies: we can "prove" that he was an anarchist, a totalitarian, even a classical liberal.[4] In the context of his real concerns, though, his position appears to remain admirably constant and coherent throughout his career. The word which describes it most accurately is one that Kaufmann – and Nietzsche himself (EH I 3) – used: he was anti-political.

As it stands, of course, this statement tells one almost nothing; I will have to explain what "anti-political" must mean if it is to be applied to Nietzsche's views. This task brings special difficulties with it, since Nietzsche never spelled out his political views with anything like the elaborateness he gave to his discussions of various moral and aesthetic questions. It is as if he found the subject too distasteful for sustained attention. My method will have to consist in identifying the parts of the theory of the state which he explicitly presents and in making informed guesses as to the connections between them. This method is obviously a risky one, but it is worth the risks because Nietzsche's unique and interesting view of the state cannot be unearthed in any other way.

BURCKHARDT AS EDUCATOR

Several ideas which seem to lie beneath a good deal of what Nietz-sche says about politics and the state can be found in a series of lectures that Jacob Burckhardt delivered at Basel the year after

Nietzsche arrived there as a young professor.[5] These lectures are an attempt to view all of history as a struggle between three different "powers": culture, religion, and the state. Running throughout his account is a principled contempt for the state, and especially for the "centralized modern state, dominating and determining culture, worshipped as a god and ruling like a sultan" (p. 199). Of the three powers, his strongest sympathies are obviously on the side of culture. The basis of both his contempt and his sympathy lies in the way he conceives both culture and the state, and in the moral principles he applies to them as well. The distinguishing characteristic of the state, for Burckhardt, is mere coercive power, and such "power is of its nature evil, whoever wields it" (p. 164; also p. 208). Though he never says so explicitly, he seems to believe that coercive power necessarily violates human individuality in a way that makes it morally suspect at best (see pp. 174–5).

So far, he is espousing familiar classical liberal doctrines, but they have somewhat unfamiliar implications when set beside his definition of culture. Religion and the state, he tells us, satisfy "the political and metaphysical need" of human beings and "may claim authority at least over particular peoples, and indeed over the world." Culture, on the other hand,

> which meets material and spiritual needs in the narrower sense, is the sum of all that has *spontaneously* arisen for the advancement of material life and as an expression of spiritual and moral life – all social intercourse, technologies, arts, literatures and sciences. It is the realm of the variable, free, not necessarily universal, of all that cannot lay claim to compulsive authority.
>
> (pp. 95–6).

Moral conduct is part of culture insofar as it is not a response to threats of punishment in the afterlife (p. 227). Forms of social organization, such as corporations, are part of culture if they arise because of the way individuals perceive their needs and not because they are imposed on them by political authority (p. 159). It is obvious why someone with Burckhardt's liberal principles would regard culture as nobler than the state: by definition, culture is that which arises in a "free marketplace of ideas" (*freier geistiger Tauschplatz*, p. 193), in which no one can coerce others into accepting his or her innovations. It is also clear enough why he should think there is a natural antagonism between them. If the state expands, coercive power increases, and this destroys the necessary condition of culture, which is freedom. On the other hand, freedom is the only thing that can enable an entire culture to flourish (pp. 191–3), and this requires a curtailment of state power.

Now, it would be a serious mistake to attribute all these ideas to Nietzsche, who once described himself as "not by any means 'liberal'" (FW 377). As we shall see, the differences between Nietzsche and Burckhardt are at least as interesting and illuminating as the similarities. But several of these ideas can be found in Nietzsche's writings throughout his career as a philosopher.

In *Schopenhauer as Educator*, published three years after Burckhardt delivered his lectures on history, Nietzsche considers the "doctrine that the state is the highest goal of mankind and that there is no higher duty for man than to serve the state." He responds to it by contrasting it with the attitude which underlies the pursuit of the aims of culture.

> I am concerned here with a type of man whose teleology envisions something above the good of the state, with the philosophers, and with them only in regard to a world which on the contrary is more or less independent of the state – namely, culture. Of the many interlocking links which constitute the human community, some are of gold and others are of cheap alloy. (U III 4)

Apparently, culture and the state compete in some important way for our attention. Fourteen years later, in *Twilight of the Idols*, he states the same theme more generally and more bluntly: "Culture and the state – one should not deceive oneself about this – are antagonists" (G VIII 4). Finally, during the last months in which he is still able to write, he makes a remark that assumes the same antagonism between culture and the state, and shows the same preference for culture. This time, in fact, he refers to all three elements of Burckhardt's trichotomy:

> Not only have the German historians utterly lost the *great perspective* for the course and the values of culture; nor are they merely, without exception, buffoons of politics (or the church) – but they have actually *proscribed* this great perspective. (EH III W 2)[6]

Like Burckhardt, Nietzsche views the modern state with a special repugnance, as something which threatens to acquire the position of an earthly god. In *Schopenhauer as Educator* he traces the development of the modern state back to the Middle Ages, when the church served, with its immense power, to harmonize the conflicting, hostile forces which are always part of human nature and to "in some measure assimilate them to one another." When the power of the church began to pass away, the state prevented the chaos which seemed about to erupt by stepping in to occupy the same central role in human life that the church had occupied, as the bond that holds us together; but "this means that it wishes the people to practice toward it the same idolatry that they once practiced toward the church" (U III 4). Later on, he says that the extensive state power we see around us is not really necessary in order to prevent chaos, it only seems so to us because our demand for security is so high: we wish to "make society safe against thieves and fireproof and endlessly amenable to every kind of trade and traffic" (M 179).[7] The ancient Greeks had a genuine need for "the idolization of the concept of the state" because they had strong destructive impulses which required being held in check, but it is not necessary for a tame people, like ourselves, "whose lust for power no longer rages as blindly" as theirs did (M 199). In investing the state with as much power as we have, "what is being effected is the very opposite of universal security, a fact our lovely century is undertaking to demonstrate" (M 179).

As a source of social order, the church had at least one advantage over the state: it is an institution "that *believes* in the power of spirituality to the extent of forbidding itself the use of all the cruder instruments of force; and on this score alone the church is a *nobler* institution than the state" (FW 358). But "the time will come when institutions will arise" which are superior to both church and state, and will put their "prototype, the Catholic Church, into shadows and forgetfulness" (MAM 476).

Nietzsche clearly accepts the two important political conclusions I have found in Burckhardt – that culture and the state are by nature antagonistic, and that the state is inferior to culture – as well as the corollary which accompanies them: that the modern state, which possesses *par excellence* the characteristics which make the state inferior, is an especially ignoble institution. This is true even though, as one can probably already see from the passages I have quoted, Nietzsche does not simply reproduce these ideas, but develops them in his own way.

A moment's reflection will suggest another, perhaps more interesting fact: that in giving reasons for these conclusions, Nietzsche will probably be a good deal more independent of Burckhardt. One should expect that the reasoning with which Burckhardt himself supported these conclusions will not be available to Nietzsche. It is well known that Nietzsche doubted that many people – at least, up to the present stage of human development – have ever been free. Thus he may not be able to discuss culture on the assumption that it always arises from a condition of freedom. Indeed, he never does define culture in terms of the conditions from which it arises; he understands it instead in terms of its *purpose*. The "purpose of culture," he says, is "to demand the formation of true *human beings*, and nothing besides" (U III 6). Indeed, the Nietzschean and Burckhardtian conceptions of culture are so different that it might be misleading to use the same word for both ideas. For Burckhardt, culture is a relatively mundane effort to supply us with the wherewithal to survive, and also to satisfy our "spiritual need in the narrower sense"; Nietzsche, on the contrary, conceives it almost entirely as a challenge to a heroic quest for self-development. When Nietzsche speaks of culture he seems to mean "high" culture, especially the fine arts; "culture" certainly does not refer to technology and social institutions, as in part it does when Burckhardt uses it. So when he says that culture and the state are antagonists he is making a rather different sort of statement from the one Burckhardt is making.

Since Nietzsche's idea of culture is not immediately, definitionally connected with the idea of freedom, he cannot have the very same reason that Burckhardt had for thinking that culture and the state are antagonistic and, with equal force, he cannot have the very same reason for preferring one to the other. His preferences are especially likely to be differently grounded, since it is doubtful that he shares the traditional liberal values which Burckhardt applies to culture and the state, at least in their traditional form. It is possible to disagree about what precisely Nietzsche's views on the use of coercion were, but he did say that every society that leads to "the enhancement of the type 'man'" is a society which "needs slavery in some sense or other" (JGB 257),[8] and that if the principle of "refraining mutually from injury, violence, and exploitation" is "accepted as the *fundamental principle of society*, it immediately proves to be what it really is . . . a principle of disintegration and decay'' (JGB 259). For the Nietzsche of the 1880s, the fact that an institution rests on coercive power cannot by itself cast any doubt on the value of that institution.

THE PHENOMENOLOGY OF CITIZENSHIP

At one point Nietzsche argues, in effect, for both of the political conclusions we have been considering by basing them on a single psychological assumption. In *Twilight of the Idols*, he explains why ''German culture is declining'' on the basis of the hypothesis that ''no one can spend more than he has.'' He claims that, applied to cultural concerns, this hypothesis means: ''If one spends oneself for power, for power politics, for economics, world trade, parliamentarianism, and military interests – if one spends in *this* direction the quantum of understanding, seriousness, will, and self-overcoming which one represents, then it will be lacking for the other direction.'' It follows that the state and culture are antagonists: ''what is great culturally has always been unpolitical, even *anti-political*.'' If, as he goes on to say at this point, culture is always ''what matters most,'' then the other conclusion follows as well (G VIII 4).

He is assuming, of course, that the amount of one's motivational energy, so to speak, is fixed, and that any amount of it that is directed toward one object is thereby used up and not available to any other object. To those who do not accept this psychological principle, the argument which rests upon it will undoubtedly prove unconvincing, and this is clearly a principle which some would not accept. Why is it not possible for artists to find inspiration in the glorious causes which they think their state represents, so that political concerns can lead to cultural greatness? More generally, why cannot one object of motivation create new sources of seriousness, will, and self-overcoming that can then be spent on other objects? An attempt to answer these questions would probably shed more light on Nietzsche's psychology than on his political views, which are our present concern.[9] Fortunately, he does give another argument for the same conclusion. It is considerably more complex than the one I have just rehearsed but since it does shed light on his political views, it is worthwhile for our purposes to discuss it at some length.

The core of this argument is to be found in the section ''On the

31

New Idol" in *Zarathustra*. His language in that section is angry and bitter, and several of the things he says there are paradoxical and mysterious. He claims that the state is a source of death or, more exactly, he speaks as if all states somehow collude in the self-destruction of their subjects: "State I call it . . . where the slow suicide of all is called life." To speak of the state is to speak "about the death of peoples." The state is also a source of self-alienation: "state, where all lose themselves, the good and the wicked." He says that it gives the people "a hundred new appetites" and mentions two of them: "They want power and first the lever of power, much money." The state is, oddly enough, "the sin against customs and laws." "Confusion of tongues of good and evil" is "the sign of the state." Twice he speaks as if the state makes claims about itself. It says: "I, the state, am the people." It also says: "On earth there is nothing greater than I: the ordering finger of God am I." Both statements are lies: "whatever it says it lies." Finally, he tells us that it is "where the state *ends*" that we can see "the rainbow and the bridges of the overman" (Z I 11).

Though the shrill tone of these remarks might lead one to suspect otherwise, I believe it can be shown that their author means them all seriously and more or less literally. Indeed, if one accepts certain other things he believes, they are all fairly plausible as well.

It is probably already obvious that some of these remarks resemble anti-statist comments I have quoted from works that preceded *Zarathustra*. One of them recalls another theme from the earlier writings, one which, until *Zarathustra*, had not been connected with the anti-state motif. This is the paradoxical remark that the state is "the sin against customs (*Sitten*) and laws." In *Daybreak*, Nietzsche had written at length about an idea he called the "concept of morality of custom" (*Begriff der Sittlichkeit der Sitte*). This earlier discussion was his attempt to account for morality as a purely social phenomenon: "morality is nothing other (therefore *no more!*) than obedience to customs," where customs are simply the "*traditional* way of behaving and evaluating" that has arisen in a particular community (M 9). Morality is a social phenomenon in a particularly strong sense: it is created by the community itself by means of a gradual evolutionary process. The "morality which prevails in a community is constantly being worked at by everybody" (M 11) and represents the accumulated "experiences of men of earlier times as to what they supposed useful and harmful" (M 19). These ideas are present in *Zarathustra* as essential parts of the critique of the state presented there. Zarathustra explains why the claim "I, the state, am the people" is a lie by saying: "It was creators who created peoples and hung a faith and a love over them: thus they served life" (Z I 11). The creators created peoples *by* hanging a faith – a code of values – over them: "No people could live without first esteeming; but if they want to preserve themselves, then they must not esteem as the neighbor esteems." A common code serves to distinguish one group of people from another, making them the unique community that they are. Until apparently quite recently, these creators were the groups themselves: "First, peoples were creators; and only in later times, individuals. Verily, the individual himself is still the most recent creation" (Z I 15).

It is in this context that Zarathustra situates the idea of the state. In the section "On Great Events," he talks about aspects of human life which, because they produce a great deal of "noise and smoke," distract us from a great truth: "Not around the inventors of new noise, but around the inventors of new values does the world revolve; it revolves *inaudibly*." The state is one of the most powerful sources of distracting noise: the state "likes to talk with smoke and bellowing – to make himself believe . . . that he is talking out of the belly of reality. For he wants to be by all means the most important beast on earth, the state; and they believe him" (Z II 18). Insofar as there is a belly of reality, it is the creator of new values – which for the most part is the people themselves. The state naturally tends to displace, in the consciousness of its subjects, the position which is usually rightfully occupied by the people. This would be at least part of the reason why the state represents the death of peoples.

At this point, two questions must be answered before one can appreciate Nietzsche's position – or even understand it. Why does he think this displacement of the people occurs? And why does he view it with such alarm?

Nietzsche never gives a systematic and fully developed answer to the first question, but he makes enough suggestive remarks to enable us to guess what he probably had in mind. He usually looks at the state as a source of beliefs about how we should act: by means of laws and other directives it tells us supposed truths about what we ought to do. A question to which he returns several times is: Why do we ever believe that these supposed truths *are* true? He identifies two sources of this faith in the state. One source is tradition or custom (*Herkommen*). "Where, however, law is no longer custom, as with us, it can only be *commanded*, it can only be force; we, all of us, no longer have a traditional sense of justice, thus we must submit to *arbitrary laws*" (MAM 459). Here he seems to be saying that if law is not identical to custom, it must be perceived as something imposed on us by a being that is distinct from ourselves. Before the separation of law and custom, the question of why we should believe what law tells us cannot arise, because it merely tells us what we all already believe; afterwards, obviously, it can. He mentions one solid source of faith in the state which could conceivably survive this separation. He says that, while the faults of the state will make insightful people skeptical about it, "the uninsightful will suppose it proper to see the finger of God, and to patiently resign oneself to directives from *above* (in which concept the divine and human types of government usually merge)." This attitude, which views the state in terms that are essentially religious, is necessary to the life of the state. In part, this is due to the relationship between religion and custom. "The power which lies in the unity of the perceptions of the people, in the same beliefs and purposes for all, is something which religion protects and puts its seal on" (MAM 472).

There is a much deeper reason, though, why religion is necessary for the state:

> the interests of tutelary government and the interests of religion go hand in hand so that, when the latter begins to die down, the foundations of the state are convulsed. The belief in a divine arrangement of political things, in a mystery in the existence of the state, has its source in religion: if religion atrophies, the state will unavoidably lose its old veil of Isis and cease to inspire respect.
>
> (MAM 472)

If people can see things from a religious point of view, if they are capable of seeing some part of reality as sacred, then they can believe that the sort of authority which the state must claim to be can exist; they can even believe in the rightness of despotic laws if they see them as coming from an agent with the divine ability to make a directive right merely by issuing it. To the extent that they cannot see the world from a religious point of view they cannot believe such things.

For Nietzsche, the weakening of religion – a process which he believes has now been going on for several centuries – produces for the state a crisis of legitimacy which cannot ultimately be decided in its favor. The ultimate outcome will be the one he predicts in the ironically Hegelian passage I quoted early on: the death of the state. Until then, it is obvious that the state will defend itself against the unavoidably fatal outcome. Nietzsche never explicitly attempts to catalogue the various ruses that the state can use to this end, but all of the characteristics of the politics of his day to which he objected so loudly are obvious examples: the building of nationalistic empires, the various other methods of providing the people with reasons to feel national pride, identifying the state with morally attractive causes, idolizing ordinary politicians as great men. He does explicitly mention one method which he believes the state will resort to eventually, the most desperate method and the worst:

> Socialism is the fantastic younger brother of nearly decrepit despotism, from which it intends to inherit . . . and since it cannot even count any longer on the old religious piety toward the state, but must on the contrary work involuntarily and incessantly for its elimination – because it works for the elimination of all existing *states* – it can only hope to exist for short periods of time, here and there, by means of the most extraordinary terrorism.

(MAM 473)

The means by which the modern state defends itself are, among other things, highly effective methods for attracting the attention of their subjects and thus displacing other objects from their minds (see MAM 481). In fact, all states are very effective at distracting us from the objects that interest Nietzsche most. The social processes which he believes are usually the real source of beliefs about how we should act – the sorts of processes which he describes in the first two essays of *On the Genealogy of Morals* – are generally extremely difficult to discover even with careful scrutiny. They are not the product of any particular, specialized institution. The state, however, is an institution that does appear to specialize in fabricating truths about what we should do, and it is highly visible and audible. Life presents us with an optical illusion that invites us to look in the wrong place for the source of our values. The modern state simply makes this natural situation worse than it would naturally be.

Why does Nietzsche view this phenomenon with such alarm? In general, when anything political excites his animus, it is usually because of its effect on human character. At one point he refers reverently to "the old master Heinrich Schütz" as "one of the most genuine and most German musicians – German in the old sense of the word, no mere *Reichsdeutscher*" (EH III W 1). His many vicious remarks about "the Germans" are not aimed at the entire German *Volk* throughout history, but at their present political system; and he objects to this system because of what it has made of the Germans. It makes greatness of the sort that Schütz represented even more rare than it was.

What alarms him about the phenomenon we are presently considering is likewise its effect on human character. One can understand what this effect is by recalling some familiar characteristics of Nietzsche's point of view, especially as it is represented in *Zarathustra*. Zarathustra preaches the goal of human perfection, which is symbolized by the Overman.[10] To reach this goal it is necessary, as the first step along the way, to know what we are and what it is that makes us the way we are. He tells us that we are, more than anything else, beings that evaluate things: "Only man placed values in things. . . . Therefore he calls himself 'man,' which means: the esteemer." Our own evaluations make us what we are; we are therefore our own creators. Of course, for the most part we have so far only done this as members of a people, and not as individuals. But now it is becoming possible for individuals to frame new values on their own, breaking free of the herd. Zarathustra demands that we do this in such a way that we approach the goal of perfection. The realization that we frame our own values and thus create ourselves is an exciting fact, since it casts us in a heroic role, but it is also frightening, since it means that human life and the values it is based on are in a certain way arbitrary, since they do not come to us from above, "as a voice from heaven" (Z I 15). Thus, we have good reason to evade this realization.

The primary evil of the state, for Zarathustra and for Nietzsche, is the fact that it provides us with a very attractive opportunity to commit this fatal evasion. It enables us to attribute the supreme power, which really belongs to us, to an entity that appears to be above us and consequently seems to be less arbitrary than we are. To the extent that we make use of this opportunity, the state becomes a source of self-alienation, of estrangement from our true nature. In Nietzsche's view the concept of God is a source of the very same sort of self-alienation, and this is surely a large part of the reason why he insists so strongly on the analogy between the state and God: in the drama of human development, they play precisely the same growth-retarding role. And for a philosopher for whom life and growth are the same thing, this means that both are sources of death. Only where the state ends (and only when God dies) does the way to perfection become visible to us.

By now it is obvious enough, I hope, why Nietzsche thought culture and the state are antagonistic and why his sympathies were overwhelmingly on the side of culture. His conception of culture is connected more or less by definition with the notion of development toward the ideal, in that he conceives of culture as that which fosters this sort of development. He has a very definite idea of what sort of awareness must be promoted in order for this mission of culture to be achieved. On the basis of an analysis of the sort of consciousness into which those who live in states are liable to fall – on the basis of what might be called his phenomenology of citizenship – he believes that states tend by nature to interfere with the development of this sort of awareness. The state is thus antagonistic toward culture and, for all the same reasons, inferior to it.

This critique of the state is quite different from the classical liberal critique and many anarchist ones as well, in that it makes no appeal to human rights or to the idea that the use of force is a bad thing. There is also a more profound difference, one which in fact distinguishes Nietzsche's political views from all standard political ideologies. All such ideologies can be understood as answers to two questions: "How much power ought to be given to the state?" and "What ought to be done with the power that the state has?" Nietzsche's views do not supply us, to any great extent, with answers to either of these questions. For the most part, he does not object to any state because of what it does or how much, but because of how much space states in general tend to occupy in our minds; they receive too much of our energy and attention (see MAM 481 and M 179). His concerns are obviously incompatible with thinking that the state ought to have large amounts of power, but they do not otherwise clearly imply anything about what state policy ought to be.

A good part of the reason why Nietzsche's critique of the state does not have very strong implications of this sort lies in the fact that the principles that he is using are entirely teleological: he is only concerned with a certain goal which the state tends to make more difficult to attain. Such principles cannot clearly imply that the state ought to be abolished or drastically curtailed because they cannot rule out, by themselves, the possibility that such abolition or curtailment would make the goal even more difficult to attain than the state does. If his critique were based on principles which are in some way deontological – for instance, principles which assert rights to life, liberty, and property, a right to liberty of thought and discussion, the wrongness of aggressive force, the wrongness of inequality, or the necessity of autonomy – the matter would be different; then his principles would imply, immediately, that whatever state activities run afoul of these principles ought to be stopped.

He does make one statement which does seem, at first sight, to have strong implications of this kind: when he declares that his "war cry" is "as little state as possible" (MAM 473; see also M 179), he could very easily be taken to mean that the scope of the state ought to be reduced to nothing or next to nothing. This, however, is not what he means. Though he believes that the state will inevitably decay, he insists that "to *work* for the dissemination and realization of this conception is surely something else"; it would not be advisable "to lay one's hand on the plough just now" because "no one can yet show us the seeds that are afterwards to be spread on the torn earth" (MAM 472). The evil of the state is that it prevents us from doing the work which would replace it as a source of values; that work not being done, the destruction of the state would do us less than no good. The point is to turn our backs on issues of state policy altogether and take up the neglected task. In this quite literal sense of the word, Nietzsche is "anti-political."

THE REIGN OF THE PHILOSOPHER–TYRANTS

Some scholars have claimed that what Nietzsche condemns in "On the New Idol" is not the state as such but only "the ossified bureaucratized state" of the past century or so,[11] or only "the nationalistic state."[12] The reasons which lie behind such interpretations apparently have nothing to do with the text of "On the New Idol" itself: the many vicious remarks he makes about the state there are all utterly categorical. The reasons seem to arise, rather, from the need to make what he says there consistent with certain things he wrote not long afterward. At least at first glance, these later remarks do provide strong reason for reading the anti-political tone out of *Zarathustra* because, in them, Nietzsche seems to be inventing and advocating his own form of totalitarianism.

A reader who goes directly from *Zarathustra* to section 203 of *Beyond Good and Evil*, for instance, is likely to be startled by what he or she sees. There, Nietzsche asks "Where, then, must *we* reach with our hopes?" and replies: "Toward *new philosophers* . . . toward men of the future who in the present tie the knot and constraint that forces the will of millennia upon *new* tracks." He adds that this man of the future must put an end to "the monstrous fortuity that has so far had its way and play regarding the future of man" by seizing control of the future: he must "teach man the future of man as his will, as dependent on a human will." A few pages later he adds: "The time for petty politics is over: the very next century will bring the fight for the dominion of the earth – the *compulsion* to large-scale politics" (JGB 208). He seems to be imagining and hoping for a degree and kind of state power that the world did not know until the twentieth century.

Certainly, an author who is as anti-political as Nietzsche appears to be in "On the New Idol" could not have hoped for such things. In order to avoid concluding that he changed his mind with bizarre abruptness – the writing of *Beyond Good and Evil* came a mere three years after that of "On the New Idol" – we must interpret away the apparent meanings of *some* of the things he says. The way in which this is probably most often done is to suppose that when he says "state" in *Zarathustra* he does not mean quite what we usually mean by the word. This way of doing it is made rather unattractive by the fact that "On the New Idol" appears, in the context of his earlier writings, to be merely a summary and completion of many clearly anti-political remarks which are scattered throughout them. There is, though, an alternative way to accomplish the needed interpretive task: it is, so to speak, to suppose that when he says "politics" in "large-scale politics" he does not mean what we ordinarily mean by the word.

In a note written during the time of *Beyond Good and Evil*, he calls for the creation of "a master race, the future 'masters of the earth' . . . philosophical men of power and artist–tyrants" who will "employ democratic Europe as their most pliant and supple instrument for getting hold of the destinies of the earth." He concludes the note with: "Enough: the time is coming when one will learn politics all over again" (WM 960). The last statement – *die Zeit kommt, wo man über Politik umlernen wird* – is ambiguous. It could mean "time is come for us to transform all our view about politics":[13] that is, we must change our opinions about what should be done about the process which we generally call politics (the control of human beings by means of the state). On the other hand, it may mean that we must change the very meaning that "politics" has for us.[14] We can imagine circumstances which would provide us with good reason to change the meaning of "politics." For instance, we might become interested in certain activities which, because they are ways of controlling human beings, resemble what we usually call politics, except that they do not involve the state. If we believe that they are very important and powerful sources of order, we can express their importance and power by expanding our concept of the political to include them, in addition to the activities of the state. If these forms of control extend beyond national boundaries (which are the present limits of most of the activities of the state) and if they accomplish ends which are greater than anything within the reach of the state, we may want to distinguish them from state politics by calling them "large-scale" or "great" (*grosse*) politics. I believe that this is the sort of conceptual and linguistic change that Nietzsche is attempting to legislate here.

In another note from the same period he identifies the principal instrument to be used by the artist–tyrant: "Law-giving moralities are the principal means of fashioning man according to the pleasure of a creative and profound will, provided that such an artist's will . . . can . . . prevail through long periods of time, in the form of laws, religions, and customs" (WM 957). Apparently, the politics practiced by this tyrant is not the work of a head of state at all, but of an individual with a powerful influence over all social institutions, the state merely being among them. This leaves open a very important question: to what extent do the methods which are distinctive of the state play a role in the means by which the philosophical man of power molds the character of future generations? Even though he will not be a head of state, it is still conceivable that those who do directly control the state will implement his ideas by imposing them on democratic Europe by brute force. How would he mold human character?

In yet another note from the same period he gives a perfectly explicit answer to this last question. There he tells us that a philosopher can only "draw up to his lonely height a long chain of generations" if he possesses "the uncanny privileges of the great educator":

> An educator never says what he himself thinks, but always only what he thinks of a thing in relation to the requirements of those he educates. He must not be detected in this dissimulation; it is part of his mastery that one believes in his honesty. He must be capable of every means of discipline: some he can drive toward the heights only with the whips of scorn; others, who are sluggish, irresolute, cowardly, vain perhaps only with exaggerated praise. Such an educator is beyond good and evil; but no one must know it.
>
> (WM 980)

As the last sentence indicates, Nietzsche expects this idea to be shocking, but if it is shocking it is not because it offends principles which we would normally think of as political, since the methods he is advocating are not those which are distinctive of the state at all. Rather, the principle it offends is the traditional view of the role of the philosopher, as one who speaks only with a view to expressing the truth. The new philosopher would use the same sort of language as the traditional philosopher, he would speak as if to tell us the objective values of things, but in fact he would only speak with a view to altering the future of human life. He does not use the methods of the state for the ends of philosophy, he uses philosophical means – ideas and language – for ends that are truly political, political in the great sense. The reign of these philosopher–tyrants would realize fully and more or less literally one of the most Nietzschean of Nietzsche's ideas: "Thoughts that come on doves' feet control the world" (Z II 22).

4

CHAOS AND ORDER

CONTROL

There is something in Nietzsche's description of the methods of the new tyrants, with which I just ended Chapter 4, that might strike one as surprising. One thinks of tyrants as using weapons much less ethereal than the "whips of scorn" used by Nietzsche's tyrants. These rulers are apparently not tyrannical in the modern sense of using brutal methods, but in the Greek sense of lacking a legitimate right to rule. In the context in which the concept of tyranny originally had its home, true monarchs were thought of as ones who could base their right to rule on a criterion of value that was external to their own thoughts and desires: namely, their royal birth. A tyrant was one who lacked this sort of legitimacy. In an extended sense, Plato's philosopher–kings were true monarchs, since they could claim that they ruled by right of objective values which they discovered and did not invent. Nietzsche's philosophers develop their "law-giving moralities" as instruments for the creation of a new and higher type of human being. They do not discover these values, they create them for this purpose. Thus these values cannot provide them with the legitimacy that Plato's philosophers gained from the morality to which he appealed. Accordingly, Nietzsche's philosophers are not philosopher–kings, but philosopher–tyrants.

The relationship between Nietzsche and Plato brings with it another and deeper surprise. Despite the obvious differences between these two philosophers, both envision a world ruled by philosophers. In the context of Nietzsche's anti-state bias, the order which is imposed by philosophers is to be contrasted with the order which is imposed by the state. He looks forward to a world in which life is ordered fundamentally by ideas and speech rather than prisons and guns. This vision of how the future ought to be is surprising in an author who wished his readers to see him as a hard-headed and cold-hearted realist. It has a distinctly idealistic and utopian character. This obviously presents something of a problem for anyone who wants to understand Nietzsche's social and political views. One needs to explain why precisely this vision of the future would be his.

In this chapter, I will suggest that the explanation is to be found in two attitudes which are tangled up with a good deal of what he thinks and feels. One is the anti-state animus that I have already described. The other is his deeply ingrained notion that someone – or some group of people – really ought to be in control, somehow, of human life in general. People who believe that someone should be in charge usually look to the state as the source of control. It is because of this that so many of the things Nietzsche said have a totalitarian sound to them, which in turn explains why the totalitarian interpretation of his political views continues to have adherents, despite his many anti-political pronouncements. Of course, he could not turn to the state as the source of control, and had to find an alternative. He chose to look instead to new philosophers who would impose their grand design on the natural course of events.

NATURE AND CHAOS

Nietzsche has a deep suspicion toward fortuity (*Zufälligkeit*) in human affairs, toward any aspect of human life which does not occur by design. This suspicion is a persistent theme throughout his writings. His expression of horror, in *Beyond God and Evil*, at "the monstrous fortuity which has so far had its way and play regarding the future of man" (JGB 203) is anticipated already in *Schopenhauer as Educator*, when he expresses his hope that "we will be the true steersmen of our lives and not concede that our existence resembles a thoughtless fortuity" (U III 1).

It is not easy to say exactly why he has this attitude. The fact that his expressions of it were frequent, intense, and generally unexplained inevitably gives the impression that it was, as he would say, "instinctive" – that is, not based on reasons at all. It is clear enough, though, that it is related, logically, to at least one other idea which is very deeply a part of the way he sees things. This is the idea that chaos, or mere disorder, is both a great evil and a permanent possibility for human life. Midway in his career he makes the following important statement:

> The greatest danger that always hovered over humanity and still hovers over it is the eruption of madness – which means the eruption of arbitrariness in feeling, seeing, and hearing, the enjoyment of the mind's lack of discipline, the joy in human unreason.

He adds that the opposite of madness, so defined, is not "truth and certainty" but "the universal binding force of a faith." Consequently, the "greatest labor" of the human race "so far has been to reach agreement about very many things and submit to a *law of agreement* – regardless of whether these things are true or false" (FW 76). The prospect of chaos is either such a great evil or such a strong likelihood – or both – that even an order which is based on illusion is preferable to it.

Nietzsche's suspicion toward *Zufälligkeit* is also locally related to another idea which is very important to him. It is one that many of his readers probably do not realize he held at all, though it is undeniable that he did. This is his notion that nature is not by any means a norm to be trusted and followed, that it should in fact have something like the opposite significance for us. There are times when this idea, too, seems to be merely "instinctive" with him. At any rate, it is difficult to doubt that he is expressing an intense personal experience when he makes remarks like this one:

> To hang on to life madly and blindly, with no higher aim than to hang on to it; not to know that or why one is being so heavily punished but, with the stupidity of a fearful desire, to thirst after precisely this punishment as though after happiness – that is what it means to be an animal; and if all nature presses towards man, it thereby intimates that man is necessary for the redemption of nature from the curse of the life of the animal.

> (U III 5)

Perhaps Nietzsche's idea that nature should be redeemed rather than followed as a guide has some deep unconscious source; but it is certainly also logically connected with other ideas which he consciously holds, most obviously with the ideas of fortuity, chaos, and control. In one of his critical remarks about nature, he tells us: "Nature, estimated artistically, is no model. It exaggerates, it distorts, it leaves gaps. Nature is *chance* [*Zufall*]'' (G IX 7). He also tells us that "every morality is, as opposed to *laisser aller*, a bit of tyranny against 'nature'" and adds that "what is essential 'in heaven and earth' seems to be, to say it once more, that there should be *obedience* over a long period of time and in a *single* direction" (JGB 188; see also G IX 41). Apparently, nature, in the sense in which it is no model, is the course which events take when they are not interfered with. In this sense, it is the *same thing* as thoughtless fortuity or "letting go" (*laisser aller*).

To understand his views on these matters, we must ask why Nietzsche believes that fortuity (or chance or "letting go") is such a bad thing. In case the alternative way of putting the question is helpful, we should also probably be prepared to ask why he thought that nature, in the relevant sense, is such a bad thing. The remarks I have just quoted only faintly suggest an answer to either question.

PREVENTING CHAOS

The remarks I quoted in the previous section do suggest one reason why Nietzsche has these attitudes. He thinks, at least in certain moods that were very characteristic of him, that "letting go" leads immediately to chaos of some sort or other. He persistently maintains that, as he says in *Twilight of the Idols*, all order in human life depends on the existence of institutions, that to have preferences which are incompatible with the existence of institutions is to "prefer what disintegrates, what hastens the end." In the same passage, he describes the preferences and intentions which are required by institutions:

> In order that there may be institutions, there must be a kind of will, instinct, or imperative, which is anti-liberal to the point of malice: the will to tradition, to authority, to responsibility for centuries to come, to the solidarity of chains of generations, forward and backward *ad infinitum*.
>
> (G IX 39)

What he means by this is illuminated – at least in part – by the example he goes on to give: the institution of marriage. He claims that marriage was being undermined in his own time by the growing insistence that mates be selected by the marriage partners themselves on the basis of love, rather than being selected by the families involved for other reasons. "Never, absolutely never, can

an institution be founded on an idiosyncrasy.'' Marriage can, on
the other hand, be founded on "the drive to dominate, . . . which
needs children and heirs to hold fast . . . to an attained measure
of power, influence, and wealth, in order to prepare for long-range
tasks.'' Marriage can also be founded on "the sex drive'',
(considered as a desire to procreate), and on "the property drive
(wife and child as property)'' (G IX 39).

Nietzsche seems to be thinking here of the sort of marriage in
which one deliberately founds a family of one's own, where the
family is conceived as a succession of generations, like a dynasty.[1]
Each of these drives leads one to have many different preferences
and intentions. But in each case, if the drive is to be satisfied in
the long run the intentions involved must include ones which have
as their object the continuing existence of the institution one is
using. To do something like found a dynasty, one must intend that
marriage will exist for some time to come. Nothing like this is true
of love, which focuses on a single individual and is "merely
momentary'' (G IX 39). Marriage can only exist as an institution
if things are done to preserve it, and only if they are *intended* to do
so. If something exists because of human actions that are intended
to cause or maintain its existence, it exists by design and not
fortuitously. In general, institutions can only exist if many things
are done *in order to* preserve them. Consequently, they exist by
design and not fortuitously. This means that a world in which
people merely attend to their private concerns, relating to other
people one at a time as individuals, with no attempt to exercise
control over society as a whole now and in the future, would be a
world in which there are no institutions at all. It would also be a
world in which there is no order at all, a chaos.

At this point we may draw a further conclusion if we ask whether
everyone should be equally in control, or whether there is an elite
who are more qualified to have "responsibility for centuries to
come'' than others are. Nietzsche would say that the answer to this
question is obvious.

THE CASE AGAINST NATURE

Is this argument a good one? Rather than try to answer this question now, I will pass on, for a while, to another argument Nietzsche
gives for the same conclusion. As far as I know, it is the only other
argument he gives for the idea that there is something inherently

dangerous about letting nature take its course. Part of the interest of this other argument lies in the fact that it has a strong bearing on the question of the merits of the argument I have just discussed. At a crucial point, the two arguments are inconsistent and, at least at this point, the other argument seems to me to be obviously the more plausible of the two. Thus it indicates a reason why the argument in the *Twilight* is not a good argument. This is particularly interesting because, surprisingly, it is to be found much earlier in Nietzsche's writings.

The earlier argument occurs in *Schopenhauer as Educator*, in the context of an urgent plea for the "purpose of culture," which is "to demand the formation of true *human beings*, and nothing besides" (U III 6). In this essay, he recognizes two sources from which modern Europe draws its ethical ideals: Christianity and "the moral systems of antiquity." Long ago, he says, Christian supernaturalism taught us to regard the naturalism of the ancients with "antipathy and disgust." Eventually, when Christian ideals "proved unattainable" we were unable to rely on them with much confidence, either. Today we live in an "oscillation between Christianity and antiquity." In this confused state of mind, we have so far been unable to invent new ideas with the power that these older ones once had: "what we are in fact doing is consuming the moral capital we have inherited from our forefathers, which we are incapable of increasing but know only how to squander" (U III 2).

The present situation is an emergency: something must be done about it. He assumes throughout this discussion that what is needed, in general, is that philosophers effectively educate people to lead better lives. At one point, he adds that, more specifically, we must find out how we can increase the effect that the philosopher has: "What would have to be devised to make it more probable that he would produce some effect on his contemporaries? And what obstacles would have to be removed so that above all his example should again educate philosophers?" Having asked these questions, which seem lucid enough, he immediately begins, rather mysteriously, an extended attack on "nature." He says that, although the fact that "nature has wanted to make existence . . . significant to man through the production of the philosopher and the artist is, given nature's own desire for redemption, certain," it is also certain that "the means it employs seem to be only probing experiments and ideas it has chanced upon (*zufällige Einfälle*)." "Nature launches the philosopher into humanity like an arrow; it

47

does not take aim, but it hopes that somewhere the arrow will stick fast. Thus she errs countless times and is dismayed." For this reason it "often seems that the artist and in particular the philosopher is *fortuitous* in his age" (U III 7).

It is not easy to know what to make of this at first. He speaks of nature as having desires, and as desiring its own redemption. But nature satisfies its desires in bumbling ways. It has targets, but it does not "take aim" at them. What, exactly, does this mean? And why does he say these things at this point in the *Meditation*?

The answer is probably to be found earlier in the same essay, where he says, obviously very disturbed, "how extraordinarily sparse and rare" knowledge of the purpose of culture is. Enormous effort is spent on cultural activity and very few people have any notion that the point of the activity is to produce more perfect human beings. He then imagines an interlocutor raising an objection to the general drift of his comments:

> Does nature attain its goal even when the majority misunderstand the objective of their endeavors? He who has accustomed himself to thinking highly of the unconscious purposefulness of nature will perhaps experience no difficulty in replying: "Yes, that is how it is! Men may reflect and argue about their ultimate goal as much as they like, in the obscure impulse in the depths of them they are well aware of the rightful path."
>
> (U III 6)

Both Nietzsche and his interlocutor are expressing a certain conception of what nature is. Though it is not very clearly expressed by either of them, the conception itself is not an unreasonable one. Each natural object tends, though imperfectly, to behave in the same way as other members of its species. For instance, if they are alive, members of the same species tend to grow in the same way, to develop into a state of maturity that has the same characteristics throughout the species. It is possible, though misleading, to call the order to which natural beings tend their "purpose." But to avoid being utterly misleading, one must specify that this tendency is not present because there is a conscious intention to bring its end state about. Nature is a tendency toward order that is not guided by consciousness, and in living things it is a tendency on the part of members of a species to develop into a final, mature state. This is the conception of nature on which Nietzsche and his interlocutor agree. Early on in the *Meditation* Nietzsche tells his reader: "your true nature lies, not concealed deep within you, but immeasurably high above you, or at least above that which you usually take yourself to be" (U III 1). What he calls one's "true nature" here is the end state toward which one's nature stupidly tends. To arrive there by conscious design would be to redeem nature.

By now, it is perhaps obvious in what way this line of reasoning is inconsistent with the one I attributed to Nietzsche in the preceding section of this chapter. That argument had among its conclusions the idea that a world in which no attempt was made to control it would be a world with no order at all. Here, he is implicitly denying this. He conceives of nature precisely as a certain order which arises without attempts to control the course of events. This suggests that something might be wrong with one of the premises of the other argument: namely, the assumption that institutions cannot exist unless people consciously try to maintain them. In the Schopenhauer *Meditation* he is saying that individuals have tendencies to develop in certain ways and that they have these tendencies as individuals, not as a result of the social systems in which they live. He is also saying that *to some extent* these tendencies support the pursuit of culture. There might also be specific institutions which are undergirded by tendencies which individuals have and consequently do not need our vigilant support. This could be true of certain forms of the institution of marriage. It could also provide arguments in favor of those institutions of which it is true. One could argue, for instance, that if certain changes were made in the institution of marriage it would run up against human nature less often than it now does, thus becoming a more stable institution and, in that respect, a better one.

This way of thinking poses a threat to the position Nietzsche ultimately wants to take. To the extent that there are sources of order in human life which are independent of conscious human control, the need for an elite of philosophical geniuses seems to be undermined. Such a supposition would fatally injure the case he makes for such an elite insofar as that case rests on the idea that "letting go" leads immediately to pure chaos. What is particularly threatening about this way of thinking is the fact that it is obviously true that order can arise spontaneously, in the absence of deliberate interference.[2] One way (among others, perhaps) in which Nietzsche could defend himself against this threat would be to change the issue at stake; instead of claiming that the regime of nature is a state of mere chaos, he could raise doubts about the quality and the quantity of the order that arises naturally. This is the strategy that he adopts against the interlocutor in the *Meditation*. He admits that nature can produce order of a sort and even admits that this order can be benign. But he also claims that, when it does produce a desirable sort of order, it does so in a highly inefficient and unreliable way. As we have already seen, he thinks it is very bad at producing philosophers and putting them to best use. Nature is not good at producing human greatness.

Beyond that, he also claims that natural order is often not desirable at all. Shortly after his mysterious attack on nature, he launches an even longer attack on state-supported universities. His attack is based on the prediction that massive infusions of tax money would enable "a number of men to *live* from their philosophy by making it a means of livelihood." This would eventually attract all philosophers into the universities, so that independent philosophers like Schopenhauer would no longer exist. The philosopher who would flourish in the new system would be, like Kant, "cautious, subservient and, in his attitude toward the state, without greatness." Such philosophers might have radically critical attitudes toward everything else, but not toward the state: upon the state itself "a *noli me tangere* is inscribed" (U III 8). As he describes it, the eventual engulfment of philosophy by the state does not take place as a result of some conscious intention to bring it off, it is the result of letting nature take its course in a system of more or less blind social and political forces. Somewhat paradoxically, the most powerful instrument of control – the state – grows in power either because no one possesses or no one will use the power required to stop it. The resulting situation is quite "natural," in the sense in which Nietzsche uses that word here. It is also, in Nietzsche's view, disastrously bad.

We are now in a position to understand why the attack on nature occurs where it does, immediately after the two questions he asks about what must be done. The questions, as you may recall, concerned what must be devised in order to increase the likelihood that philosophers will have the proper effects on their contemporaries, and what obstacles must be removed in order to make these effects possible. The diatribe against nature serves to emphasize and justify these questions by indicating what they are not about. They do not ask which unconscious tendencies of human nature support philosophers in their task, or which complexes of blind social forces can help them to have the effects they should have. They concern conscious, personal relations between individuals, as individuals. The problem is how certain individuals can exercise power, by cultural means, over other individuals. In this context, the social institutions which have accumulated fortuitously over the centuries are important mainly as obstacles. Nietzsche's only recommendation for institutional reform in the Schopenhauer *Meditation* is that university philosophy departments be abolished (U III 8). If there are any institutions which are positively useful to the philosophers they will apparently be ones which the new philosophers have deliberately designed.

When he eventually tells us what can be done to make it more likely that people will receive the message of philosophy with the greatest benefit, he says a good many things but, as he points out, they can be summarized easily. The recipient must be in a certain set of circumstances. These are: "free manliness of character, early knowledge of mankind, no scholarly education, no narrow patriotism, no necessity for bread-winning, no ties with the state – in short, freedom and again freedom." These are, quite generally, "the conditions under which philosophical genius can at any rate come into existence in our time despite the forces working against it" (U III 8).

He represents these conditions as elements of freedom, and it is not surprising, in light of what we have seen, that the freedom involved is freedom of a particular sort. Each of the elements is an instance of freedom in the sense that each gives one a measure of independence from the world around one. Each one enables the individual to stand apart from the mountains of detritus which the blind forces of social evolution have piled up. This is true of knowledge and "manliness of character," and more obviously true of the other cases. Freedom, considered as independence, is valuable because it is a condition of genuine social progress. This, in turn, is because the conception of social progress Nietzsche is employing is essentially a heroic one: genuine advances, to the extent that they do not occur fortuitously, are literally the doing of great individuals, and they are done intentionally.

ASSESSING NIETZSCHE'S CONCEPTION OF ORDER

In the argument in the Schopenhauer *Meditation* Nietzsche is sorting and grading the causes of order. On the one hand, there is the order that arises naturally; on the other hand, there is the order that exists by design. The latter includes especially the order that is imposed by philosophers. The sort of order that nature produces is either malevolent or, when it is benevolent, so imperfect that the good it does is nearly accidental. At best, what it produces is a degraded sort of order, or a diluted kind of chaos. Nature is not something which we should be glad to entrust with the great task of improving the human race. Since the other sources of order-by-design (such as the church and the state) can be ruled out for one reason or another, we are left with the option of putting all our trust in Nietzsche's philosophers.

What should we think of this? As I have suggested, this argument is, at least, more forceful at one point than the one I found in *Twilight of the Idols*. It does not require us to believe that pure chaos follows whenever people let go of their control of the course of events. Still, this argument is a fallacy as it stands. There is a missing premise. From the fact – if it is a fact – that one principle of order is inadequate it does not follow that we should place all our trust in some other principle. One must also assume, at least, that the other one – the activity of Nietzsche's philosophers – *is* a reliable source of the right sort of order, so much more reliable than the sources of natural order that they have no significant contribution to make.

Whether the missing premise is true or not, it is at any rate not obviously true. Some of us have reason to doubt it on the basis of experience. Everyone who has tried to teach important ideas to others knows that it is an extraordinarily weak and loose method for controlling the behavior of one's audience. Further, a little reflection can convince one that Nietzsche may face a problem which is often encountered when one attempts to impose an order on human life which is not naturally there. Such attempts frequently require knowledge which one does not and perhaps cannot have. Suppose, for instance, that I wish to pursue the goal Nietzsche envisions in the remarks in *Twilight of the Idols* I quoted earlier: namely, to make the institution of marriage more secure than it would be without my efforts. If I am not married already, what might I do to pursue this goal? The most obvious answer is that I should get married, and thus send others a message to the effect that marriage is a worthwhile institution, deserving of our support. But if I am then unhappy in my marriage – and this is probably made more likely if I marry for the reason that I am now envisioning – I may well end up sending the sort of message which is the opposite of the type I want to send. On the other hand, if I decide on these grounds not to get married, and this turns out to be the right decision as far as my private well-being is concerned, I may also give others the very impression I wish to avoid. If I am already married and am tempted to get divorced, the same dilemma confronts me. Here, as often happens, I do not know enough about the eventual social effects of my actions to produce a particular effect intentionally.[3] Indeed, as this example suggests, there may be types of social order that are best supported by the individual who, as Nietzsche says scornfully, "lives for the day, . . . lives very irresponsibly" (G IX 39) – or, to put it more neutrally, by individuals who do not attempt to create social order at all, but only attend to their private concerns.

In *Schopenhauer as Educator*, and, indeed, in the relevant passages I discussed in the last chapter, Nietzsche is very inexplicit about the nature of the ideals that his philosophers are to provide for the rest of us. This obviously makes it very difficult to say, at this point in my argument, whether they would be able to do what he asks them to do. I will have to set this issue aside until Chapter 7, when I will discuss more fully his conception of the ideal. Before I do that, though, I can still make a certain amount of progress in assessing the merits of the missing premise in the argument of the Schopenhauer *Meditation*. This assumption is a claim about the relative merits of natural order and a certain sort of order by design. It would certainly help, in deciding whether we should accept Nietzsche's assumption, if we could decide whether he was too quick in dismissing the contribution which natural order can make. I will spend most of the rest of this chapter trying to settle this issue. First, though, I will pause to place the problem in a wider context.

THE LIBERAL CONCEPTION OF ORDER

Most of us have reason to at least hope that something, somewhere, is wrong with what I have made Nietzsche say in this chapter so far. The reason I have in mind, however, is perhaps not easy to see.

We have seen him say something which is at first surprising, coming as it does from someone who claims that his ideas are "anti-liberal to the point of malice": he has made a very energetic case for freedom. He has said that freedom is valuable in that it is an absolute requisite for genuine advances in human development, and that this is true because it must be possessed by those who are to develop "philosophical genius." It is important to realize that this belief in the value of freedom is a theme that persists throughout his writings. Later on, he praises Brutus on the ground that the motive that led him to kill Caesar represented "the most awesome quintessence of a lofty morality." He describes this morality as a love of "independence of soul," a love of "freedom as the freedom of great souls" (FW 98).

Nietzsche's admiration for Caesar is apt to mislead us about the nature of his politics unless we remember that he admired his assassin more, and precisely for assassinating him. But we will be misled in another direction if we fail to notice the nature of his admiration for the hero of republicanism. His admiration depends on his belief in freedom as the freedom of *certain* people. Freedom is valuable, for him, because it is an indispensable good for people who are ready to undergo certain radical characterological transformations, and this is the only ground for the value of freedom which he ever acknowledges. As we will see (Chapters 6, p. 99; 7, pp. 138–42) he denies that most people can have either the desire or the opportunity to undertake this heroic task. He does not think that most people should be "free," in any interesting sense of that word. Thus, he lives up to his promise to deliver ideas that are decidedly not liberal. But most of us are probably liberal enough to think that there is some reason why everyone should be free. So we should, as I have said, want to depart at some point from the reasoning which led him to think quite differently on this subject.

Perhaps it will be illuminating to consider at what point the liberal tradition itself deviates from Nietzsche's way of thinking. One crucial difference lies in the way one conceives of what Nietzsche calls "nature." Consider, for instance, Burckhardt's definition of culture as "the sum of all that has *spontaneously* arisen for the advancement of material life and as an expression of spiritual and moral life." Culture is spontaneous social order, an order that characterizes the behavior of communities and is not intentionally imposed on them by anyone. This makes it an instance of "nature."

But it is obviously understood as a sort of order which is characteristically benign and desirable. This already marks a difference between the liberal Burckhardt and Nietzsche. But there is a deeper difference that underlies it. Burckhardt regards this particular sort of order as characteristically desirable because it arises in a free marketplace of ideas. This means that the order involved, though not intentionally brought about by anyone, arises from the interaction of a group of people. It is the product of a system and not an individual. Burckhardt believes that, within systems in which the elements are the behavior of different individuals, an order can arise which was not intentionally imposed on it by anyone; and that, at least for certain systems, this order tends to be a desirable one. One might call this belief "the liberal conception of social order."

On the other hand, when Nietzsche thinks of natural order as something which is to some extent desirable, he thinks of it as a product of certain tendencies which individuals have as individuals, apart from the social systems in which they live. Given that, it is not surprising that Nietzsche had little faith in the power of nature to achieve something good. What he had in mind, to the extent that he thought it had such power at all, was a certain vague tendency toward the good that exists in the individual psyche prior to its contact with ideas, institutions, or other people – something like a natural unconscious desire. This is not a force for the good that we would care to rely on very much at all; if anything, he is too generous toward it. But if we think of natural order as emerging from social systems, a different picture begins to emerge.

Consider, for instance, some systems that have been dear to the hearts of liberals. Perhaps the most obvious example is the competitive market, as many economists have explained it. According to long-familiar theories it is a system in which individuals who are attending only to their private concerns hit upon broad social effects which they need not want, and certainly lack the knowledge, to bring about intentionally; the system finds the price at which the consumers are willing buy up the available goods and services, and it allocates scarce resources to their most highly valued uses. To take another obvious example: the adversary system in courts of law pits lawyers against each other in their efforts to argue their own side of a case. They are not trying to be fair and balanced, and they are not supposed to; they each are merely supposed to support one side by all the honest means available. Of course, this means that they are not really aiming at justice, which would require precisely that they try to be fair and balanced. But a familiar liberal theory maintains that justice, with its fairness and balance, is what tends to emerge from their behavior. It arises from a system in which it is not part of the aim of the primary active participants. Again, according to certain theories, the system of periodic political elections works in something like the same way. It opposes factions and parties to one another and is said to achieve results which are more fair and reasonable in the long run than would be achieved if any one faction (even the one with the best intentions) were left to its own designs.

Finally, consider an example which is closer to the issues with which Nietzsche is concerned: Ralph Waldo Emerson's defense of what might be called pluralistic communities.[4] Emerson's argument begins with the claim that we are all subject to a certain serious danger which follows from the human inclination to imitate others, and from the even stronger desire to be imitated by others. These drives create a "perpetual tendency to a set mode." "Each man . . . is a tyrant in tendency, because he would impose his idea on others." Fortunately, this dynamic runs up against "Nature, who . . . has set her heart on breaking up all styles and tricks." He states the same idea more concretely and more clearly like this:

> Jesus would absorb the race; but Tom Paine or the coarsest blasphemer helps humanity by resisting this exuberance of power. Hence the immense benefit of party in politics, as it reveals faults of character in a chief, which the intellectual force of the persons, with ordinary opportunity and not hurled into the aphelion by hatred, could not have seen.

In a society in which people are free to adopt and express their own point of view, those who would impose their idea on others become opposed to each other in something like a public debate, and although "no one of them hears much that another says, . . . the audience, who have only to hear and not to speak, judge very wisely and superiorly how wrongheaded and unskillful is each of the debaters to his own affair." Such a community "is morose, and runs to anarchy, but . . . it is indispensable to resist the consolidation of all men into a few men."

In each of these examples, a beneficial effect is said to arise from a social system and not from individuals as individuals. The liberal conception of order does not assume that individuals have a reliable innate conatus toward the ideal. Nor, obviously, does it assume that all systems have such benign tendencies, either. Throughout the nineteenth and the late eighteenth centuries, the liberal program was to abolish various institutional systems – including monarchy, the landed aristocracy, the established church, and franchised business monopolies – on the ground that such systems have precisely the opposite sort of tendency. The liberals wanted to replace them with ones which would bring out what is best in people, whether those people are in themselves good, bad, or indifferent. Their conception of social order enabled them to hope that people would behave well without relying on the natural goodheartedness of the human race and without setting up wise leaders to tell people what to do.

If the liberal conception of order has much to be said for it, then the missing premise in *Schopenhauer as Educator* is not true. To the extent that it is true, there is a reliable alternative to Nietzsche's preferred source of desirable order. What reason might he have had for rejecting the liberal conception? One possible reason has to do with the fact that, at least for the most part, the social goals which liberals have claimed are promoted by their favored sort of order have been radically different in kind from the goals that interest Nietzsche. They have been much more modest and banal. Burckhardt says that what he calls culture promotes "the advancement of material life" and satisfies spiritual needs "in the narrower sense" – a qualification which is meant to distinguish the spiritual ends of culture from the more radical spiritual ends of religion. He is not prepared to promise that culture will replace humans as we know them with radically new and better types of beings. Most of the examples of liberal order I have just discussed promote ends which are even more modest than Burckhardt's, such as producing goods and services at least cost, ensuring that our jails contain only people who have committed some crime, and preventing fanatics from winning too much political power.

Few would claim that markets, courts, and elections breed business people, lawyers, and party leaders who are examples of genuine virtue. It can easily be argued that they do the very opposite. Perhaps they produce their valuable social effects at the sacrifice of individual character.[5] But the development of character is the only thing that Nietzsche is interested in. It looks as though he has good reason for rejecting the liberal conception of order.

This impression is reinforced if we take a second look at

Emerson's account of pluralistic communities. At first glance, it looks more promising from a Nietzschean perspective than the other examples, because it rests on a certain appeal to the importance of character. But on closer inspection we can see that it appeals to a concern for character which is very different from the sort of concern which guides Nietzsche. Emerson is describing a system that prevents something bad from happening – namely, that all human beings become absorbed into one character-type; he is not claiming that it makes any existing type *good* in some positive way. Indeed, given what he says, it may well be that he *should* not make such a claim. What he says, essentially, is that a community should be a sort of debating society in which the claims that individuals make to represent the good life are subjects of dispute. People who participate in public debates are typically driven further apart by the heat of argument. Rather than bringing them together, the debate preserves their differences. If this is how such communities work, we can expect that in them the exemplars of different ethical ideals would, each one of them, represent only part of the good life. In that case, the good would tend to be fragmented, in that probably no one would represent it whole and intact.

Emerson would not mind this result because he is convinced that no one could possibly embody the whole of human perfection anyway. The impression we have that some people do embody the whole of the good is the result of something like an optical illusion:

> All persons exist to society by some shining trait of beauty or
> utility which they have. We borrow the proportions of the
> man from that one fine feature, and finish the portrait
> symmetrically; which is false, for the rest of his body is small
> or deformed.[6]

Emerson can accept the prospect of living in a world in which the most outstanding human beings, like the "representative men" he writes about elsewhere, are excellent in only one way because he thinks it is the only possible world.

Nietzsche agrees that this is the way the actual world is. As a matter of fact, he describes this aspect of our world in words that are strongly reminiscent of Emerson, but in a very different tone of voice:

And when I came out of my solitude and crossed over this bridge for the first time I did not trust my eyes and looked again, and said at last, "An ear! An ear as big as a man!" I looked still more closely – and indeed, underneath the ear something was moving, something pitifully small and wretched and slender. And, no doubt of it, the tremendous ear was attached to a small thin stalk – but this stalk was a human being! . . . But I never believed the people when they spoke of great men; and I maintained my belief that it was an inverse cripple who had too little of everything and too much of one thing.

He apparently does not think that this is the only possible world. At any rate, he clearly does not find it an acceptable one: "Verily, my friends, I walk among men as among the fragments and limbs of men. This is what is terrible for my eyes, that I find man in ruins and scattered as over a battlefield or a butcher-field" (Z II 20). Certainly, he has reason to reject a system that seems to help preserve the incompleteness of the individual as we see it in the world around us.

It seems a fairly safe generalization to say that the liberal conception of order, as we know it so far, does not answer to Nietzsche's needs. As a matter of historical fact, its proponents have used it in such a way that Nietzsche would regard them as having committed themselves to an ethically second-rate sort of world, in which greatness is sacrificed in order to avert one disaster or another. In order to defend the liberal conception in a way that would answer to his purposes, one would have to show that this historical fact is not also a logical necessity. One would have to show that there is a system which arguably would have a tendency to spontaneously produce the sort of excellence he desires. In the next section I would like to suggest that there is such a system. Indeed, we find it in Nietzsche's own works, in one of his earliest writings.

"HOMER'S CONTEST"

In the unpublished fragment, "Homer's Contest," written before the *Untimely Meditations*, Nietzsche sets forth some ideas which bear an unexpected resemblance to the liberal ideas I have just discussed. In the present context, his notion of "contest" (*Wettkampf*) inevitably brings to mind the economic concept of competition (*Wettstreit*), and the things he says about it resemble in interesting ways standard liberal theories of competition.[7] But there are differences as well which, for our purposes, are equally interesting.

Nietzsche's purpose in this fragment is to explain what he takes to be a great achievement of Greek culture. The achievement was the solution to a specific problem, which had to do with a peculiarity of the Greek psyche. He believed that the myths of the Greeks indicate that they were marked by "a trait of cruelty, a tigerish lust to annihilate [*Vernichtungslust*]," which was stronger in them than it is in many other peoples – especially including ourselves. The earliest of their myths indicate that in the pre-Homeric world this *Vernichtungslust* ran unchecked and unsublimated: in such a world "combat is salvation; the cruelty of victory is the pinnacle of life's jubilation." He assumes that the Greeks found such a world horrifying, just as we do. This creates the problem. The problem is not how to tame the urge to annihilate (though taming it turns out to be part of the solution); the problem is how to avoid a certain evaluational attitude which might spring from this horror. Since the *Vernichtungslust* was ubiquitous in Greek life, the most immediately appealing response would probably be the one which the Orphics took: namely, disgust. They responded with "the idea that a life with such an urge at its root was not worth living." The problem is how to avoid this response. The Greek solution was a new evaluation of the facts: they "tolerated the terrible presence of this urge and considered it *justified*" (H). What concerns us here is how this transformation from the pre-Homeric world came about.

Nietzsche finds the key to the authentically Greek view of these matters in a "remarkable" passage in *The Works and Days* of Hesiod in which the poet describes the true nature of Eris, a goddess who personifies conflict. He claims that it is wrong to think that Eris, as such, is evil. There are actually two Erises. One Eris, "who builds up evil war, and slaughter," is indeed bad.[8] The other, however, is good:

> She pushes even the unskillful man to work, for all his laziness. A man looks at his neighbor, who is rich: then he too wants to work; for the rich man presses on with his plowing and planting and the order of his state.
> So the neighbor contends with the neighbor who presses on

toward wealth. Such an Eris is a good friend to mortals. Even the potter resents the potter, and the craftsman resents the craftsman; tramp envies tramp, and singer envies singer.

Nietzsche comments that this Eris is good because "as jealousy, resentment, and envy, [she] spurs men to activity: not to the activity of fights of annihilation but to the activity of fights which are *contests*" (H).

The event which separated the Greek world as we know it from the brutal pre-Homeric world was a complex evaluation of the *Vernichtungslust* – which of course is what Nietzsche takes Eris to represent – together with a revaluation of certain other mental states associated with it. The good Eris is good precisely because, under certain circumstances, it becomes jealousy, resentment, and envy. These in turn are good because of the quality of the activity which – under those same circumstances – they are able to inspire. They elicit something of value even from the unskillful and give reason to hope that even tramps might do something worthwhile. Nietzsche is attributing to the Greeks a view which is an alternative to a certain sort of ethical dualism. The good and bad Erises are not entirely distinct and separate principles of action. The good Eris is the same urge as the bad one. The urge merely assumes a benign form.

The circumstances that enable this to happen were created by a shared belief that the Greeks held, that all of life is a contest. More exactly, "the command of Hellenic popular pedagogy" was the principle that "every talent must unfold itself in fighting." Once accepted, the principle created a social system in which everyone is a contestant in a struggle, not to undo, but to outdo others. "Even the most universal type of instruction, through the drama, was meted out to the people only in the form of a tremendous wrestling among the great musical and dramatic artists." As it is transformed in the context of such an agonistic community, the ultimate object of the *Vernichtungslust* is still, in a literal sense, denial or negation (*Vernichtung*) of some sort. In this context, it takes the form of negating the value of the achievements of others by doing something even better oneself. Thus, in order to seek the same general object that was pursued in the pre-Homeric world, one must also seek excellence of some sort. This is an important part of the reason why outstanding excellence was so widespread in Greek culture. It is also an important component of the reason why the Greeks were able to judge life favorably, not in spite of, but in part because of their belief that Zeus had set a certain potentially terrible force "in the roots of the earth and among men" (H).

As Nietzsche describes it, this entire complex transformation was only possible because of the social situation in which the primordial urge happened to express itself. This point becomes clearer when one considers what, according to him, generally happened in Greek life when the system broke down. Under it, the individual's potentially destructive urge is turned toward constructive forms of expression by the vivid presence of other individuals who have achieved something excellent; one feels oneself in need of proving oneself against them. Thus "the Hellenic notion of the contest . . . demands, as a *protection* against the genius, another genius." In that case, what should we suppose will happen if one achieves pre-eminent greatness of some sort – for instance, unequalled wealth or popularity or military prowess? The contest is only possible if the contestants are of comparable status; a *Wettkampf* is, literally, not just any sort of fight (*Kampf*), but one that is equal or even (*wett*). If one sees no one who is comparable to oneself, then one is no longer challenged by the excellence of others, in which case one no longer has the only reason the system gives for acting in a constructive rather than destructive manner. Then Eris collapses back into its brutal form as if the intervening agonistic culture had never happened. Nietzsche claims that the historical record shows that when a Greek was "removed from the contest by an extraordinarily brilliant deed" the result was "almost without exception a terrifying one" (H).[9]

One can see what Nietzsche is saying here as an explanation of a certain idea which was apparently common among the Greeks but seems rather curious to us: the idea that unequalled greatness brings with it overweening thoughts and actions, which bring in their turn catastrophe for oneself and others. We know that success gives one a fat head but, in the context of our culture, the Greek version of this idea sounds like a melodramatic exaggeration. Nietzsche is saying that, in the context of their culture, it tended to be literally true.

Nietzsche has presented us with a model which, as I have said, has several interesting characteristics. It describes a system of behavior that is generated by a certain social fact about the individuals in the system, a certain shared belief about life. The system serves, in part, to specify and direct the purposes with which the individuals act. It focuses a generalized drive toward negation of some sort in such a way that the drive is transformed into various more specific psychological states, such as resentment and envy; these are also directed in such a way that the agent seeks to be excellent in some way or other. These states are effects which the system itself tends to have, to some extent independently of anyone's trying to bring them about. While Nietzsche's model does require that the agents in it act with the intention of accomplishing certain ends, the results which it attributes to the system are mostly not among the objects of the intentions which are needed to make the system work.

Among the most important results is one which actually tends to defeat the intentions of the individual participants. As individuals contend with one another, they present each other with more and more difficult challenges to be overcome, and consequently with greater and greater reasons to achieve more and more. Thus they help, together, to ensure that excellence is relatively widespread in their community. But this result is in tension with the individual's own purpose, which is to be the best.[10] Nietzsche attributes another result to the system, one that is even more important than this one. By changing the terrible force in the roots of life into something which is powerfully and visibly good, it makes possible the Hellenic love of life which he believes was the greatest achievement of Greek civilization. This is a result which no one involved in the system could even have foreseen, much less intended.

It is obvious by now that Nietzsche's model is an instance of what I earlier called the liberal conception of order. It represents a system of behavior that tends to generate a desirable sort of order which is not intentionally imposed on it by anyone. But the model also attributes to the system a characteristic which was not to be found in the traditional versions of the liberal conception: the spontaneous creation of character. In pursuing the sort of activity which the system supports – in contending with one another in the pursuit of excellence – the individuals within it are working to change themselves. They are trying to become more excellent individuals. One cannot predict what form this development will take. They may acquire greater courage, boldness, ambition, or self-control; or, since creating new ideas about life is one conspicuous form of human excellence, they may develop in unheard-of new directions. The one thing Nietzsche's model does predict is that the inhabitants of such a system will acquire a view of the world that enables them to love life as it is, and if one does that one already is, according to him, a different person and lives a better life.

There is one more point that is more or less obvious by now. To the extent that Nietzsche's use of the liberal conception of order has any plausibility – and it surely does have some – it cuts into the plausibility of the missing premise in the argument in *Schopenhauer as Educator*. If the model he builds in "Homer's Contest" is correct, it identifies a source of order that is distinct from the efforts of value-positing philosophers and that reliably generates a type of order that is desirable by his own standards.

Of course, the model does indicate that people who formulate new values have a positive contribution to make to the formation of character. But it also indicates that the precise nature of this contribution is quite different from what Nietzsche, later in his career, typically takes it to be.

In "Homer's Contest," the system he describes is created by a certain belief which its participants share, and he does seem to think that this idea was created by certain intellectuals (apparently including Homer and Hesiod). This indicates a way in which value-legislators can have a profound influence on subsequent generations. People have the character they have, in part, because of the institutions in which they live and, since institutions are constituted by relevant shared beliefs, people who formulate relevant beliefs and convince others to accept them can be said to be fashioning institutions. But, as we saw in Chapter 3, Nietzsche eventually develops a fondness for saying that such people are not merely fashioning institutions, they are also making human beings of a certain type; they are "fashioning man according to the pleasure of a creative and profound will" (WM 957). In the world of "Homer's Contest," as I have described it, this is not what they are doing at all. If a procedure can correctly be called "fashioning" or "making" something, then the individual who is executing the procedure must at least have a fairly clear and *accurate* notion of what that something is which will be produced by the procedure. If Nietzsche's philosophers use the procedure he describes in "Homer's Contest" they can have no such accurate notion. The attitude they take regarding the power they have over the materials they work with should not be the attitude potters take toward their clay. They cannot simply alter these materials according to the pleasure of their will. They initiate a process which is thereafter largely out of their control, and the best they can do is to have reason to believe that, wherever it leads, it will be to something good. Perhaps they will learn something about what is good by waiting and seeing what happens. Maybe their materials will talk back and teach them something.

"Homer's Contest" suggests the interesting possibility of a Nietzschean liberalism. By analogy with the political slogan, "socialism with a human face," one is tempted to call it "liberalism with teeth." One thing that generally blunts the rhetorical bite of traditional liberal social theories is that they rely, in order to work, on human drives which their authors seem to admit are shabby or, at best, second-rate: democracy is said to work because politicians will strive to garner votes if they must do so in order to stay in power; the adversary system in the courts works because lawyers can be trusted to use every available trick to advance their careers; the market works because economic agents struggle to get the greatest income at least cost to themselves. To rely on motives in this way is the reward them, and to reward them is to encourage and foster them. The human types encouraged by these systems appear, in themselves and as types, to be second-rate at best. The types are generally defended for their beneficial consequences only.

Such ideas suffer a disadvantage when they compete with authoritarian plans to transform everyone into really *good* human beings. In certain ways, the good is more attractive than the merely practical. Someone who did not know Nietzsche's later writings might well suspect that in this early fragment he is beginning to develop a form of liberalism which avoids this problem. Although the motive which drives the system in his model is generally held to be bad, he plainly does not accept his culture's evaluation of it. He thinks that the original drive is – ethically – good or evil depending on its subsequent development in the activities that arise from it. He regards these activities, and the character-types which are constituted by them, as good in themselves and not merely productive of good consequences. If he could develop an ethical theory which would justify him in saying that drives and activities can have this sort of value,[11] he could defend free institutions without appearing to foster the second-rate for the sake of the merely practical. In the fight against its totalitarian alternatives, a Nietzschean liberalism would have a weapon at its disposal which the traditional versions lack.

THE AFTERLIFE OF "HOMER'S CONTEST"

Of course, despite the interesting potential leads in "Homer's Contest," Nietzsche never did develop these ideas in this way. For nearly all of his subsequent career, he was strongly attached to the heroic–authoritarian views I have taken some pains to describe.

"Homer's Contest" remained a fragment, unpublished until after its author's death. When ideas from it were eventually used in works he published himself, they were ones that did not reflect the theme which I have focused on here: the theme of social relations characterized by a positively benign natural order. In one such passage, the idea that survives from his early manuscript amounts to little more than the platitude that a little healthy competition is a good thing (MAM 170). In another, he says that it is because "the will to triumph and eminence" is an ineradicable part of human nature that "the Greek state sanctioned gymnastic and musical contest among equals": they thereby "marked off the boundaries of an arena where that drive could discharge itself without endangering the political order" (WS 226). Here he is attributing to the *Wettkampf* the purely negative value of allowing a potentially dangerous force to discharge or relieve itself (*sich entladen*) in a harmless way. He is also focusing on it as a tool of social engineering, ignoring the fact that, if it can be used in this way, it will also have a certain tendency to make further interference in people's lives unnecessary.

Somewhat later, in *Daybreak*, we find an aphorism that typifies the way in which his ethical thinking eventually developed. There, he says that any drive acquires its status as good or evil only

> as its second nature, only when it enters into relations with drives already baptized good or evil. . . . Thus the older Greeks felt differently about *envy* from the way we do; Hesiod counted it among the effects of the *good*, beneficent Eris . . .: which is comprehensible under a condition of things the soul of which is competition; competition, however, was evaluated and determined as good.
>
> (M 38)

Nietzsche is providing a partial explanation of how competition can cause a drive which is potentially bad to produce action that is good in itself. This means that he is starting to do something that needs to be done in order for his earlier theory to be complete. But at the same time he is turning away from the subject-matter of the earlier view in a way that indicates things to come in his later writings. In the early view, the contest was discussed as a social fact, a fact about how people interact with one another. In this passage, competition (*Wettstreit*) is a *drive*, a fact about the inner workings of the individual. The theory in "Homer's Contest" is a sociological one; here Nietzsche is doing motivational psychology and not sociology. This shift indicates in miniature a change which characterizes his work as a whole. As his mental habits develop, he looks less and less to the unique dynamics of interpersonal relations in order to explain human events, and more and more to the facts of psychology (see JGB 23).

This is obviously a very important change. Part of its importance lies in the fact that sociology – like economics – is a science of natural order. The norms which sociologists use in their explanations generally do not exist because someone intended that they should exist. They are not designed by anybody. Typically, a sociological explanation does not explain things, ultimately, by showing that someone intended them to happen. But a psychology that explains events on the basis of "drives" – and that is the sort of psychology Nietzsche develops – explains events precisely by showing that they *are* intended. The intentions involved may be unconscious, but they are intentions all the same. To the extent that one explains things in this way, one will tend not to look for natural social order and not to see it when it is there. To such a person, the heroic conception of social progress will tend to be very congenial, perhaps self-evident.

But why does Nietzsche drop the idea of a social system which naturally produces benign order? Whatever the reason might have been, it seems to have happened before he wrote *Schopenhauer as Educator*. There, he argues as if he had not already used the idea in "Homer's Contest." I suspect that part of the reason is that he did not quite realize what sort of idea he had his hands on when he wrote "Homer's Contest" in the first place.

This suspicion is borne out by some remarks in the early piece in which he is contrasting the pedagogy of the ancients with that of the moderns. He says that the Hellenic principle that every talent must unfold itself in fighting contradicts the modern view which "fears selfishness as the 'evil in itself.'" The Greeks thought that selfishness "mainly receives its character as 'good' and 'evil' from the aim toward which it exerts itself."[12] Then, apparently in order to explain why the typical Athenian can be seen to "develop his self in contests" only up to the point that it was "of the greatest use to Athens" and brought it the "least harm," he tells us toward what aim the Athenian exerted himself:

> Every Greek experienced in himself, from childhood, the burning wish to be, in the contest of the cities, a tool for the welfare of his city; within these bounds his selfishness ignited, within these bounds it was curbed and confined.

In other words, Greek competitiveness tended to bring the most good and the least harm to the community because that is what the contestants intended it should do: "the Greek youth thought of the wellbeing of his native city when in rivalry with others he ran or threw or sang" (H).[13] He does not seem to realize that, in effect, he has already offered a different explanation of the benign tendencies of the Greek competitive urge: that it is played out within the bounds of a social system that to some extent works independently of, and even frustrates, the intentions of the individual participants. Of course, the two explanations are mutually compatible, but they are quite different. As he thinks of them, however, they seem to be blurred together; one of the most interesting features of the model he builds in "Homer's Contest" appears to be concealed from him.

It appears that Nietzsche was not clearly aware of the liberal conception of order at all. This, as I have said, appears to be a good part of the reason why this idea disappears from his writings. But this lack of lucid awareness is itself rather odd and requires some further explanation. Not only did he use the idea early in his career, but he must have seen Emerson and Burckhardt – two authors whom he greatly admired – using it in their works. The only available explanation seems to be the one that is suggested by various remarks that I quoted from Nietzsche early on in this chapter (pp. 43–45). They suggested that he regarded all events that are not controlled by human intelligence and will with a deep, personal repugnance. Throughout this chapter, I have tried to see to what extent this attitude is the product of some sort of rational inference on his part. The final result of this attempt seems to be that, although it is logically related to certain other views he holds, it is not fully explicable in this way. Early in his career, he has his hands on an alternative to his notion that fortuitous events are inherently bad, and he does not seem to realize that this is what he has.

Nietzsche apparently does not reject the alternative consciously and on the basis of evidence. The only available explanation seems to be that it was simply crowded out of his mind by a personal repugnance which influences his thinking in a way that is, in some measure, independent of reason and evidence. The suspicion he bears toward *Zufälligkeit* is, to some extent, "instinctive." Someone who has this instinct will see events which are not products of human intentions as "fortuity," "chance," "madness," and "chaos." An idea which suggests that we might do well to trust such events will to that extent be unattractive. In that respect, the idea will not seem to be worthy of one's most lucid and careful attention. Probably, people with Nietzsche's instincts will only take such an idea seriously if they are faced with some inescapably salient need which no other idea could satisfy. As a matter of fact, we will see later (Chapter 7, pp. 134–41) that there is evidence that he does begin to formulate his own version of the liberal conception of order at the end of his career. But this only happens after he develops certain theories in ethics and moral psychology which more or less force it on him.

5

VIRTUE

A CONCEPTION OF VIRTUE

The chapter *Von den Freuden- und Leidenschaften* in Part I of *Zarathustra* is Nietzsche's most general discussion of the nature of virtue. As is indicated by its untranslatable title – Kaufmann's "On Enjoying and Suffering the Passions" is probably about as close as one can come – this chapter is also about the passions. The claim he makes there about the passions is embodied in a play on *Leidenschaft* (passion) which turns on the fact that *leiden* means "to suffer," both in the sense of suffering pain and in the sense of, more generally, undergoing something or permitting something to happen. The English word, "passion," hints at the same double meaning, though more indirectly, through its Latin ancestor, *passio*, and through its audible etymological relationship to "passive." These hinted meanings hint in turn at something deeper, a very old and very natural attitude toward the emotions. This is the view that the passions are simply things that we undergo, that happen to us, as if they were the weather of the soul; its storms may be endured or escaped (as one can come out of the rain) but they are not really things that we *do*. The passions would therefore be to some extent incompatible with human power and freedom. In this chapter Nietzsche claims that this view is not true. While our passions are usually *Leidenschaften*, they can also be *Freudenschaften* – a coinage of his which would mean things which are the opposite of painful and also, because of the other meaning of *leiden*, things which are the opposite of passive. The passions can become instruments of freedom and power.

This liberating transformation does not occur by means of the sort of moral discipline in which passion is simply eliminated, nor does it happen by an exercise of will power in which passion is

70

controlled and its expression in one's behavior is suppressed. According to Nietzsche, it occurs by means of a certain process, distinct from all these, in which the passions are transformed into virtues:

> Once you suffered passions [*hattest du Leidenschaften*] and called them evil. But now you have only your virtues left: they grew out of your passions. You planted your highest goal in the heart of these passions: then they became your virtues and passion you enjoyed [*Freudenschaften*].

Passions become virtues, and thereby lose their character as something merely passive, when they contribute to the pursuit of one's highest goal. "And whether you came from the tribe of the choleric or of the voluptuous or the fanatic or the vengeful, in the end all your passions became virtues and all your devils, angels" (Z I 5).

It becomes obvious that this idea has broad implications for Nietzsche when, in the penultimate sentence of this chapter, he invokes one of the principal themes of *Zarathustra* as a whole. He has Zarathustra say, as if to explain the point of what he has said so far: "Man is something that must be overcome [*überwunden*]; and therefore you shall love your virtues, for you will perish [*zugrunde gehen*] of them" (Z I 5). With this startling statement Nietzsche is sounding the *Überwindungsmotiv*, the theme of overcoming. This theme is worked out in *Zarathustra* by means of a system of rather mysterious and sometimes annoying plays on several different words, each of which has a literal meaning that suggests either upward or downward motion. The words involved include *Übermensch* or overman and *überwinden*, which means to overcome, to conquer, and to subdue. The other important ones are: *untergehen*, which would literally mean to go under, while its dictionary meanings include to set (when applied to the sun), to perish, and to be annihilated; and *zugrunde gehen* (literally: to go to the ground), which means to perish and to be ruined. Zarathustra's many plays on these words generally suggest, as they do in the passage I have just quoted, that there is some intimate connection between overcoming, destruction, and creation – in this case the creation of virtue.

Probably, we can most easily achieve lucidity about what this connection is by going directly to a discussion of Nietzsche's doctrine of the will to power. As we shall soon see, the "overcoming" that he says is involved in the creation of virtue is the same thing as the will to power. When we have understood this, we will see why he speaks of the virtues as something that will destroy us, and why he seems to think that we should welcome this fact. We will also see more clearly why the process in which virtue is created is also one in which *Leidenschaften* are converted into *Freudenschaften*.

THE WILL TO POWER

Nietzsche's remarks on the will to power often suggest – as does his talk about overcoming in Zarathustra – that it amounts to something like a desire to manipulate and control something or someone. This is the sort of thing the English and German words, "power" and *Macht*, most naturally bring to mind. At such times what he says seems to have disturbing implications, as he clearly intends it should. At other times he suggests, less disturbingly, that the will to power is more like a desire to exercise one's powers, as for instance one's powers of speech, or one's capacity to think or invent. Here the will to power seems to be a drive to realize one's potentialities as an end in itself.

For instance, in one important statement about the will to power, Nietzsche says:

> Physiologists should think before putting down the instinct of self-preservation as the cardinal instinct of an organic being. A living thing seeks above all to *discharge* its strength – life itself is *will to power*; self-preservation is only one of the indirect and most frequent *results*.
>
> (JGB 13)

To say, as he does here, that living things seek "above all" to discharge their strength and do not do so because the environment forces them to is to say that they do things simply because they *can* do them. Life in that case would be spontaneous activity; it requires pretexts and not reasons. This would mean that the will to power is a drive to *act*, spontaneously.

Which of these two possible conceptions of the will to power does he mean: that it is a drive to manipulate and control, or that it is a drive to spontaneous activity? We can find the answer in the most complete statement of the idea of the will to power in the works that Nietzsche prepared for publication, two sections in the middle of *On the Genealogy of Morals*. There he indicates fairly clearly that he means both of them.

The passage I have in mind occurs in the context of his long and complex discussion of the development of punishment as a social institution. He pauses in the midst of this discussion to dispel a certain confusion which he believes would stand in the way of our grasping the history of any important human fact. This is our tendency to explain the origin of such facts by referring to the purposes they serve. He tells us that "the cause of the origin of a thing and its eventual utility, its actual employment in a system of purposes, lie worlds apart" (GM II 12). Two aspects of punishment must be carefully distinguished: "on the one hand, [there is] that in it which is relatively *enduring*, . . . the 'drama,' a certain strict sequence of procedures" which are simply various different acts in which something painful or harmful is done to someone; on the other hand there is "that in it which is *fluid*, the meaning, the purpose, the expectation associated with the performance of such procedures." He adds that the procedures involved antedate the purposes, which are spuriously used to explain their origins. Interestingly, he makes this point by saying that "the procedure itself will be something older, earlier than its employment *in punishment*" (GM II 13; emphasis added). Apparently, only something that has the "meaning" or "purpose" (these words apparently mean the same thing here) of punishment could *be* punishment, so that the procedures must also antedate punishment itself as its first ancestor.

Nietzsche describes the process by which punishment acquires its meaning as the process that continually produces whatever meaning there is in the world of living things:

> whatever exists, having somehow come into being, is again and again reinterpreted to new ends, taken over, transformed, and redirected by some power superior to it; all events in the organic world are a subduing, a *becoming master*, and all subduing and becoming master involves a fresh interpretation, an adaptation through which any previous "meaning" and "purpose" are necessarily obscured or obliterated.

What Nietzsche calls "interpretation" is the process which creates the meaning of something. It is a relation which has three terms: there is a subject-matter that acquires a new meaning, there is the purpose toward which it is directed and which constitutes its meaning, and there is the agency that projects the purpose and imposes it on the subject-matter. Wherever there is meaning, "a will to power has become master of something less powerful and imposed upon it the character of a function.'' Finally, he tells us that we can only acknowledge the existence of ''spontaneous, aggressive, expansive, form-giving forces that give new interpretations and directions'' if we also admit the reality of ''that which dominates and wants to dominate.'' If we do not make this admission, we have discarded an indispensable presupposition of ''a fundamental concept, that of *activity*'': in that case, the closest we can come to having this fundamental concept is to have a notion of ''an activity of the second rank, a mere reactivity'' (GM II 12). Apparently, he means by this, at least in part, that only a dominant force is able to determine the meaning that its circumstances have for it; forces that are not dominant have to accept meaning as something that is simply given. Thus a drive to spontaneous activity – as contrasted with mere reactivity – is also a drive to manipulate and control.

The process Nietzsche describes in his theory of virtue is clearly an instance of what he calls interpretation. When virtue is created, the subject-matter which acquires a new meaning is the passion – that of the fanatic or the vengeful person, for example. The agency which projects and imposes the purpose is apparently some part of the individual human being that is able to envision ideals and make them effective, thus imposing on the passion the character of a function. This constitutes its ''overcoming'' the passion. What perishes in the process is, in the first instance, the passion with which it began. By being directed toward one's highest goal, the passion of the fanatic, for instance, ceases to have the meaning it formerly had and becomes something quite different. What it was has been destroyed and supplanted by something else. In this way, *Leidenschaft* gives way to *Freudenschaft*.[1] But since our passions are inextricable parts of our personal identity, we ourselves perish in the formation of our virtues; something that was essential to our old selves is annihilated in favor of something new. In changing our character we view ourselves as plastic material which is to be given up to the creation of something new: ''This ghost that runs after you, my brother, is more beautiful than you; why do you not give him your flesh and your bones?'' (Z I 16).

AN APPLICATION

So far, I have stated Nietzsche's view of the nature of virtue in very abstract language, and this must leave its exact meaning in doubt.

I will try to make it clearer by showing how it can be used to explain the nature of specific traits as he understood them. This should also help to show the power and plausibility of the view as I have stated it, since – obviously – one of the principal tests of the value of a theory of virtue is the extent to which it can be used to illuminate the actual phenomena of character and conduct.

A case which is particularly useful for these purposes is the discussion of justice in *On the Uses and Disadvantages of History for Life*, the second *Untimely Meditation*. It was written some years before Nietzsche had developed his general conception of virtue and clearly indicates the sorts of considerations from which the conception in *Zarathustra* must have evolved. It is very likely that he arrived at his general conception of virtue in an attempt to explain phenomena like the ones he brings to light in the *Meditation* on history.

The discussion in the earlier work occurs in the context of an inquiry into the value of the study of history. Having pointed out many bad effects that historical culture can have on life, he considers a certain defense of it which amounts to claiming that it is in a certain respect intrinsically good. This defense states that the "well-known 'objectivity'" of the historically cultured person makes such a person more just, "and just in a higher degree than men of other ages" (U II 6). The sort of justice referred to here is an intellectual virtue,[2] a certain excellence in the use of one's mind, especially in one's judgements about the past. Nietzsche responds to this defense, in part, by claiming that objectivity is not the same thing as justice and, in fact, is not a virtue at all.

This is true, he claims, even if we take "objectivity" in "its highest interpretation," according to which "the word means a condition in the historian which permits him to observe an event in all its motivations and consequences so purely that it has no effect at all on his own subjectivity." It is a state of consciousness which contains no passions or volitions, only an awareness of the events being observed, so that they "photograph themselves by their own action on a purely passive medium." Nietzsche points out that this definition describes a person "to whom a moment of the past *means nothing at all*" and he apparently would deny that something that differs from ordinary consciousness only in the fact that meaning and everything it presupposes have somehow been removed from it can have any intrinsic value. While he is careful to avoid saying that objectivity is a bad thing as such, he denies that it is always admirable; it is sometimes simply the "lack of feeling and moral strength [that] is accustomed to disguise itself as incisive coldness and detachment." Seeing the truth is only admirable if the truth is seen through "the outwardly tranquil but inwardly flashing eye of the artist," and this is what genuine justice supplies. Of "the just man" he says:

> If he were a cold demon of knowledge, he would spread about him the icy atmosphere of a dreadful suprahuman majesty . . . but . . . [he] is from the start only a poor human being; . . . for he desires the truth, not as cold, ineffectual knowledge, but as a regulating and punishing judge.

Justice is the way human beings, as opposed to gods, seek the truth. The difference he sees between justice and objectivity then becomes apparent when he compares – rather than contrasts – the judge and the fanatic. He tells us that there is nothing that distinguishes them at all, other than the fact that the judge aims at and achieves "correct judgement" while the fanatic possesses instead only a "blind desire to be a judge" (U II 6).

The "just man" apparently shares the passions of the fanatic, and this is what explains his "inexorable disregard of himself"; part of the difference between them lies in the fact that in justice these passions are directed at a different goal: namely, the truth. Of course, the fanatic is one of the types Zarathustra mentions to illustrate the possibility that all our passions can become virtues. Here Nietzsche indicates that the virtue that fanaticism can become is justice. He also reveals an aspect of his view of virtue which is not explicit in the discussion in *Zarathustra*: the idea that virtue requires passionate intensity because of the nature the goals which it seeks.

> There are many truths that are a matter of complete indifference; there are problems whose just solution does not demand even an effort, let alone a sacrifice. In this region of indifference and absence of danger a man may well succeed in becoming a cold demon of knowledge.

But these are not the truths with which the supposed virtue of historical objectivity has to contend. To put out the effort needed to seek truths which are achieved only in the face of danger and sacrifice, mere receptivity is not enough; one needs a positive drive toward the truth. In particular, one needs a "great sense of justice . . . the noblest center of the so-called drive to truth" (U II 6).

Nietzsche believes that the goals of virtue in general are difficult to achieve. This belief enables him to see virtue in traits which he probably could not otherwise admire, including everything that is symbolized by the figure of the camel early in Zarathustra: all submission to externally imposed discipline. "What is difficult? asks the spirit that would bear much, and kneels down like a camel wanting to be well loaded." Thus it can be admirable, for instance, to submit to ancient customs, even though doing so means "letting one's folly shine to mock one's wisdom" (Z I 1). Though it is unenlightened, the enthusiastic submissiveness of the human camel is admirable because it indicates a dedication to an ideal of some sort. In this respect it is superior to the objectivity which is attributed to the enlightened historian.

THE PROBLEM OF INDETERMINACY

Nietzsche's theory of virtue, as I have described it, is a definition of virtue. It is not, so far, a very clear definition. Aside from the fact that it does not tell us which goals are the highest, it does not tell us which passions contribute to their pursuit and, consequently, it leaves undetermined the identity of the particular traits to which it refers. It does not enable us to decide – at least in the absence of some supplementary theories concerning somewhat different subjects – which traits are virtues. This, in fact, is not unusual for definitions of virtue, but certain aspects of Nietzsche's theory render this indeterminacy more troublesome than it usually is.

Aristotle's definition of moral virtue – that it is a disposition governing choice which observes a mean, determined by reason, between excess and defect[3] – is obviously "indeterminate" in the same sense of the word. But of course his theory of the virtues consists of more than a mere definition. He also gives us a list of a dozen moral virtues which is apparently meant to include all the excellences of character there are. Assuming the accuracy of the list, we need not wonder which traits the definition refers to. Although the definition by itself does not settle this question for us, the entire rather messy theory does. Thomas Aquinas determines the reference of his very similar theory in the same way, but introduces some elegance by arguing that all the other virtues are subspecies of four basic or "cardinal" virtues: prudence, fortitude, temperance, and justice.

Nietzsche does not solve the problem of indeterminacy by giving a list of the virtues and would insist such a solution is illegitimate. A list can only solve this problem if it is complete, and he believes that no list of the virtues could be complete. One important reason for this appears in the first sentence of "On Enjoying and Suffering the Passions": "My brother, if you have a virtue and she is your virtue, then you have her in common with nobody." Each occurrence of a virtue is different in kind from all others. There really is no virtue other than "the peculiar virtue of each man" (FW 120). This idea in turn rests on several other ideas, one of which can be found by looking behind Zarathustra's explanation of the fact that this idea is not generally believed. He claims that the fact that we do not normally realize the uniqueness of every occurrence of virtue is due to an illusion which is caused by ordinary language; having a virtue, "you want to call her by name" and consequently "you have her name in common with the people and have become one of the people . . . with your virtue" (Z I 5). As he says elsewhere,

> To understand one another, it is not enough that one use the same words; one also has to use the same words for the same species of inner experiences; in the end one has to have one's experiences in *common* [*gemein*].
>
> (JGB 268)

A language, to have meaning for all its users, must refer to things which are both shared and ordinary (Nietzsche's word, *gemein*, means both these things). Things that are shared are generally ordinary because things that are good tend to be unusual. Thus the good tends to elude the grasp of language.

But the idea that good things tend to be unusual does not fully explain why Nietzsche thinks that *every* occurrence of a virtue is different from *all* others. Rarity is not the same thing as absolute uniqueness. Some plausible theories of virtue would in fact imply that, though they may well be rare, no virtue could be possessed by only one person. Suppose, for instance, that virtue is simply a disposition to act on some ethical principle, and that one can only learn such principles by taking the conduct of others as an example. This is at least close to Aristotle's view. This would mean that a virtue can only be acquired in a community in which others (perhaps many others) possess the same trait. Nietzsche does not need to draw this conclusion because he believes that principle, and reason in general, are not important parts of virtue. Zarathustra tells us that virtue has "little prudence in it, and least of all the reason of all men" (Z I 5).

To see why he actually draws more or less the opposite conclusion, we must look again at the things that he does think are important parts of virtue. He only tells us that virtue has two components: a certain passion and a certain goal. He cannot think that individual virtues are unique on the grounds that the goals of individuals differ, because he believes that people do sometimes share the same goals: "A thousand goals have there been so far, for there have been a thousand peoples. Only the yoke for the thousand necks is still lacking: The one goal is lacking" (Z I 15). He believes that goals at least sometimes are socially acquired, in much the same way that principles are in the theory I have just imagined. In fact, he clearly believes it is desirable for all people to share the same goal. The absolute uniqueness of virtue, then, has nothing to do with a divergence of goals.

This leaves us with passion as the factor that uniquely individualizes the virtues. And, in fact, it is only a few sentences after he tells us that each person's virtue is unique and inexpressible that Zarathustra introduces the idea that our virtues grow out of our *Leidenschaften*. His idea seems to be that the passions of different individuals are different and thus lend to the way in which they pursue common goals characteristics which divide their individual pursuits into different traits.

This does not mean that it is wrong to attach the same name to the traits of several different individuals, at least if we remember that such names "do not define, they merely hint" (Z I 22). In many contexts the similarities – especially the shared goals – are what matters most, and the rest can be safely forgotten for the moment. We can even give lists of the virtues that are the most important, as Nietzsche does in two different places.[4] But because we cannot foresee the infinitely diverse ways in which passion can distinguish an individual's pursuit of the good, we cannot give a *complete* list of the virtues.

Nietzsche, then, would refuse to determine the reference of his definition of virtue by Aristotle's means. This does not, by itself, mean that there is anything wrong with his account of virtue. After all, to accomplish this end *simply* by adding a list to one's definition – without any principle for selecting the things on the list – is an unsatisfyingly *ad hoc* method anyway. (Aristotle surely only does it because he is convinced that there is no better way.) Especially, it does not mean that Nietzsche is unable to supply us with procedures for distinguishing virtues from non-virtues. We will see in Chapter 7 that he does claim to be able to do just that. But he also thinks that the work of making these distinctions can never be finished. The definitive catalogue of the virtues can never be compiled.

NIETZSCHE'S THEORY OF VIRTUE AND ITS PREDECESSORS

Nietzsche's theory of the virtues is obviously quite different from the most familiar of the earlier accounts of the same subject. These differences, in fact, are even greater than they seem at first. In one interesting instance, his own choice of words makes his view sound much more similar to one of its predecessors than it actually is. His description of the formation of virtue as a process of "overcoming," and the fact that the passions are what one overcomes, give his account a very misleadingly Kantian sound. It is strongly suggestive of acting *contrary* to one's passion and controlling the inclinations which spring from them, as when courageous people "overcome" their fear. But in Zarathustra's sense of the word, what the courageous people "overcome" is not fear but whatever drives them to their goals. Nietzsche believes that Nietzschean overcoming tends to make the Kantian sort of overcoming unnecessary. Shortly before he began to work on *Zarathustra* – and, apparently, before the word "overcoming" began to acquire a special meaning for him – he wrote: "At bottom I abhor those moralities which say: 'Do not do this! Renounce! Overcome yourself!'" That the sort of overcoming he rejects here is the Kantian kind becomes obvious as he goes on to defend his antidote to these moralities:

> But I am well disposed toward those moralities which goad me to do something and do it again . . . as well as I alone can do it. When one lives like that, one thing after another that simply does not belong to such a life drops off. . . . What we do should determine what we forgo; by doing we forgo – that is how I like it, that is my *placitum*. But I do not wish to strive with open eyes for my own impoverishment; I do not like negative virtues – virtues whose very essence is to negate and deny oneself.
>
> (FW 304)

Rather than acting contrary to something, one acts *in favor of* something else.

Zarathustra strongly emphasizes another difference between his account of virtue and some distinguished older ones. He tells us that having more than one virtue is "a hard lot" because one's virtues will inevitably conflict with one another (Z I 5). He is opposing, in a startling way, an old doctrine – held in one form or another by Plato, Aristotle, Aquinas, and Kant – called the unity of the virtues. This is the idea that the virtues are a single trait, or at least that they cannot be possessed separately from one another. Most of us probably come close enough to this doctrine to at least believe that the virtues are at any rate more closely connected than vices are: while one cannot ordinarily be successfully lazy and successfully greedy, one *can* be both temperate and just. But Nietzsche does not come even this close to this old idea.

Against the unity of the virtues he preaches the enmity of the virtues, or what he calls "the fight among your virtues"; "Behold how each of your virtues covets what is highest: each wants your whole spirit that it might become *her* herald; each wants your whole strength in wrath, hatred, and love" (Z I 5). Probably, part of his reason for thinking this lies in his account of the nature of action in general, and not merely virtuous action. He holds that it is an important fact that the will to power does not merely appropriate and assimilate certain things, but excludes other things as well. At the moment one is at work on one project, one must exclude other possible projects, and all irrelevant facts, from one's mind. All action in this sense rests on a "decision in favor of ignorance" (JGB 230). Where Plato identifies virtue with knowledge, Nietzsche declares that virtuous action rests on a sort of ignorance, simply because all action does. "Every virtue inclines toward stupidity; every stupidity, toward virtue" (JGB 227).

This would seem to imply a certain sort of conflict among the virtues: it would mean that, at the moment one acts on the basis of one virtue, the concerns that are not its concerns – including everything in which one's other virtues take an interest – are excluded from one's attention. It would thus explain part of what Nietzsche is saying in his doctrine of the enmity of the virtues. But it does not seem to explain why he sees the conflict as arising between the *traits* themselves, and not merely between possible actions. More obviously, it fails to explain his curious claim that, if one virtue loses a conflict with another virtue, it begins to destroy itself:

Each virtue is jealous of the others, and jealousy is a terrible thing. Virtues too can perish of jealousy. Surrounded by the flame of jealousy, one will in the end, like the scorpion, turn one's poisonous sting against oneself. Alas, my brother, have you never yet seen a virtue deny and stab herself?

(Z I 5)

He does not explicitly give a reason for this claim, but one can plausibly be drawn from his conception of virtue and, once again, from his conception of action in general. His theory of the will to power indicates that an action is a certain relation between an agent, a goal which the agent seeks, and certain materials the agent employs in seeking the goal. In each action, then, there is a factor which can provide the agent with a standard by which to evaluate the act. Having sought a goal, one can judge one's act favorably if it achieves one's goal, unfavorably if it does not. The same is true of his conception of virtue, which is an application of the idea of the will to power. To act virtuously is to possess a standard of value by which things can be measured, and the *only* standard it involves is the goal which it seeks. For Nietzsche, the passion which is also a part of the virtue is simply a source of energy which drives the agent toward the goal.

Consider what would happen, then, if one has more than one virtue, provided that one's different virtues aim at different goals. Then possessing one's virtues implies possessing several standards of value, every one of which is a goal. Now, measured by the standard of any particular goal, any given resource can only be considered worthwhile if it leads to that goal. Similarly, anything which interferes with the pursuit of a given goal must be regarded as a bad thing – and this includes every usable resource which is diverted to the pursuit of other goals. A gain on the part of one goal tends to represent a loss on the part of the others. This means that there is something like a conflict of interest among one's goals and, consequently, among one's Nietzschean virtues. By the standards of any one virtue, worthwhile materials which are used for the ends of another virtue are to be regarded as pure losses.[5]

But a conflict of interest is not the same thing as active enmity. How do we explain his idea that the virtues fight among themselves, and his curious claim that the fight can end with the self-destruction of one of them? Perhaps the easiest way to do this is to think in terms of a specific example. Consider, for instance, how

Nietzsche can explain the development of a religiously motivated skeptic, like Pascal. Such a person could begin his development possessing two strong virtues: a scientific love of truth and, at the same time, Christian piety. The goals of these two traits conflict, as all goals do, at least because resources which are devoted to one of them are lost to the other. In addition, Nietzsche would think that they also conflict in a more direct manner. The truths which the scientific love of truth produces tend to undermine beliefs which are presupposed by the objects of one's piety. On the other hand, the concerns toward which one's piety is directed would imply that the search for scientific truth is worldly vanity and not worthy of the great sacrifices which the love of truth demands. If I were faced with such a conflict, I would find that my religious activities call into question the value of my scientific activities, which would do precisely the same thing in return. I would be of two minds about my own way of life. Each of my principal goals would imply beliefs which would imply in turn that there is something faulty in the activities which serve the other one.

In Nietzsche's conception of virtue, there appears to be only one way an inner conflict like this can be resolved: one goal might come to occupy exclusively the privileged position of one's highest goal. In that event, various different things might happen next. The individual might stop pursuing altogether the goal that has lost the contest. Perhaps more likely, since mental habits die hard, is the possibility that it will be pursued, but as a means to the highest goal. This implies that the trait which pursues the inferior goal would no longer be practiced as a virtue in Nietzsche's sense, because its goal would no longer be among one's highest goals: its end will have been demoted to the status of a mere means. But the trait would persist in a distorted form. For instance, if one's piety finally engulfs one's scientific love of truth, the latter trait would serve the ends of piety by seeking out problems and paradoxes which show the futility of reason, thus eliminating an obstacle to piety. In that case, one's love of truth will have turned its poisonous sting against itself. In the same way, one's courage can drive one to face the fact that courage is foolish, one can make it a point of honor to realize that one's love of honor is primitive and stupid, and one can come to know out of honesty that honesty is often less profitable than illusions and lies. Such things can happen when a weaker virtue is enslaved by a stronger one.

The fact that Nietzsche believed in the enmity of the virtues while many of his predecessors believed in their unity rests on a deeper difference between his theory and theirs. The philosophers who believed in the older doctrine all also believed that the virtues are produced by an intellectual ability of some sort, such as what Aristotle called *phronesis* or practical wisdom, which is the ability to form correct opinions about what constitutes "doing well" or "good practice" (*eupraxia*). It often makes sense to think of an intellectual ability as an indissoluble whole which must be possessed entire or not (really) possessed at all. Consider, for instance, our ability to add numbers together. If one is capable of doing sums, one can in principle add any column of numbers (given enough time); if one can do certain sums but not others that means that one has not quite mastered the ability to add numbers together. Similarly, we might well think that if I possess generosity but not justice I do not possess it as a result of practical wisdom. If virtue is produced by practical wisdom, this would mean that I do not possess generosity *as* a virtue at all. This is Aristotle's view; it is his version of the doctrine of the unity of virtues.[6] Similar views were held by most of the others who held the doctrine.[7] It rests on what might be called the doctrine of the unity of practical reason.

It is not surprising, then, that the idea of the unity of the virtues holds no appeal for Nietzsche, since he denies the doctrine which traditionally lies at its root. He claims that virtue has little prudence or cleverness (*Klugheit*) in it. The factors which he thinks are important in accounting for the nature of virtue are goals and passions. And while it is somewhat plausible to think that an intellectual ability like prudence will have an indissoluble unity which can then be passed on to the virtues if such an ability is the source of virtue, there is certainly no reason to expect that one's goals and passions will cohere at all. As we have seen, goals actually conflict just in case they compete for the same resources. All goals which are sought as ends in themselves do compete, at least for one's time, and thus Nietzsche was quite right, given the nature of his account of virtue, to repudiate the unity of the virtues and, beyond that, to insist that their mutual enmity is inevitable. Any account in which the virtues are viewed simply as states in which one seeks different goals must yield the same result.[8]

CAN WE ACCEPT NIETZSCHE'S ACCOUNT OF VIRTUE?

It should prove to be a useful first step toward deciding how much truth there is in Nietzsche's account of virtue if we can first decide to what extent we already see virtue as he sees it. Then we can consider whether, on the points where we differ from him, it is he who is in the right or ourselves.

His view certainly at least bears some resemblance to the way we see certain virtues. For instance, generosity, as we ordinarily understand it, seems to consist mainly in seeking a certain goal: a generous person seeks the good of others as an end in itself. There are other traits which we seem to regard in the same way. We probably think of industriousness as a certain tendency to actively seek opportunities for expending effort, and not so much as a capacity to passively accept what must be done.

However, there are also ways in which the broad implications of his account are not consistent with the way most of us view life. While probably few people believe in the unity of the virtues – as is obvious from the fact that we often think that someone possesses one virtue while lacking another – few of us would go so far as to think that people who have more than one virtue are condemned to suffer a war among the parts of their character until only one of their virtues is left alive. As a matter of fact, the difference between Nietzsche and our everyday ethical thinking goes even deeper than this, as we can see by considering our respective views on the nature of courage, a virtue about which both Nietzsche and the rest of us seem to have fairly definite opinions.

The most revealing indication of Nietzsche's conception of courage – and of the great importance that trait has for him – can be found in "The Vision and the Riddle," the chapter in which Zarathustra first states the idea of the eternal recurrence of the same things. There, as elsewhere (see MAM 572), Nietzsche sees courage as something which is good for the people who have it, in that it enables them to win contests which they would lose without it. He says that man is "the most courageous animal," and this fact has enabled man to overcome all the other animals *mit klingendem Spiele*, a phrase which means something like "with flying colors" but also connotes play (*Spiel*). The association of courage with play suggests that there is something novel in the conception of courage involved, and the same thing is suggested by the thing he chooses to contrast it with: "there is something in me that I call courage [*Mut*]: that has so far slain my every discouragement [*Unmut*]." The contrast between courage and *Unmut* – which literally refers to ill-humor and a peevish sort of anger[9] – suggests that courage is really a sort of playful spiritedness. In fact, *Mut* also means "spirit," but the fact that he does have courage in mind here is made clear enough when he tells us that *Mut* is "the best slayer" and names, as one of the things it slays, an emotion which is a form of fear: "the dizziness at the edge of abysses." He also tells us that it "slays even pity," which is "the deepest abyss." Later in the chapter, Zarathustra has a vision of a shepherd into whose mouth a snake has crawled. The snake has sunk its fangs into the shepherd's throat, and it proves to be impossible to kill it until the shepherd's courage enables him, despite his "nausea and pale dread," to bite the reptile's head off and spit it out. Zarathustra's vision is telling him what he will need in order to realize the idea of the eternal recurrence: "Courage . . . is the best slayer . . . for it says, 'Was *that* life? Well then! Once more!'" (Z III 2).

Courage is something which enables us to act in the face of emotions which would normally prompt us to recoil from action, including not only fear but pity, horror, and disgust. How does it accomplish this? Nietzsche does not answer that question in this chapter, but in an earlier aphorism he writes: "Courageous people are persuaded to an action when it is represented as more dangerous than it is" (MAM 308). Courage includes a positive desire to face danger,[10] and in *Zarathustra* it apparently also includes a desire to face all things which are difficult to face, including the disgusting and the horrible. It apparently does so because it involves seeing such things as challenges.

The trait which Nietzsche calls courage bears some resemblance – at least insofar as it is applied to situations involving danger – to what we call courage. Courage, as we know it, is typically something which is good for the person who has it (we think that cowards get less out of life than brave people do) and, clearly, the trait we call courage enables one to act when fear either does or at least could prompt one not to act. But this, I think, is as far as the resemblance goes. In ordinary life we are apt to need what we call courage in order to do a wide variety of things: to ask the boss for a raise, to express an unpopular opinion, to "come out of the closet" with unconventional behavior, to approach someone in whom one is romantically interested, and so forth. Such things are always done for some purpose, but they are clearly not always done *with the purpose of* facing danger. Sometimes, danger may indeed be part of the agent's goal, but more often it is merely accepted as the burdensome but indispensable means to one's goal, which may be any one of many different things.

Ordinary courage differs from Nietzschean courage in that the former does not include, as an essential part of itself, the pursuit of any particular goal, while the latter does. This difference is partly responsible for another and deeper one: courage as we know it requires more wisdom, is less compatible with folly (that is, the lack of wisdom), than is the case with Nietzsche's version of courage. The fact that an act is done in pursuit of a particular end is, so far, compatible with almost any sort of folly and stupidity. The only sort of unwisdom with which it cannot coexist is that of not recognizing the value of that end. Aside from that, it can be miscalculated and wastefully self-destructive. Since what Nietzsche calls *Mut* simply is an authentic and passionate desire to face the dangerous and the difficult, the only wisdom it requires is that of knowing that this particular end is good.

On the other hand, although ordinary courage can be shown in pursuit of many different goals, we do not call an act courageous unless we think that the goal involved, whatever it might be, is really worth pursuing. For instance, some people think that honor and glory are absolutely without value and that pursing such things is foolish. Because of that, someone who definitely holds such a view would not think of the actions of a person like Shakespeare's Hotspur, who braves danger precisely for honor and glory, are characterized by what we call courage. Ordinary courage is incompatible with the folly, in general, of pursuing ends that are no good at all. Beyond that, we sometimes refrain from judging an act to be courageous even when it is done in pursuit of some good. Suppose that I were to embark on a venture in which I really have no purpose other than acquiring a rather small amount of money. Suppose, also, that I have plenty of money and that my project involves putting my own life seriously in danger. I doubt that it would occur to anybody to call such an act courageous. People might say "That took guts," or they may call it rash or foolish. One can argue about whether such behavior should be condemned or not – rashness and folly are vices, while "guts" seems to be neither a virtue or a vice – but it seems clear enough that "courageous," as we ordinarily mean it, is the wrong word to use here.

These facts can be explained if we make a simple assumption about the way in which we ordinarily understand courage. Situations which are occasions for courage in this sense of the word are ones in which the agent is facing a certain sort of problem: namely, the problem of what to do when one's goals *conflict*. Safety is a goal that everyone seeks. Sometimes one of one's other goals can only be pursued by forgoing the goal of safety to some extent. That is what it means to call the situation dangerous. For an act to be courageous *this* problem must be solved well. This requires that several things be the case. First, if one forgoes safety for the sake of the goal that conflicts with it, that other goal must be something which is worth seeking. To forgo a good for the sake of something worthless is not an instance of solving this sort of problem well. In addition, and for the same reason, if the goal which is alternative to safety is sought, it must be something which can at least reasonably be believed to be worth the sacrifice of safety involved.

Courage, as we ordinarily see it, is not simply a goal-directed trait. It is a problem-solving trait in which one's behavior is made consistent with the relative importance of one's diverse goals. Thus, the sort of unwisdom with which it is incompatible goes beyond the folly of not knowing which ends of action are worth pursuing. It is also incompatible with a certain sort of ignorance regarding the *relative* worthwhileness of one's goals. This fact is clearly relevant to the broad problem of the enmity of the virtues. It is true that, as Nietzsche points out, virtues which are simply states in which one seeks a certain goal will inevitably conflict with one another. But we are not stuck with his conclusion that there is an inevitable and perpetual war among all the parts of one's character. Some of the virtues in which we believe – courage is one and there are presumably others – serve to *settle* conflicts among our ends. On this view, virtue manages to some extent to eliminate its own conflicts.

This, of course, does not settle the question of whether Nietzsche is in the right or we are. Nietzsche's most likely answer to what I have said is suggested by the passage from *The Gay Science* (FW 304) which I have already quoted on page 80 of this chapter. The answer would state that courage as it is ordinarily understood is a "negative virtue" in that it consists in observing a requirement that one forgo something. A system of ideals that contains negative virtues is to that extent inferior to one in which they have been supplanted by positive ones, virtues which do not tell us to forgo something but tell us rather to pursue something else. Instead of wasting our resources by negating parts of ourselves, we accomplish the same results by turning our whole selves toward something good. This is exactly what Nietzsche's conception of courage is supposed to do.

It is essential to this argument that one assume that positive virtues can accomplish the same results that negative ones do. But we can see from the case of courage that this is not always so. This argument may well be plausible if one has in mind the sort of negative virtue that tells us to avoid seeking a certain goal altogether – as a certain sort of chastity does, for instance. But courage as we ordinarily understand it is not this sort of negative virtue. It consists, in part, in an appreciation for the proper *ranking* of the goals one does seek. That goods must be ranked, and that some rankings are better than others, is something that Nietzsche appreciates very well in other contexts. But it plays no role in his conception of virtue. The mere fact that one is committed to a particular goal cannot, as such, settle the problem of the value of the goal *in relation to* the many other goals one pursues.[11] To do that, one needs traits that are negative in the way that ordinary courage is. A trait which performs this indispensable function would clearly be a virtue, and consequently an ethical system that lacks such traits is thus far inferior to one that does not.[12]

Nietzsche's failure to acknowledge virtues like ordinary courage does not represent a mere oversight on his part. He is more or less required to do so by his determination to keep reason, as far as possible, out of his conception of virtue. As I have said, virtues that are negative in the way that ordinary courage is are traits that – unlike generosity or industriousness – essentially serve to solve certain problems. And the sort of problem they solve cannot be solved consistently well without intellectual principles of some sort and some significant amount of thinking. Exactly when should one respond to the promptings of fear, annoyance, disgust, and physical pleasure? When should one bite through them, like the shepherd in the vision? Even at their best, passion and desire are not very reliable guides here. One must also think. This requires us to let something into our account of virtue that Nietzsche wishes to keep out.

6

JUSTICE AND THE GIFT-GIVING VIRTUE

HOW FAR DOES NIETZSCHE GO?

In aphorism 103 of *Daybreak*, Nietzsche makes an alarming statement which he repeats many times with variations throughout his
published and unpublished writings: "I deny morality as I deny
alchemy. . . . I also deny immorality: not that countless people feel
themselves to be immoral, but that there is any true *reason* so to
feel." He then adds an explanation that is apparently intended to
calm his reader's alarm somewhat:

> It goes without saying that I do not deny – unless I am a fool
> – that many actions called immoral ought to be avoided and
> resisted, or that many called moral ought to be done and
> encouraged – but I think the one should be encouraged and
> the other avoided *for other reasons than hitherto.*

Of course, this explanation does not tell us nearly enough to
enable us to decide whether we should find his denial of morality
alarming or not. In the first place, it leaves open the question that
is most likely to concern us in this context: which actions does he
believe are to be done and which does he believe are to be avoided?
It is conceivable that, while his beliefs on this issue would agree
with most of ours, he might make a few crucial and disturbing
changes. What is perhaps more important, though, is the fact that
this explanation introduces and leaves open a deeper question, one
that could easily pass us by unnoticed: What are the new reasons
for action that he proposes? Where moral issues are concerned, the
reasons can seem as important, though in a different way, as the
actions which are based on them. If this fact is not sufficiently
obvious, imagine a world that differs from one's own view of the
way things ideally ought to be only with respect to the reasons for

which things are done. Suppose that everyone in this world always behaves exactly as they ought to, but not at all because they care about the interests, feelings, or rights of people other than themselves. They are absolutely indifferent to such considerations. They act as they do because they have a superstitious fear that if they were to do otherwise they would immediately suffer from severe headaches. Their only reason for behaving morally is to avoid physical pain. Such a world would be much safer to live in than ours is, but the point or meaning of moral conduct would otherwise be largely obliterated. A change in the reasons for which one acts can be enormously important, even when one's outward behavior remains the same.

Nietzsche ends *Daybreak* 103 with this declaration: "We have to *learn to think differently* – in order at last, perhaps very late on, to attain even more: *to feel differently*." It is possible that, quite aside from which actions he advocates, he may advocate that our actions be grounded in ways of thinking and feeling which, given our fundamental moral beliefs and expectations, we ought to find quite disturbing. In this chapter I will try to show that certain recommendations he makes do in this way give us some cause for alarm. Only in later chapters will I be able to say how alarming they are. Ultimately, in Chapter 9, I will claim that Nietzsche should find them disturbing, too.

THE GIFT-GIVING VIRTUE

It is obvious, from what we have seen in Chapter 5, that Nietzsche's conception of virtue or excellence of character is a very important part of his ethical theory. This suggests that there is at least one promising way to get a revealing first impression of how far Nietzsche's ethical radicalism goes: we might ask what Nietzsche thinks the greatest virtue is like. This approach is particularly promising because he actually gives a direct answer to this question in the section of *Thus Spoke Zarathustra* called "On the Gift-Giving Virtue" (Z I 22). There he tells us that "a gift-giving virtue is the highest virtue."

The name he gives to this trait rather suggests that what he has in mind is what we call generosity. It is natural to think that this is what he means, since Nietzsche's admiration for generosity, and for the closely related virtue of mercy,[1] is a theme that remains fairly constant throughout his writings. A few years before he wrote

Zarathustra, he had written: "*Honest* towards ourselves and whoever *else* is a friend to us; *courageous* towards the enemy; *generous* towards the defeated; *polite* – always; this is what the four cardinal virtues want us to be" (M 556). A few years earlier than that, he had written: "The means of changing your iron duty into gold in everyone's eyes is this: always do a little more than you promise" (VMS 404). However, it would be incorrect to identify generosity with Nietzsche's "gift-giving virtue." The latter includes an extremely broad range of psychological phenomena. Indeed, the words "a gift-giving virtue is the highest virtue" (*eine schenkende Tugend ist die höchste Tugend*) is ambiguous between saying that there is a certain virtue which is the highest and saying that there are a number of virtues (including, perhaps, generosity as we know it) which become the highest when practiced in a certain way. We shall presently see that, if the latter is what Nietzsche means, then the "way" he has in mind has enough unity to justify speaking of it as a virtue, provided that we keep in mind that we are talking about a psychological structure that can include many other traits, one of which may be generosity as we ordinarily understand it.

Surprisingly, in "On the Gift-Giving Virtue" Zarathustra identifies one important aspect of this structure as a form of selfishness, and shows what it is like by contrasting this sort of selfishness with another, "degenerate" form. "You force all things to and into yourself that they may flow back out of your well as the gifts of your love. Verily . . . whole and holy I call this selfishness." Zarathustra describes this sort of selfishness as taking things in order to be able to give. He contrasts it with "another sort of selfishness, an all-too-poor and hungry one that always wants to steal – the selfishness of the sick: sick selfishness." Sick selfishness is predatory and destructive: "with the greed of hunger it sizes up those who have much to eat." It sees the whole world only in relation to itself, it is "a degenerate sense that says, 'Everything for me.'" On the other hand, the sort of selfishness which is whole and holy sees itself only in relation to what it can do for the world: "This is your thirst: to become sacrifices and gifts yourselves; and that is why you thirst to pile up all the riches in your soul" (Z I 22).

The "gift-giving" Nietzsche is praising here includes an attitude that has a very broad scope. It is a certain attitude toward acquisition in general, including apparently the acquisition of ideas and experiences: one wants to pile up all riches in one's soul. It is also about all sorts of giving, and seems to include action in general as a sort of giving, in which something of value is bestowed upon the world. Despite its breadth, though, this gift-giving does have enough unity to justify treating it as a single trait and a single virtue: in it one acquires things in order to act and give, and one acts and gives from a sense of superabundance. "When your heart flows broad and full like a river, a blessing and a danger to those living near: there is the origin of your virtue." In an extremely important statement, Zarathustra declares that in the gift-giving virtue one experiences no internal needs and apparently recognizes no necessities at all, except for the imperative that one must have no needs: "When you will with a single will and you call this cessation of all need 'necessity': there is the origin of your virtue" (Z I 22). It seems that occasions for exercising this virtue are not seen as representing necessities, but simply as presenting *opportunities* to expend superfluous energy.

Zarathustra's description of super-healthy benevolence is an inspiring one and it has interestingly unusual ethical implications as well. The benevolence he describes is not ultimately a result of altruism, but of successful egoism. Nietzsche seems to be saying that, if we can pile up spiritual riches by living the sort of healthy life he describes in his books, then the problems of distribution that altruists and Moralists try to solve by laying down their iron duties would take care of themselves. Healthy human beings, who are not creatures of duty at all, are naturally a blessing to others. "Physician, help yourself: thus you help your patient too" (Z I 22). He is advocating what might be called a supply-side ethics.

The novelty of the position that Nietzsche takes in "On the Gift-Giving Virtue" is greater than it might seem at first sight. Zarathustra reveals one of the more important, though perhaps less obvious, difficulties a few pages earlier when he says: "But how could I think of being just through and through? How can I give each his own? Let this be sufficient for me: I give each my own" (Z I 19). As Zarathustra suggests, the gift-giving virtue differs considerably from the moral virtue of justice.[2] In a just act, something good or bad is given to someone for a certain sort of reason; the giver believes that there is some characteristic of the recipient (and of course the many theories of justice differ on what this characteristic can be) in virtue of which it is right that the recipient should be given this thing, where the notion that it is right to give this thing implies that it would be *wrong* to omit giving it. In this sense, the thing is given because doing so is seen as necessary. In the gift-giving virtue what is given is apparently not given because of any characteristic of the recipient at all, but because of some characteristic of the agent, and the giving is clearly not seen as necessary.

Nietzsche is parting with the tradition (most notably including Plato) which holds that justice is either the only or the highest virtue that regulates our relations with other people, but his reason for doing so separates him from a great deal more than this particular tradition. The standard ethical theories take the position that what the moral agent does is to find the act which is the right thing to do, in that it would be wrong to omit it. This is one point on which utilitarian and deontological theories generally agree. According to these theories, good conduct always includes what Kant calls a "necessitation" of the will.[3] Nietzsche is proposing an ethical ideal that is quite different from this.[4]

His proposal draws a certain amount of its appeal from the fact that in some respects our ordinary ethical thinking actually conforms to his view rather than to the traditional ones. As I hinted earlier on, the familiar notion of generosity seems to be closely related to Nietzsche's gift-giving virtue. Generous behavior is ordinarily understood to be a form of good conduct that is not necessary. To do something that one has promised to do is, at least in typical cases, the sort of thing that philosophers call just, and this characterization implies that the act is necessary, that it would be wrong to omit it. To do *more* than one has promised is at least in some cases the sort of thing we call generous, and to call it that *means* (among other things) that one did not have to do it.[5] It was a good thing to do but one could have blamelessly omitted it. Theories that depict good conduct as doing what one must do are not compatible with the ordinary notion of generosity, but Nietzsche's view plainly is. It even suggests an interesting psychology of the generous person, which would claim that generous people give from a sense of "having overmuch of the good" (Z IV 1).

JUSTICE

However, while Nietzsche can accommodate the idea of generosity, it is well known that he raises doubts concerning whether he can make room for other ideas which are at least as important to the way we see things. When Zarathustra admits that he cannot give to each his own he would seem to suggest that the gift-giving virtue and *not* justice ought to regulate one's relations with other people. There is an important reason why we expect what might be called the category of moral necessity to be applied to a very broad range of relations between persons. We need to believe that there are things people are capable of doing to us – actions, for instance, in which we are victimized by means of physical violence – which they must avoid doing because it would be wrong to do them. That is, we need to require that people refrain from doing them and that they refrain because it is morally necessary. If the gift-giving virtue is the only virtue that regulates one's relations with others, then if people who possess this trait refrain from killing me and running off with my goods, this means that their not murdering me is a free gift they make to me, like a Christmas present.[6] This means that, even if a world governed by the gift-giving virtue rather than justice and related traits were a world without theft and murder, it would be a world in which non-victimizing behavior does not have the meaning that we ordinarily find in it. Kant tried to explain what this meaning is by means of the ideas of dignity and treating people as ends, and many people who are not Kantians hold what is in broad terms the same idea: human beings have a special status and this status cannot be observed unless certain things are not done to them and in fact are not done because they would be wrong. If Nietzsche thinks that the gift-giving virtue is the only virtue which should regulate relations between people, he cannot consistently accommodate the idea that any human being has this status.[7] This would certainly mean that his way of thinking is disturbingly different from our own.

As a matter of fact, Nietzsche does believe that justice should play a role in relations between people, and the difference between his point of view and ours is consequently not as great as Zarathustra's admission seems to suggest. In order to understand how we stand in relation to Nietzsche, we must understand the nature and extent of the role that he envisioned for justice and the way in which he connected justice with the gift-giving virtue. As we shall see, his views on these issues were complicated and not fully worked out. We shall also see that they do not entirely prevent his doctrine from having some quite disturbing consequences.

Nietzsche's discussion of justice and revenge in *On the Genealogy of Morals* (GM II 11) contains some remarks which have

95

illuminating implications concerning the relationship between justice and the gift-giving virtue. There he tells us that justice and revenge, contrary to what one might think, are very different traits and are in fact characteristic of opposite sorts of people. The reason why this must be so is the fact that "the just man remains just even toward those who have harmed him (and not merely cold, temperate, remote, indifferent: being just is always a *positive* attitude)." The only person who can be fully just, consequently, is the one who "has absolutely no need to take a false and prejudiced view of the object before him." This person is the "active, aggressive, arrogant man" whose way of thinking and feeling is typified by "the truly *active* affects, such as lust for power, avarice, and the like." Revenge, he tells us, is not at all typical of this sort of person because it is a "reactive affect," like "hatred, envy, jealousy, mistrust, [and] rancor" (GM II 11). What the reactive affects have in common is the fact that each one of them proceeds from a felt need to protect oneself from some threat represented by another person, and the protection includes thinking of the other person in a way that falsifies what they really are. The person who can be just even when it is most difficult to do so is the one who perceives no such threats and feels no such needs. In other words, justice proceeds from the complex of traits that Zarathustra groups together under the name of the gift-giving virtue.

Justice, then, is a case of abundant, aggressive vitality imposing limits on itself, limits which it can afford to observe. But Nietzsche recognized that such vitality is a very different sort of trait, in itself, from justice, and this fact has a sobering implication which he also recognized. He states this implication in the form of a remark about law, which he believes makes justice possible by training people, including "the injured person himself," to make "an ever more *impersonal* evaluation" of criminal conduct. He remarks that

> legal conditions can never be other that *exceptional conditions*, since they constitute a partial restriction of the will of life, which is bent upon power, and are subordinate to its total goal as a single means: namely, as a means of creating *greater* units of power.

Since "'just' and 'unjust' exist . . . only after the institution of the law," this would mean that the conditions in which these categories apply are themselves "exceptional" (GM II 11). Necessarily, most of life will not be just.

THE PROVINCE OF JUSTICE

What we wish to know, at this point, is how far he thinks the limited province of justice extends. One might still hope that what he means by limiting it to exceptional conditions is something fairly harmless. In that case one's hopes would be disappointed. Elsewhere in the *Genealogy* he says of the "noble" peoples who create "master moralities" that

> the same men who are held so sternly in check *inter pares* [among equals] by custom, respect, usage, gratitude and even more by mutual suspicion and jealousy . . . once they go outside, where the strange, the *stranger* is found, they are not much better than uncaged beasts of prey.
>
> (GM I 11)

Of course, here he is describing certain anthropological facts and not prescribing what anyone should do; but when in *Beyond Good and Evil* he states the normative conclusions he draws from these facts, what he says is simply a more humane version of the idea that justice only applies *inter pares*, among people who "are actually similar in strength and value standards and belong together in *one* body" (JGB 259). There, he tells us that "one has duties only to one's peers" and that "against beings of a lower rank, against everything alien, one may behave as one pleases or 'as the heart desires,' and in any case 'beyond good and evil' – here pity and like feelings have a place." The "like feelings" that he has in mind here include

> the happiness of high tension, the consciousness of wealth that would give and bestow: the noble human being, too, helps the unfortunate but not, or almost not, from pity, but prompted more by an urge begotten by excess of power.
>
> (JGB 260)

When the noble human being is benevolent toward people who are less than his equals, it is an instance of the generosity that flows naturally from the gift-giving virtue.

This is the position which Nietzsche consistently maintains in the *Genealogy* and *Beyond Good and Evil* (see, in particular, GM II 8). It leaves us with the same problem that was initially raised by Zarathustra's apparent admission that he could not be just, except that the scope of the problem is now limited to relations between people of unequal strength. Unfortunately, limiting the problem in this way does not make it much easier for us to sympathize with what he is saying. Nietzsche believes that the test of justice is whether one will be just toward those who have harmed one. We might well be inclined to add that there is another test which is just as important: whether one will be just toward those who do not have the power to make us regret it if we do not. To us, it is a very important fact that principles of justice compel us to grant the status of human beings to people whom we could profitably treat as less than human. A theory which says that it is logically impossible to be just toward the weak lacks something in our eyes, and it cannot correct this sort of deficiency by adding that they can be the recipients of generosity instead.

There is reason to believe that Nietzsche himself eventually came to perceive this as a deficiency in need of correction. In the works of 1888 – not very long after he wrote *Beyond Good and Evil* and the *Genealogy*[8] – he sketched out a theory that does provide a correction. Though, as we shall see, it does not lay all related problems to rest, the nature of the change he introduced at this point, during his last productive year, is a very interesting one. Part of the interest lies in the fact that it reveals a way in which the *inter pares* theory is inconsistent with one of Nietzsche's most beloved ideas: his conception of an aristocratic society. In attacking the idea of equality in *Twilight of the Idols* he says that it seems to be preached by the idea of justice itself, whereas it really is the termination of justice, " 'Equal to the equal, unequal to the unequal' – *that* would be the true slogan of justice" (G IX 48). Of course, to say that justice requires that unequals be treated differently from equals is quite different from saying that there can be no justice between unequals. What he is saying here might be spelled out in terms of rights and duties by saying that everyone does have rights and, while they do not have the same rights, the strong do have duties to the weak – namely, to observe the rights of the weak. This in fact is how he does spell it out, later on, in *The Antichrist*. There he describes his ideal of a "healthy society," which embodies "the order of castes . . . the highest law of life" and, in describing the conduct of the members of the highest caste toward members of the others, he says: "When the exceptional human being treats the mediocre more tenderly than himself and his peers, this is not mere politeness of the heart – it is simply his *duty*" (A 57). This is clearly a retraction of the earlier *inter pares* idea – the phrase "mere

politeness of the heart" even recalls the "as the heart desires" of
Beyond Good and Evil 260 – but the contradiction between the position he takes here and the earlier one goes deeper than this, as we
can see from a brief look at his description of his caste society and
his defense of his new theory of rights.

He describes a system of three castes. In the highest caste are the
"most spiritual human beings," whose "joy is self-conquest;
asceticism becomes in them nature, need, and instinct." They have
"the privileges of the fewest: among them, to represent happiness,
beauty, and graciousness on earth." In the second caste are those
who are "preeminently strong in muscle and temperament." They
"are the guardians of the law, those who see to order and
security." The third and lowest includes the enormous majority of
the people, those for whom "to be mediocre is their happiness;
mastery of one thing, specialization – a natural instinct." It is their
place to carry out most of the functions of economic, social, and
cultural life: "Handicraft, trade, agriculture, *science*, the greatest
part of art, the whole quintessence of *professional* activity" (A 57).[9]

He explains his conception of rights in terms of this distinction
between classes. "The *inequality* of rights is the first condition for
the existence of any rights at all." The reason for this, apparently,
is that there can be no rights without society and "the separation
of the three types is necessary for the preservation of society." The
members of each class are separated – that is, their class
membership is defined – by the rights they possess, each class
having different rights. "A right is a privilege. A man's state of
being is his privilege." One might think that it is no "privilege"
to belong to the lowest caste, since to belong to this group is to be
"a public utility, a wheel, a function." But we must not "underestimate the privileges of the mediocre." The people in the higher
strata work under heavier burdens: "As one climbs *higher*, life
becomes ever harder; the coldness increases, responsibility
increases" (A 57).[10]

Apparently, the rights which each person possesses are ones that
enable one to perform the tasks of one's caste. Society is preserved
by the fact that these rights are observed. This would require that
everyone has a duty to observe the rights of all others – to not
interfere, at least, with the performance of their tasks. In the sense
in which justice is observing the rights of others, it cannot apply
merely *inter pares*. If it did, the structure that Nietzsche admires
would fall apart. Thus the ideal of aristocratic society, of rule by

the best as he now understands it, is incompatible with his earlier theory of justice.

JUSTICE AND POWER

Obviously, it is more than possible to disagree with the theory of 1888. As Nietzsche would insist, it is incompatible with the standard democratic, liberal, socialist, and anarchist ideologies. But at least it does not do violence to the basic assumptions of traditional ethics in the way that the earlier theory did. Everyone is granted rights which others are bound to respect; no one is at the mercy of someone's heart's desire.

However, the change in Nietzsche's views does leave him with a serious problem. As he points out (GM P 4), the earlier position grew out of ideas that he had been developing since his earliest aphoristic works. These ideas culminate in the complicated reasoning of the *Genealogy* and constitute a sort of argument for the position he takes there. Nietzsche never answers this argument and does not seem to be aware of having changed his mind. Of course he has a perfect right to change his mind and had good reason to do so in this case, but for the sake of the cogency of his system he must be able at any rate to answer the argument which leads to the rejected position and away from the new one without rejecting any ideas which he would need to keep. Perhaps we can gain some insight into whether he can do this by identifying the ideas that form the basis for the earlier position.

Central to this position is the idea that the most fundamental moral concepts and sentiments originated in "the oldest and most primitive personal relationship, that between buyer and seller, creditor and debtor," and in the contracts that arise from this relationship (GM II 8). For instance, punishment originated when "the debtor . . . pledged that if he should fail to repay he would substitute something that he 'possessed' . . . for example, his body, . . . his freedom, or even his life" (GM II 5). After originating in relationships between individuals, "the budding sense of . . . guilt, right, obligation, settlement, first *transferred* itself to the coarsest and most elementary social complexes" (GM II 8).

"Our duties," he tells us, "are the rights of others over us." Others acquire these rights in relationships of trade in which they concede rights to us in return. Clearly, they can only enter such relationships by "taking us to be capable of contracting and repaying," which means that they must attribute to us a certain measure of power. Once it has been entered, the relationship itself tends to provide evidence that this attribution was a reasonable one, because when "we fulfill our duty . . . we justify the idea of our power on the basis of which all these things were bestowed upon us" (M 112). For this reason, the trade relationship tends to be self-maintaining once it is established. The stability of the relationship is further enhanced by the fact that it is one in which individuals use their power to mutual advantage: "One gives another what he wants, so that it becomes his, and in return one receives what one wants" (MAM 92). This means that to some extent my partners in trade have a motive to help me to maintain the power they have admitted I have. "My rights – are that part of my power which others have not merely conceded me, but which they wish me to preserve" (M 112). Because of the nature of the relationship, then, the partners will act to preserve the conditions on which it rests.

This, however, does not explain how the relationship can come into existence in the first place. Throughout much of history, "the trader and the pirate . . . are one and the same person: where the one function does not seem expedient, they carry out the other" (WS 22). Until fairly recently, those who entered into peaceful trade did so in preference to another option, which is to get what one wants by violent predation. Nietzsche gives several possible reasons why people who have such an option might choose the more peaceful alternative: because "they expect something similar in return," because they "consider that a struggle with us would be perilous or to no advantage to themselves," and because they wish us to have enough power to be useful in "an alliance with them in opposition to a hostile third power" (M 112). The reason which Nietzsche favors as the best explanation is the second of these: "where there is no clearly recognizable predominance and a fight would mean inconclusive mutual damage, there the idea originates that one might come to an understanding and negotiate one's claims" (MAM 92); thus "prudence created justice to put an end to feuding and *useless* squandering between similar powers" (WS 26).

What happens when one is faced with a predominant power and would lose a fight should one occur? In his early discussions of justice and rights, Nietzsche mentions one, and only one, reason why one might be granted some rights by the superior power.

On the Right of the Weaker – Whenever anyone, such as a besieged city, submits to the stipulations of a greater power, there is the possibility of stipulating in return that one will destroy oneself, burn the city, and thus cause great damage to the more powerful one. Hence arises a sort of *equalization* upon which rights can be established.

He adds that to this extent slaves can have rights against masters: "The *right* originally extends *as far as* the one *appears* to the other to be valuable, substantial, unlosable [*unverlierbar*], unconquerable" (MAM 93). This idea is in the spirit of Nietzsche's early thinking on rights and justice. The rights of the weaker arise in an extremely rudimentary trade relationship in which, in a way, both sides benefit – the stronger parties gain a right to exploit the weaker and in return accept a duty not to give the weaker parties reason to annihilate themselves. This relationship is established because, since the subjected ones still are able to destroy themselves, both sides have some power. Indeed, given the assumptions to which Nietzsche has committed himself at this point, it is difficult to conceive any other way in which the weaker could acquire rights against the stronger. But this line of reasoning plays no role in Nietzsche's position as he spells it out in the *Genealogy*, and it is not hard to guess why. It only means that the greater power will have a "duty" to make the life of the weaker marginally better than death. Since the stronger would generally have no motive to violate this duty anyway, the "right" it implies would in general have no effect.

From this brief survey of Nietzsche's early views we can see that it is connected very obviously with what eventually became one of his central ideas: the idea of the will to power. In this context, the will to power functions as a psychological doctrine, as a theory of motivation. Because this idea also eventually becomes his ethical doctrine as well, his standard of value, it would seem to be very natural for him to accept as just any equilibrium that arises when power plays against power, which would mean that the weak either have no rights at all or have "rights" that do them no good. Justifying the theory of 1888 may well be no simple matter.

I will be discussing this problem, in connection with others that are related to it, at length in Chapter 9. For the present, I will merely make one tentative suggestion regarding how it might be solved.

In the development of the early theory, the idea that people are valuable to one another is at least as important as the idea of power, and the two ideas are related in an odd way. In the social mechanism from which, according to this theory, rights and duties arise, one person's power over another functions to a certain extent as a *measure* of the one person's value for the other. People only think that it would be beneficial to enter relationships of trade with others if they fear the others are too *strong* to be beaten in a fight. The stronger only acknowledge the value of the weaker to the extent that they can be coerced into doing so through the threat of self-destruction on the part of the weak. This is not a very plausible way to measure the value that one person has for another. I may be of greater value to you than I can terrify you into realizing. This way of measuring the value of persons would systematically tend to underestimate it.

It is perhaps not surprising that Nietzsche would employ a standard that systematically undervalues persons. As he admits during his last active year: "*Nausea* over man, over the 'rabble,' was always my greatest danger" (EH I 8). He shows a strong tendency to rate very low, and surely too low, the value that "lower" persons have for "higher" ones. This bias may reach its nadir in an unpublished note of 1884: "The great majority of men have no right to existence, but are a misfortune to higher men" (WM 872).

By 1888, however, he had gone far enough in reversing this tendency to write: "A high culture is a pyramid: it can stand only on a broad base; its first presupposition is a strong and soundly consolidated mediocrity" (A 57). In a note written in 1887, he indicates that he realizes what this implies about the value which the lower offer to the higher:

> Main consideration: not to see the task of the higher species in leading the lower (as, e.g., Comte does), but the lower as a base upon which a higher species performs its *own* tasks – upon which alone it can stand.

> (WM 901)

Starting from this premise, it could even be argued that the lower are more valuable to the higher than the higher are to the lower. What the productive mediocre have to offer Nietzsche's ascetic artist–philosophers is the wherewithal to survive; what they get in return is something for which Nietzsche thinks they feel all too little need.

The higher might do well to come to an understanding with the lower and negotiate their claims. If this idea is added to the basic assumptions of the earlier theory and reworked accordingly, it might perhaps yield the result that when the higher treat the lower more tenderly than themselves it is simply their duty. This, at any rate, could be one way to carry out a justification of the theory of 1888 on more or less Nietzschean grounds. But Nietzsche never did rework his theory in this way and, as I have indicated, probably did not see the contradiction between his later and earlier theories of justice. Had he noticed this problem, he might not have solved it in this way at all. As we shall see later on (Chapter 7, pp. 139–40), when he tells us how the higher human beings would justify their claims against the lower ones, he simply says that they would base it on an appeal to the authority of ancient customs. This suggests, to me at any rate, that he sees them as confronting no special difficulties in justifying their system to the lower orders, as if it would be obvious that it is a system from which everyone gains something.

The problem of justifying Nietzsche's last thoughts on justice rests on top of a deeper problem, which I have had to ignore in this chapter. I have presented his views on justice as ways of protecting Nietzsche from committing himself to saying that our relations with others are to be regulated entirely by the gift-giving virtue. The problem is whether, given his conception of virtue, he is entitled to have a conception of justice at all, at least if it is to claim that justice is a virtue. I will argue in Chapter 9 that he is not, and that the problem remains whether one is thinking in terms of the *inter pares* theory or the caste theory of 1888. It has to do with characteristics which all conceptions of justice have in common,. and with the nature of Nietzsche's theory of virtue. If I am right about this, the possibility of social relations that are regulated only by the heart's desire will rise to alarm us again, and I will give a reason why it should disturb Nietzsche, too. Before I try to show any of this, however, I should complete my account of his theory of virtue. This (among other things) is what I will now do in Chapter 7.

7

WHICH TRAITS ARE VIRTUES?

THE QUESTION

We have seen, here and there, isolated examples of traits Nietzsche admires. These include, most recently and perhaps most importantly, the one he calls the "gift-giving virtue." Of course, my account of the positive, substantive part of his ethical theory will not be complete until I go beyond discussing isolated examples and say something about the principles by which he proposes to distinguish between those traits that are admirable and those that are not. What general response does he have to the question: Which traits are virtues? We will see in this chapter that his response is by no means a simple one. It does not take the form of a direct answer to it at all. As we have already seen (Chapter 5, pp. 77–9), he does not claim to give us a complete list of the virtues and thinks that this cannot be done. But he does give us a set of procedures for determining which human traits are genuinely virtuous.

It will be a while, though, before I will explicitly say anything about his response to this important question. In order to understand his ethical values, one must first understand three important principles: his experimentalism, his vitalism, and his relativism. Further, in order to understand any one of these principles fully, one must understand how all three of them hang together. Obviously, this will take some time. In order to help the reader avoid feeling lost, I will begin by making some preliminary comments on his experimentalism and some rather dogmatic remarks about how the three principles are related to one another. The reasoning behind these remarks will gradually emerge as I try to say exactly what each of these principles are.

EXPERIMENTALISM

Nietzsche places tremendous importance on the idea of experimentation. He claims that his own attitude is in some way fundamentally that of an experimenter, saying that he no longer wishes to "hear . . . of all those things and questions that do not permit of any experiment" (FW 51). He even suggests that, at the present moment in history, everyone is an experimenter (GM III 9). Unfortunately, aside from the fact that he thought that it is important, there is not much that we can be entirely certain of regarding his views on this subject. Though they are numerous and often suggestive, his remarks on experimentation do not add up to anything like a thoroughly worked out methodology. There is one thing, however, of which we can be certain. It is that he believes that if the new morality he calls for is to be created, it will be constructed on the basis of experimentation. At one point, after predicting that science, especially the social sciences, will eventually demolish "the whole nature of moral judgements to date," he raises "the most insidious question of all": namely, "whether science can furnish goals of action after it has proved that it can take such goals away and annihilate them." The answer he offers is that, after scientific theories have demolished the old moralities, scientific *method* can build something new in its place: "then experimentation would be in order that would allow every kind of heroism to find satisfaction – centuries of experimentation that might eclipse all the great projects and sacrifices of history to date" (FW 7).[1]

I will call Nietzsche's idea that a morality (in the inclusive, lower-case sense of the word) can be based on experimentation his "experimentalism." If this idea is interpreted in the most immediately obvious way, it raises a serious problem, especially for someone who holds meta-ethical theories like the ones that Nietzsche holds. We can take a step toward the correct interpretation of Nietzsche's experimentalism if we see how he manages to evade this problem.

The problem arises from the fact that, if the analogy between moral and scientific experimentalism is to be exact, then acceptable moral principles would have to be supported by experimentation, as acceptable scientific theories are; and this means that they would have to be supported by observation – namely, one's observations of the results of one's experiments. But, as Gilbert Harman pointed out some years ago, moral principles cannot be supported by observation in anything like the way that scientific theories can.[2] It is possible, at any rate, to find something that one can call a moral observation, at least if we suppose that an observation is "an immediate judgement made in response to [one's] situation without any conscious reasoning having taken place."[3] A scientist, looking in a cloud chamber, observes, "There goes another vapor trail with that curlicue shape." I see some children mistreating a cat and I make a similarly immediate judgement to the effect that what they are doing is wrong. Both are observations in the sense just specified. The scientist's observation will support some theory about subatomic particles only if the best explanation of the scientist's making the observation has to assume that the theory is true. The theory that will be supported in this way will be the one that occupies a particular position in relation to the facts: if the theory is true, it will best explain the facts asserted in the observation (i.e., the vapor trail and its shape). In the case of the moral observation, we can find a principle that occupies the same position. Perhaps the fact that what the children are doing is wrong is best explained by the fact (if it is a fact) that the un-Nietzschean principle, "Causing pain for the fun of it is always wrong," is true. To this extent, the scientific and moral realms are analogous.

Beyond this point, however, the analogy Nietzsche seems to need breaks down, because the best explanation of my making the moral observation does not require that we assume that this moral principle is *true*. It only requires that we assume that I *believe* this principle. If I do believe it, it will explain my observation very well, whether it is true or not. If I believe this principle, I will inevitably "observe" that what the children are doing is wrong. Something that is crucial for the existence of experimental evidence of the sort that we find in science is lacking in the moral realm: to have such evidence, there must be subjective events (i.e., observations) which can best be explained by the objective truth of the principle or theory that occupies the particular status I described above. Otherwise the observation will not support the principle or theory, and consequently neither will the experiment one is observing.

To see why this is particularly a problem for Nietzsche, consider what it would mean if scientific observations were explicable in this way on the basis of beliefs that scientists have. Suppose, for instance, that every time scientists "see" a vapor trail of a certain kind it is simply because they believe some theory that implies that there will be such a phenomenon to observe. In that case, these observations would be, so to speak, mere figments of the intellects of the people who make them. It is well known that Nietzsche believes that moral observations have something like this status. He says, in italics, that *"there are altogether no moral facts,"* and that "morality is merely an interpretation of certain phenomena." His reasons for thinking this apparently include an extreme version of the idea that the formation of such an interpretation is fully explicable on the basis of the psychology of the person who is doing the interpreting, that "morality is mere sign language, mere symptomatology" (G VII 1). Probably, he would only claim that *some* moralities are mere figments, utterly out of touch with reality, but he is happy to say that all moral judgements – including the ones that he approves – are to be understood mainly as expressions of the psychology of the person who makes the judgement: "Formerly, one said of every morality: 'By their fruits ye shall know them.' I say of every morality: 'It is a fruit by which I recognize the *soil* from which it sprang'" (WM 257; see also 254 and 256).

Of course, there are very large questions about what all of this means. But it seems obvious that, whatever else it means, it commits him to a view at least as strong as the one that generates the problem I have described: that particular ethical observations are, by themselves, not evidence of the truth of the principles from which they spring. There are limits, then, to the sort of experimentalism Nietzsche is entitled to advocate. He is not entitled to advocate that we should test notions about what sort of life is good or bad simply by acting on such notions and then observing whether the results are indeed instances of good or bad ways of life. What is more important is the fact that such an idea seems absurd on the face of it, anyway. But in that case, what does his experimentalism amount to? It would obviously be helpful, in answering this question, if one could find examples of Nietzschean experiments.

In view of this fact, it is rather disappointing that Nietzsche only explicitly identifies a single example of the sort of moral experiment he has in mind. Fortunately, his comments about it shed a good deal of light on the nature of his experimentalism. Even the identity of the example he selects is highly suggestive: he refers to it as "the experiment," as if it were either the only experiment or the most important one.

These comments occur in the context of a discussion, in *The Gay*

Science, of what might be called "the natural history of truth and error." "Over immense periods of time," he says, "the intellect produced nothing but errors." Among these "errors" are the belief that there are substances, the belief in free will, the belief "that a thing is what it appears to be," and the belief "that what is good for me is also good in itself." Throughout this part of his discussion, he avoids saying, or even suggesting, that the people who believe these errors ought to have done otherwise. They believed them because these errors "proved to be useful and helped to preserve the species: those who hit upon or inherited these had better luck in their struggle for themselves and their progeny." That is apparently good enough reason for them to believe such things. Eventually, an important change took place. It was found that one could sometimes argue about the merits of conflicting ideas without calling the "basic errors" into question. Also, one noticed that some ideas, "though not useful for life, were also evidently not harmful to life." For some issues, it was possible, innocently, to discuss ideas with a view to finding the truth, without regard for their impact on our happiness or survival. As an unforeseen result of this, a new drive was born, which gradually became stronger as one indulged it, and "knowledge and the striving for the true found their place as a need among other needs" (FW 110).

Nietzsche makes it plain that he thinks this development represents a considerable advance, that this striving for the true is an admirable drive. But there is a good reason why human beings were for so long entirely unconcerned with truth as good in itself: it tends to clash with things that we have believed in order to be happy and stay alive. Thus, we cannot take it as obvious how far we should pursue this growing need for truth. Today, its progress has resulted in a crisis: "A thinker is now that being in whom the impulse for truth and those life-preserving errors clash for their first fight, after the impulse for truth has proved to be also a life-preserving power." This conflict raises "the ultimate question about the conditions of life . . . and we confront the first attempt to answer this question by experiment. To what extent can truth endure incorporation? That is the question; that is the experiment" (FW 110).

What is determined by this experiment? Directly, at any rate, it determines how much truth we are able to assimilate. But a good deal more hangs upon this direct result. Consider, again, the fact that although Nietzsche admires the striving for truth he also refrains from saying, generally, that people ought to strive for the truth. This might strike one as somewhat odd, but it follows from two mutually consistent principles that Nietzsche firmly holds. On the one hand, he believes that the degree to which one can assimilate the truth and survive determines one's rank as a person: "How much truth does a spirit *endure*, how much truth does it *dare*? More and more that became for me the real measure of value" (EH P 3; see also WM 1041 and A P). On the other hand, he believes that one should not assimilate more of the truth than one can endure, "that one might get hold of the truth *too soon*, before man has become strong enough, hard enough, artist enough" (JGB 59).

But strength, hardness, and artistry are, roughly, the characteristics that, according to Nietzsche, determine one's personal worth. This means that the question of one's rank is, so to speak, prior to the ought-question, the question of how much truth one ought to incorporate. More exactly, Nietzsche must believe that the factors that determine one's worth as a person also determine what one ought to do, so that not everyone ought to do the same thing. This belief is what I will call Nietzsche's relativism.

Now one can see what, ultimately, is and is not decided by the experiment Nietzsche has described. The two ethical principles involved are the idea that the ability to assimilate truth is a standard of worth and the idea that one should only assimilate as much truth as one can endure. These principles are *not* being tested by this experiment. As we shall see, the former principle is derived, more or less *a priori*, from Nietzsche's vitalism, and the latter probably, though more problematically, comes from the same source. This means that this experiment does not run aground on the problem I have posed about moral experimentation in general. If this experiment is representative of the sort of experimentation Nietzsche has in mind, his basic principles are apparently not to be supported by such means at all. But the nature of his ethical theory leaves several ethically important issues that *can* be decided in this way. First, his ethic estimates the worth of persons on the basis of their character, and not merely on the basis of their actual overt behavior. To determine one's value as a person, it is not enough to survey one's behavior so far; one must also make sure that one attempts[4] to achieve the ideals which are the standards of value. What is perhaps more important is the fact that his relativism implies that one cannot know *a priori* how these ideals apply to oneself in terms of what one ought to do. One cannot know how much of Nietzsche's kind of truth one ought to accept until one makes the relevant attempts. In other words, the experiment ultimately decides the answers to the question of rank and the ought-question. This is the part of morality that experimentation is able to support. It can do this because the issue that is directly decided by the experiment – namely, how much truth one can incorporate – implies answers to these questions if one assumes, independently of the experiment, that the relevant principles are true.[5]

VITALISM: AN EARLY ARGUMENT

Nietzsche's use of the idea of life as a standard of value lies at the bottom of many of his defenses of the things he admires. Concerning the sort of morality he approves, he says:

> Every naturalism in morality – that is, every healthy morality – is dominated by an instinct of life; some commandment of life is fulfilled by a determinate canon of "shalt" and "shalt not"; some inhibition and hostile element on the path of life is thus removed.
>
> (G V 4)

Morality, properly, stands in relation to life as means to end. In perhaps his broadest brief characterization of the sort of morality he opposes, he says that it makes "a means to life into a standard of life; instead of discovering the standard in the highest enhancement of life itself," it employs "the means to a quite distinct kind of life to exclude all other forms of life, in short to criticize and select life" (WM 354).

One commits this error of transforming a mere means into a sovereign standard when one treats anything other than life as an end in itself:

> If one severs an ideal from reality one debases the real, one impoverishes it, one defames it. "The beautiful for the sake of the beautiful," "the true for the sake of the true," "the good for the sake of the good," – these are three forms of evil eye for the real.
>
> Art, knowledge, morality are *means*: instead of recognizing in them the aim of enhancing life, one has associated them with the antithesis of life, . . . [one regards them] . . . as the

revelation of a higher world which here and there looks down
upon us through them.

(WM 298)

Life is the only thing that is good in itself, and is the standard
by which the value of everything else is to be measured; this is what
I will call Nietzsche's vitalism.

We can see, from the remarks I have just quoted, that Nietzsche's vitalism is in some way crucial to his aesthetics and his
epistemology as well as his ethics, to his view of the beautiful and
the true as well as the good.[6] Unless we can understand this principle and the reasoning that lies behind it, a good deal of what he
has to say will very likely pass us by. Perhaps the most natural way
to begin would be to look closely at Nietzsche's formulations of
vitalism to see what it would mean to take the enhancement of life
as a standard of value. But as the examples I have just quoted
suggest, his formulations of the principle are all disappointingly
sketchy. I think it will be more fruitful to begin by examining the
arguments he offers in favor of it, and then trying to determine
what the principle must mean – or should mean – by considering
what these arguments could be taken to prove.

We can find Nietzsche using the idea of life as a standard of value
very early in his career, as is indicated by the title of the second
Untimely Meditation: *On the Uses and Disadvantages of History for Life*.[7]
In that work we also find his first attempt to justify this idea. He sets
the argument up by first asking: "Is life to dominate knowledge and
science, or is knowledge to dominate life? Which of these two forces
is the higher and more decisive?" The argument which immediately
follows these questions is a curious one, but I think it can be read
in a way that at least makes it worth looking into. In order to do
that, I will interpret it somewhat along the lines of my earlier discussion of his doctrine of the enmity of the virtues (Chapter 5, pp. 81–
4). I will suppose that what he is asking is whether one drive is to
dominate another drive, and I will also suppose that he assumes that
for one drive to dominate another is for its end to be ranked higher
than the end of the other drive. This would mean that he is asking:
which is to be valued more highly, knowing or living? In light of
these suppositions, consider the argument he gives:

There can be no doubt: life is the higher, the dominating
force. For knowledge which annihilated life would have
annihilated itself with it. Knowledge presupposes life and thus

112

has in the preservation of life the same interest as any creature has in its own continued existence. Thus science requires superintendence and supervision.

(U II 10)

He seems to be saying that if life were not valued more highly than knowledge, knowledge would somehow pose a threat to the continued existence of life, and that this would be absurd because knowledge requires life in order to exist. I do not suppose that Nietzsche, in his pre-nuclear innocence, is saying that if knowledge were valued too highly it might bring an end to all life. What does worry him throughout the *Meditation* on history is the fact that a wrong ordering of one's values can seem to justify choices which are actually not justifiable. Perhaps he is thinking that, if one values some other good at least as highly as life then it is rational, in terms of one's values, to prefer the existence of that good to the existence of life. One can see Nietzsche's argument as an attempt to defend a certain ordering of one's values on the grounds that the alternative rankings would justify choices which it is absurd to think could be justified. Stated in its most general form, the argument might in that case be reconstructed like this: Any good that is properly valued at least as highly as life could justify the annihilation of life. And any good produced by human action that justified the annihilation of life would thereby justify its own annihilation. But no good could justify its own annihilation – since anything the annihilation of which is justified is not good. Consequently, no good that is produced by human action is properly valued as much as life. This has, at any rate, the appearance of a valid argument. If one finds this argument persuasive, then probably one should also find plausible his idea that our pursuit of values like knowledge requires "superintendence and supervision," that is, that we should take care that they do not interfere with our pursuit of the greater value of life.

But Nietzsche probably wants to show more than this. He does not merely believe that such goods as historical knowledge are of less importance than life, he thinks that we should "serve history only to the extent that history serves life" (U II P). He believes this because he thinks that all the goods that human beings seek are only good to the extent that in some sense they promote life. But it is not clear how this idea is related to this argument. It can be derived from the argument's conclusion, but only if we assume that any two goods can only be ranked by regarding one as a means to the other. This assumption, however, is certainly not true.[8] I value a dollar more than I value a candy bar, as may be inferred from the fact that I am not willing to a pay a dollar for a candy bar; but I do not regard the candy bar as a means to a dollar.

But the idea that all other goods are in some way means to life is apparently an important aspect of Nietzsche's vitalism. As one can see from several remarks I have already quoted, it plays a significant part in some of his statements of the vitalist principle, and it is not difficult to see why. As I have characterized it, vitalism has two parts; the first part states that life is the only thing that is good in itself, and the second states that it is the standard by which the value of everything else is to be measured. If one grants that all goods are only good as means to life, both parts of vitalism follow by easy inferences.

That this is true of the first part is obvious. That it is true of the second part is perhaps a little less obvious, but it is no less evident if one considers a simple example. The goal that a general seeks is victory in war. There are also various other things that he regards as good for him, as a general, such as the number of soldiers under his command, the invulnerability of their armor, and the range of their weapons. But he does not regard these other things as good without qualification. He would not spend all his time trying to get more troops while the enemy is launching an attack against him. More men, sought under such circumstances, would not constitute a good at all. This is because such goods are only good for him, as a general, to the extent that they conduce to the achievement of the goal of victory, and they are bad to the extent that they interfere with it. This being the case, victory is the standard by which he determines how good or bad things are. This is always how one's goals stand in relation to their means. If there were one goal that all other goods serve as a mere means, then that good would be the standard by which all value is measured. If life is that goal, then the second part of Nietzsche's vitalism is true.

If it could be shown that life is a goal with this sort of exalted importance, establishing the truth of vitalism would be very easy. But its importance for Nietzsche's argument is not merely a matter of convenience. Without it, the argument in the *Meditation* on history does not prove that vitalism is true at all, even if the argument is perfectly sound. Recall that the final conclusion of that argument, as I have interpreted it, states that the pursuit of the various other goods should not interfere with the pursuit of life. Vitalism is a considerably stronger thesis than this. It states that all things are only good or bad in virtue of some relation they have to life. The conclusion of his argument only says that various goods should not be pursued to the extent that they interfere with a certain greater good; it does not imply that there is some single reason why they are good. In particular, it does not imply that there can be one principle that indicates which things are good and worth pursuing in ethics, art, and the sciences. But Nietzsche's vitalism is meant to have these implications. The idea that life is the one end to which all other goods are means would provide the support this strong thesis needs, by showing why the concept of life serves as a standard of all value. It also appears to be, from his scattered remarks on the subject, the foundation on which his vitalism is actually based. Consequently, he needs to give an argument that is meant to show that we should accept the idea that life is the all-encompassing end he takes it to be.

A LATER ATTEMPT

He does give such an argument, long after the *Meditation* on history, in *Twilight of the Idols*. It begins with the passage, which I have already quoted, in which he says that in every "healthy morality," in every morality that "is dominated by an instinct of life," the "canon of 'shalt' and 'shalt not'" merely removes "some inhibition and hostile element on the path of life." Immediately afterwards, he adds that there is one alternative to such a morality: "*Anti-natural* morality – that is, almost every morality which has so far been taught, revered, and preached." Anti-natural morality is defined by the fact that it "turns, conversely, *against* the instincts of life: it is *condemnation* of these instincts, now secret, now outspoken and impudent." He adds, as if to explain this characterization: "Life has come to an end where the 'kingdom of God' begins" (G V 4). Apparently, the idea is that if a morality commends goals (such as the kingdom of God) other than the goals of the instincts of life, it condemns those instincts, and thus life itself, as something bad.

He then defends vitalistic or "healthy" morality by attacking its only alternative. He does not do so by claiming that its "revolt against life" is based on false beliefs; he points instead at what he regards as "the futility, apparentness, absurdity, and *mendaciousness* of such a revolt.'' The reasons he then gives for these charges are, at least at first glance, somewhat mysterious. He says that we cannot condemn or otherwise measure the value of life because to do so one would have to take ''a position *outside* of life.'' In order to explain and justify his claim that we cannot take such a position, he says:

> When we speak of values, we speak with the inspiration, with the way of looking at things, which is part of life: life itself forces us to posit values; life itself values through us when we posit values. From this it follows that even . . . anti-natural morality . . . is only a value judgement of life – but of what life? . . . I have already given the answer: of declining, weakened, weary, condemned life.
>
> (G V 5)

This argument is perplexing. It seems to come to rest on a gratuitous assumption that living things cannot really question the value of life, and then it seems to switch abruptly to an outrageously *ad hominem* attack on his opponents. We can secure a clue to what Nietzsche has in mind if we recall that ''healthy'' morality is defined in terms of its goal: its values are intended to promote life. This means that, in order for the other sort of morality to be the only alternative, it must also be defined in terms of its goals: it must have values that are *not* intended to promote life. In order for such a morality to be ''mendacious'' and ''apparent,'' these explicit values must covertly be intended to promote life after all. When he says that anti-natural morality is ''a value judgement of life,'' he must mean that it is a judgement that is made *for the sake of* a certain life.

What the argument comes to rest on, then, is a broad psychological claim about the proponents of the alternative view. At best it is only as good as the evidence for this claim. This means that the argument is not complete as it stands; it requires that evidence be given for this psychological interpretation, and he gives none in the passage I have just discussed. However, he does give the required evidence elsewhere in his work, and at considerable length. A brief survey of the evidence he presents will go far in indicating how the argument for naturalism in morality is supposed to work.

His most sustained discussion of these matters is to be found in his discussion of ascetic ideals in *On the Genealogy of Morals*

(GM III, esp. 11–21). By "ascetic ideals" he apparently means any ideal that requires one to frustrate the basic needs of the human organism, such as the desire for material well-being, the desire to feel good about oneself, and the sex instinct.[9] The part of this discussion which is relevant to our immediate concerns is his attempt to explain what he calls "serious" asceticism. This is the sort of asceticism in which these needs – either some or all of them – are explicitly condemned as bad.[10] Since these needs are absolutely ineradicable parts of life, to condemn them and try to correct them means that one regards life itself as "a wrong road . . . or as a mistake that is put right by deeds" (GM III 11). Thus what he calls serious asceticism in the *Genealogy* is identical to what he calls anti-natural morality in the *Twilight*.

To understand his attempt to explain this phenomenon, one must realize that his explanation rests on a certain crucial assumption:

> It is plain that in this essay I proceed on a presupposition that I do not first have to demonstrate to readers of the kind I need: that man's "sinfulness" is not a fact, but merely the interpretation of a fact . . . the latter viewed in a religio-moral perspective that is no longer binding on us.

He clearly takes the same position regarding all the "paradoxical and paralogical concepts" which are most characteristic of ascetic morality, including not only "sinfulness" but "'guilt,' 'sin,' . . . 'depravity,' [and] 'damnation'" as well (GM III 16). By dropping the religio-moral perspective, he is limiting himself to offering strictly naturalistic explanations of such concepts.

This in turn imposes a further constraint on the explanations he can give. As he sees it, these concepts do not give descriptions of natural phenomena that are as such even remotely plausible. They are only plausible descriptions of anything if one first assumes a world populated by supernatural entities like souls and gods, and various supernatural powers. This being the case, he cannot explain why people possess and use these concepts by pointing to evidence which leads them to do so. People who use such concepts claim they do have evidence that supports their use; but to do so they must invoke supernatural avenues to knowledge, such as revelation, which Nietzsche's assumption rules out. The idea that one suffers from a condition of chronic sinfulness is quite different in this respect from the idea that one keeps doing things that have bad consequences and unhealthy motives. It is easy to see how one could give evidence for the latter idea within a purely naturalistic perspective; but, within such a perspective, it is difficult to say what "evidence" could even mean in connection with the idea of chronic sinfulness. The only alternative to explaining ascetic concepts on the basis of evidence for them is to look at the role they play in the economy of the psyche itself. If an idea cannot be explained as a conclusion from evidence, not even as an understandable mistake, one asks what motive someone could have for accepting it.

With this purpose in view, he notices one striking characteristic that ascetic ideals have in common. This is the fact that they all have strong effects on the feelings of those who accept them and take them seriously. Different ideals have different effects, but these effects all fall into two general categories. Some ascetic notions seem to have a hypnotic effect on the human mind and body. If carried far enough, their effect is to reduce activity to "the minimum metabolism at which life will still subsist without really entering consciousness" (GM III 17). Examples of such notions include selflessness, sanctification, various "petty pleasures" such as the pleasures of giving, and "mechanical activity" (e.g., the "blessings of work") (GM III 17 and 18). Other ascetic notions have virtually the opposite effect; they tend to cause intense paroxysms of emotion. One of the most spectacular examples is guilt, which brings with it a whole series of emotional disturbances, including "dumb torment, extreme fear, the agony of the tortured heart, convulsions of an unknown happiness, the cry for 'redemption'" (GM III 20). Psychologically, the effects of ascetic concepts resemble those of psychoactive drugs. Some are depressants and others are stimulants.

On the basis of discussions of a wide range of ascetic concepts he gives the following explanation for all of them. They are, in various ways, means of resisting a chronic feeling of displeasure. This feeling of displeasure is caused by inhibited physiological activity, which in turn is caused by physical factors outside the organism, such as disease and an incorrect diet (GM III 17). It is obvious how the concepts which have hypnotic effects can achieve this purpose: they reduce the intensity of all conscious feelings, including feelings of displeasure. But it is less obvious how ideas that cause emotional disturbances can serve the same end, since some of these paroxysms are themselves generally unpleasant. The reason Nietzsche thinks they are able to do this lies, partly, in the nature of the displeasure these ideas are supposed to resist. This displeasure is not an acutely intense pain, but rather a "dull, paralyzing, protracted pain" (GM III 19). He thinks that this pain is actually deadened by the more violent emotions that these ideas cause, on the principle that a sufficiently strong sharp pain can block awareness of a dull one (GM III 15). This can be desirable if for some reason the sharp pain is preferable to the dull one. Nietzsche believes that in this case the violent affect is far preferable to the less violent one.

The reason why this is so illuminates his diagnosis of both categories of ascetic ideas. The principal reason the dull pain is undesirable is not the fact that it is painful. The main reason lies in the fact that this affect has a powerful effect on what one's life is like and yet, since its causes are unknown to the person who suffers it, it is experienced as a form of suffering that has no meaning. It gives one a sense of living "like a leaf in the wind, a plaything of nonsense – the 'sense-less'" (GM III 28). To one in the grips of such a feeling, life itself can seem meaningless; it can seem pointless to make choices and act. There is more than one way to prevent this catastrophe from happening. On the one hand, one can reduce the offending affect. This is what the more calming or hypnotic ascetic ideas do. On the other hand, one can replace it with an affect which, though it may also be unpleasant, is produced by one's own principles and consequently is experienced as saturated with meaning. The bite of conscience is indeed painful, but the ideas that make it possible place it in the context of the drama of sin, punishment, and redemption; when suffering humanity invented this affect "life again became *very* interesting" (GM III 20). Ascetic concepts in general brought to those who needed them the sense that there is a point to making choices and acting. The individual "could now *will* something; no matter at first to what end, why, with what he willed: *the will itself was saved*" (GM III 28).

Perhaps Nietzsche's defense of naturalistic morality in the *Twilight* is less mysterious now than it was at first. On the surface, anti-natural morality is intended to promote something other than life; its explicit meaning always includes or implies some sort of condemnation of biological existence as such. At bottom, however, "life wrestles in it and through it with death and *against* death"; it is "an artifice for the *preservation* of life" (GM III 13). It preserves life by making it possible for the afflicted to go on living. Thus, the defense of naturalistic morality is not based on a gratuitous assumption to the effect that living things cannot question the value of life. It is based on an inference to the best explanation. The starting-point of the inference is an extensive discussion of the observable characteristics of anti-natural – or, equivalently, ascetic – moralities. It is not possible to convey most of the content of this discussion in the summary I have given here, so most of the power of the argument has been lost in my presentation of it – inevitably, I think. At least the structure of the argument should be apparent enough. It consists of a description of Nietzsche's observations, an explanation of them which is meant to be coherent and plausible, and an implicit challenge to others to try to present a better explanation. He is confident that, at least within the constraints imposed by a naturalistic metaphysic, no explanation that is both relevantly different and better can be given.

Nietzsche is basing his argument for vitalism on the claim that all moralities are really vitalistic. He is merely charging those who claim to disagree with him with inconsistency; to the extent that he is trying to change someone's mind, he is asking that they bring their preaching into line with their apparently unalterable practice. There is no need to demonstrate vitalism, as if to refute someone who genuinely disagrees with it.

The objections Nietzsche does raise against anti-natural moralities are not really refutations at all. Some of his objections have to do with the character of their adherents. In the intentions that deeply underlie them, anti-natural moralities assume the value of life. But these intentions are carried out by means of ideas that imply that life is merely some sort of mistake. In order to take these ideas seriously, one must conceal one's deepest intentions, and thus the true nature of one's morality, from oneself. One's revolt against life must be not merely mendacious but reflexively so: one must be self-deceived. Clearly, Nietzsche regards this sort of systematic self-deception as a serious character-flaw.[11] Further, such desperate methods are only needed in the first place because one suffers from some hidden failure in one's functioning as a living organism – from some "physiological inhibition," as he puts it. This means that one is already, before being corrupted by anti-natural morality, a less than perfect example of what human beings at their best can be. Thus Nietzsche's attack on the character of his opponents in the *Twilight* is not logically irrelevant to his defense of vitalistic morality. As he sees it, this personal attack is required by the fact that the defense takes the form of arguing that all moralities are fundamentally vitalistic in the intentions that lie behind them. The argument implies that the real intentions involved are masked by other, merely apparent ones. In the *ad hominem* attack he claims that there is something characterologically deficient, so to speak, in the way in which these moralities promote life.[12]

Nietzsche has another objection to the way in which such moralities pursue the vitalistic goal. Although it is rather different in kind from the objection I have just explained, there is a certain logical connection between them. Although this objection could be described as a "medical" one, its force is ultimately character-ological. It consists of Nietzsche's assessment of ascetic morality as a technique for solving a certain problem. He does not deny that the problem it addresses – the need to resist a certain chronic feeling of malaise – is a real problem. Nor does he deny that, considered in its own terms, the technique is a success. Indeed, his explanation *requires* that it be successful, or it would fail to explain why people use the technique.

However, although he must admit that the technique achieves its aim, he thinks it does not aim very high. The affects that it combats are caused by organic dysfunctions – a "physiological inhibition." Naturalistic morality serves to remove "some inhibition and hostile element on the path to life" (G V 4), and in a certain sense this could be said of anti-natural morality as well. But anti-natural morality solves a problem of a very particular sort: without it, its adherents might not want to go on living, and it prevents that catastrophe from happening. It does this merely by directly altering one's consciousness; more precisely, it merely blocks one's awareness of the cause of one's problem. The cause is left untouched. In this respect, it is analogous to a pain-killing drug administered to patients who might otherwise commit suicide to avoid their pain.

The situation is worse than this with regard to the ascetic ideals which cause violent emotions, since the paroxysms they induce actually add more stress to the patient's already overburdened organs. They add "a shattered nervous system . . . to any existing illness" (GM III 21). As Nietzsche points out, "the violent physiological revenge taken by such excesses . . . does not really confute the sense of this kind of medication, which . . . does *not* aim at curing the sickness" (GM III 20). Still, the realm that ascetic morality does not aim to change for the better is precisely one's character, which determines the value of one's life and actions. A morality which aims higher, and attempts to make sounder and therefore better human beings of us, would be a better sort of morality, provided it could achieve its aim.

ASSESSING VITALISM

We now have two arguments for vitalism or at least, in the case of the earlier argument, for something like vitalism. What should we think of them? There is one important aspect of the later argument which I cannot adequately discuss here. The argument rests on, among other things, Nietzsche's claim that his explanation of moralities that are not overtly vitalistic is the best one available to us. In order to decide rationally that he is right about that, we would have to conduct the same sort of investigation that he himself has carried out, examining an extensive collection of data about the contents of these moralities and their immediate effects on the minds and lives of their adherents. Such an investigation would be strongly empirical, and would take us far into the fields of psychology and cultural anthropology. What I am attempting here is, of course, a more or less purely philosophical examination of Nietzsche's ideas. One can only acquire a right to accept the later argument if one's reflections on it eventually cross the boundaries of philosophy into other domains. However, it may not be necessary to go that far. This argument faces a certain difficulty which, if it cannot be overcome, would make it unnecessary to collect empirical data. It would indicate that the argument can be rejected out of hand. In fact, roughly the same difficulty is confronted by both of these arguments, and it is moreover a purely philosophical one.

Consider, first, what the later argument states. It can be summarized, and tidied up, as follows. We ought to accept the idea that life is the highest value, in that it is the good for the sake of which all other values are good. The values that are least likely to be good in this way are those that are prized by ascetic morality. But they are really only valued because they enable those who value them to go on living. In this sense, they are only valued for the sake of life. If even these goods are valued in this way then we must, in fact, already value all goods in the same way. Since this seems to be an unalterable fact about human nature then, for the sake of consistency, we should consciously accept the idea that life is the value for the sake of which all other values are good.

The difficulty I have in mind has to do with the fact that to say that something is done or valued "for the sake of life" can mean more than one thing. First – and this is probably the most natural meaning of the expression – it can mean that the thing is valued or done for the sake of survival, in order to prolong one's life. But it could also mean that the thing is done in order to live *well*, for the sake of well-being or flourishing. If I study philosophy or get married for the sake of the effect my choice has on my life, I am probably doing it in order to make my life better, not longer. Nietzsche's claim that life is the value for the sake of which all other values are good can be interpreted in two ways. If it must be taken in one way or the other, there is little doubt about which way it should be. In the preface to *On the Genealogy of Morals*, the book I have relied on so heavily for its discussion of ascetic morality, he says that he asks, concerning the value judgements people make, "*what value do they themselves possess?*"[13] To explain how this question is to be answered, he adds: "have they hitherto inhibited or promoted human flourishing (*Gedeihen*)?" (GM P 3). He judges the worth of values by considering them as means to well-being. This should not be surprising, since the apparent alternative – namely, considering them all as means to mere survival – would clearly be more or less insane. No one would say that the highest good is simply staying alive.

There seems to be only one way to interpret the conclusion of Nietzsche's later argument. This, however, presents Nietzsche with a serious difficulty, since it appears to indicate that the premises of the argument do not support the conclusion, even if they are true. It requires him to say, a step or two prior to his conclusion, that we already accept, in some implicit way, the idea that life is the ultimate end, in the sense that promoting human flourishing is that for the sake of which all other goods are good. In that case, the explanation of ascetic morality would have to say that even apparently life-denying values aim at life as an end, *in this sense*. Otherwise, it would fail to show that we already implicitly agree with his conclusion. But this is not what the explanation says. It says that the motivation behind these values is a need to find reasons to go on living, a need that would be satisfied by any reasons at all. The ultimate end is to go on living or, in other words, mere survival. A superficial reading of Nietzsche's use of the idea of anesthesia might give one the impression that he is attributing to the adherents of ascetic morality a hedonistic conception of well-being, according to which one can make one's life better by reducing the amount of pain in it or increasing it with pleasure. But in fact it assumes that these people do not hold such a conception of well-being. It depicts them as replacing painful experiences with others which are sometimes more intensely painful, and without any compensating increase in pleasure. What justifies the greater pains, in their way of life, is the fact that it increases the impression of meaning in their lives; meaning itself is valued because it enables them to continue to function as living organisms.

As I have reconstructed it, Nietzsche's later argument appears to depend, in a way that destroys its validity, on an ambiguity in one of its terms. There are undoubtedly other ways of presenting the argument which would represent with equal accuracy what he is doing, but one suspects that they would all suffer from essentially the same problem. What Nietzsche is doing is to argue that we ought to accept the idea that a certain value is the ultimate end by claiming that we already do seek it as the ultimate end. But in fact his claim about our actual motivation appears to attribute, at least to some of us, an end that is quite distinct from the one he recommends; but so far no reason has been given, and certainly none is obvious, why those who seek the end he attributes to ascetic moralists must already also seek the one he recommends.

A look at Nietzsche's earlier argument reveals a similar problem. Essentially, that argument states that no good that depends on human action for its existence should be valued as much as life, for if such a good were valued that highly it would justify the annihilation of life and, consequently, of itself. Here, once more, certain crucial premises are about survival and not well-being. The argument begins with the idea that if certain goods were valued too highly they could justify the sacrifice of our survival. If this supports the conclusion at all, it seems the conclusion would have to mean that no good that depends on human action for its existence would be valued as highly as *survival*. But this is not very plausible, because it means that justice, freedom, and truth are less important than staying alive. If this is what the conclusion means, one is inclined to think that there must be something wrong with the argument itself. Moreover, it is not at all what Nietzsche wants to prove. The book in which the argument occurs defends the idea that intellectual pursuits like the study of history should enable us to live better; he shows no interest in making our lives longer. Once again, Nietzsche's premises seem to be more or less irrelevant to the sort of idea he wants to prove.

LIFE

It should be obvious by now that my approach to Nietzsche is based on the assumption, which I hope I have managed to justify, that he is not a fool. Whenever one finds him engaged in a line of reasoning which seems to be invalid or otherwise bad in some simple and straightforward way, there is generally something one has missed or gotten wrong, such that the argument is better and more interesting than it appeared at first. It is probably healthy to suspect that something like this has happened in regard to the two arguments I have just discussed. Especially, one's suspicions should be aroused by the fact that twice, and years apart, he seems to have made a mistake that has something to do with an ambiguity in the notion of doing and valuing things "for the sake of life." Perhaps if we examine Nietzsche's conception of life, and of doing and valuing things for the sake of life, we can find a way in which at least one of these arguments might be repaired. I would like to suggest that this is indeed the case. Nietzsche has fairly definite views on the relationship between survival and flourishing, and there is at least reason to hope that they can be used to overcome the difficulties I have presented.

Life, according to Nietzsche, is a "multiplicity of forces, connected by a common mode of nutrition" (WM 641). Moreover, it is a multiplicity of forces in which "the different contenders grow unequally," so that some of them command and others obey (WM 642). Living organisms are the only systems of "forces" that are organized in this way. As we have already seen, the end that is served by everything that is good is to bring about a certain condition of the living organism, which he has called flourishing. In a late note, he gives the following further characterization of this end:

> The entire *conscious* life, the spirit along with the soul, the heart, goodness, and virtue – in whose service do they labor? In the service of the greatest possible perfection of the means (means of nourishment, means of enhancement) of the basic animal functions: above all, the enhancement of life.
>
> (WM 674)

The end is the perfection or completion or consummation (*Vervollkommnung*) of the basic animal functions, which apparently (his wording is not very clear here) is the same thing as the enhancement of life. One needs to know what "perfection" means in this context. Fortunately, he does not leave us entirely in the dark about this:

> Greater complexity, sharp differentiation, the contiguity of developed organs and functions, with the disappearance of the intermediate members – if that is perfection, then there is a will to power in the organic process by virtue of which dominant, shaping, commanding forces continually extend the bounds of their power and continually simplify within these bounds: the imperative grows.
>
> (WM 644)

Once again, this unpublished note is less lucid than Nietzsche's published writings generally are, but the basic idea is clear enough if one remembers Nietzsche's definition of life. Life is a hierarchically integrated system the members of which have a common means of support. Perfection is the state in which this integration is fully achieved (*vollkommen*). To "enhance life," then, is to increase the extent to which this state has been achieved.

This state is the end Nietzsche uses to measure the value of all other goods. Considering the importance of this idea, his account of it is, so far, disappointingly abstract and vague. One can get a more vivid notion of what it means by considering some of the ways in which he characterizes the absence of perfection, a condition that he variously calls "declining life," "degeneration," and "decadence." He usually characterizes this condition in terms of its symptoms. He says that "license and luxury" (G VI 2) as well as "the corruption of morals" (WM 43) are consequences of decadence or degeneration. The same is true of the tendency "to choose what is harmful to oneself" (G IX 35); it is also true of the tendency to make mistakes, in the sense of doing what is harmful to oneself by inadvertence (G VI 2). In addition, "the weakness of the will – or, to speak more definitely, the inability *not* to respond to a stimulus – is itself merely another form of degeneration" (G V 2). Finally, all activity that is laborious, not easy, tends to indicate that life is on the decline (G VI 2).

The variety of these signs and symptoms is bewildering at first; one could almost think that he simply uses terms like "degeneration" and "decadence" to describe whatever he does not like. But his definition of decadence tells us what he supposes they all have in common:

But this is the simile of every style of *decadence*: every time, the anarchy of atoms, disgregation of the will, "freedom of the individual." . . . Life, *equal* vitality, the vibration and exuberance of life pushed back into the smallest forms; the rest, *poor* in life. Everywhere paralysis, arduousness, torpidity *or* hostility and chaos.

(W 7)

One can see how each of these symptoms could be seen as an indication of the disintegration of the self, of a failure of integration among the parts of the psyche. Perhaps the most obvious case is weakness of will. Its presence indicates that one's conception of what one should do has failed to overcome contrary impulses and produce action. That is, a certain principle of order within the self has proved to be too weak to control certain other elements of the self. The same is true of the corruption of morals, at least if it represents a mere outbreak of licence and not the emergence of a new morality, except that here the failing source of order is moral principle.

Concerning the tendency to choose things that are bad for oneself, Nietzsche says that the principle, "Not to seek one's own advantage," is a psychological mask for a deeper state of affairs which could be expressed by "I no longer know how to *find* my own advantage." This in turn is a consequence of the sentiment, "*I* am no longer worth anything" (G IX 35). Once again, a potential source of order – the ability to determine what is to one's advantage – has failed to function. This is due to the failure of something else which, consequently, also proves to be a source of order: the ability to believe that one deserves to be advantaged. One could say something relevantly similar of the tendency to do what is harmful to oneself inadvertently. It means that the ability to discover one's advantage, whether one has it or not, has at any rate failed to impose its own order on one's behavior. Laborious action can also be seen as an indication of the weakness of a certain ordering principle. In this case, the motives behind one's act, whatever they are, prove to be strong enough to produce behavior: they were able to overcome whatever contrary impulses they encountered. But these contrary impulses were able to create difficulties for it; greater power would have experienced no difficulties.

Nietzsche's remarks on the symptoms of declining life indicate that his notion of perfection is simply an application of his

127

conception of power. It is obviously the same conception of power Zarathustra uses in his theory of virtue, in which he depicts the transformation of *Leidenschaften* into *Freudenschaften*. In Nietzsche's view, virtue is a sort of integration of the parts of the self. It arises when one part of the self imposes order on other, potentially chaotic parts by successfully orienting the subordinate parts toward its own purposes, until "they are confidently granted freedom again: they love us as good servants and go voluntarily wherever our best interests lie" (WM 384). In his discussion of the symptoms of decline, we see him identifying some of the parts of the self that carry out this form-giving task. They include notions about what one should do, moral principles, the ability to discover one's best interests and the desire to act on those discoveries, self-esteem, and in general all the purposes for which one acts. Perfection is achieved when forces like these rule within the self while other forces submit.

We are now ready to see a way out of the difficulty I posed for Nietzsche's later argument for vitalism. As you will recall, the argument required him to show that we all accept flourishing as the ultimate end, and the problem was that he seemed to be explaining the hard cases by attributing a distinct and independent end to certain people: namely, mere self-preservation. We have just seen what flourishing is for Nietzsche. It is the consummate attainment of power. This means that to flourish is to possess, fully, what we all seek, since Nietzsche also believes that all living things strive ultimately for power. Thus, flourishing is the ultimate end for all of us. This, of course, is what he should be saying, given the logic of the later argument. This argument could be made to work if one could argue, further, that the behavior he attributes to adherents of anti-natural morality is not directed at survival as an ultimate end at all but, rather, at flourishing as he understands it. His conception that a will to power is the fundamental source of all motivation requires him to think that such a further argument is possible, and he is well aware of this fact.

> Physiologists should think before putting down the instinct of self-preservation as the cardinal instinct of an organic being. A living thing seeks above all to *discharge* its strength – life itself is *will to power*; self-preservation is only one of the indirect and most frequent *results*.
> In short, here as everywhere else, let us beware of

superfluous teleological principles – one of which is the instinct of self-preservation. . . . Thus method, which must be essentially economy of principles, demands it.

(JGB 13)

Evidently, the further argument would state that the assumption of a will to power can explain the ubiquitous fact that organisms tend to do things that support their own existence, because such behavior is just what one would expect from an organism that seeks power above all else: self-preservation would be a frequent, though indirect result of such a drive. If that is true, the drive to self-preservation is a dispensable principle, and the will to power by itself provides a simpler and therefore better explanation of the same phenomena.

It is not difficult to see how he can think that his simpler theory can explain the same facts. To achieve power is, to say it once more, to appropriate parts of the environment and incorporate them, along with the other parts of the organism, into a single hierarchial system. The most crudely obvious instance of this – namely, the physiological process of nutrition – has a tendency, which is also obvious, to be life-sustaining. On the other hand, "if this incorporation is not successful, then the form probably falls to pieces" (WM 656): failures to achieve power have a tendency to diminish one's chances for survival. This is certainly true of all the symptoms of degenerating life I catalogued a few pages back.[14]

However, it is also true that the "will to power can manifest itself only against resistances; therefore it seeks that which resists it" (WM 656). Consequently, life has a certain tendency to do things that put itself in danger. We should expect life to be somewhat less efficient in supporting itself, more willing to waste its resources and take risks, than it would be if it sought mere survival as something good in itself. Nietzsche would probably say that this is just what we do see when we look at the world around us. The fact that life by nature takes risks means that it will have a certain systematic proneness to break down. There will always be individual organisms that fail in their attempts to achieve full integration. Since life always strives for power, we should not expect these troubled individuals to give up the struggle. But if the breakdown is serious enough, the organism will only be able to continue its striving to the extent of keeping the basic physiological processes going. This will appear to the unenlightened to be a mere fight for preservation or survival. It does no harm to call it that, as long as we understand what it actually is. It is actually a fight for the only sort of power that is still available.

To carry on this fight, the individual will be willing to sacrifice everything, including other sorts of power. To see what this can mean, consider the fact that Nietzsche's conception of life, and the notion of flourishing that is based on it, make no use of the distinction between mind and body. The processes of appropriation and integration to which they refer would have to include mental as well as physical functions. Mentally, appropriating parts of the world would mean having accurate notions of what the world is like, and integration would mean conducting one's spiritual functions in ways that are consistent with what one knows. In this way, " 'the spirit' is relatively most similar to a stomach" (JGB 230), since it carries out what is really the same sort of activity. But if knowing the truth means that one will no longer be able to act at all, the organism is more than willing to sacrifice this sort of power altogether. It will dull and block its consciousness, believe in fictional beings like gods and souls, and perhaps even give itself over to powerfully distracting emotions. These are the strategies Nietzsche attributes to adherents of anti-natural morality. The difference between it and the sort of morality he recommends is not based on a difference between the ends they seek; it is based on the difference between relative failure and relative success in achieving the same end: life as will to power.

This, at last, completes my account of Nietzsche's vitalism and his arguments for it. If it still seems somewhat obscure, that might be because, as I said earlier, it can only be fully understood when one has understood its relations with the other two principles I mentioned at the beginning of this chapter: Nietzsche's relativism and his experimentalism. Before I try to provide this understanding, I must give some account of his relativism. I have so far said little about it.

RELATIVISM

Nietzsche is an ethical relativist. Ethical relativism is the idea that what counts as right or good varies from one individual to the next. It can be defined somewhat more elaborately – and, for my purposes, well enough – as a claim about the standards by which people and their actions are ethically evaluated: it states that such standards apply to individuals (that is, they are only able to indicate, correctly, their worth as persons or how they ought to act) in virtue of some fact about individuals themselves; and that, because the relevant facts are sometimes true of one person and not of others, not all standards that apply to some people apply to everyone. In an analogous way, everyone is a relativist about some standards or other. Professors do not judge the work of beginning students and graduate students by the same standards. Here the relevant fact is how much the student has had an opportunity to know. Probably most educated people are relativists about standards of etiquette. An American who visits another country and knowingly violates local customs, simply on the grounds that what is true in Wisconsin is also true in Bali, would be generally seen as an obnoxious and possibly dangerous fool. But of course many people are not relativists about morality, and there are some forms of ethical relativism that are more or less obviously absurd. It is surely not true that people visiting the head-hunting Dyaks should commit ritual murder.

There are two characteristics of relativism, in my sense of the word, which I should probably be more explicit about before going on. They are both relevant to understanding Nietzsche.

First, various different facts can determine which standards apply to a person. If it is true, as guide books say, that women visiting Balinese temples should not wear shorts, that is (in large part) because the locals believe it is true. The relevant fact can be a belief. There is a frequently discussed version of ethical relativism which says that an ethical standard applies to a person just in case they believe the standard is true, or just in case most people in the community they are in believe it. We shall see shortly that Nietzsche does not hold this form of ethical relativism.[15] But there are other sorts of facts that can be relevant in this way. Professors do not select the standards they use when evaluating freshman term papers on the grounds that the freshmen believe those standards. They base their choice on other facts about the individuals involved.[16]

Second, just as it is possible to be a relativist about etiquette and not about ethics, it is possible to be a relativist about some ethical standards and not others. We have already seen one standard about which Nietzsche does not take a relativist position. He evaluates the worth of persons on the basis of a single standard: the degree to which they have attained what he calls power. He does not believe that its applicability is based on facts that distinguish one person from another.

Now I will try to say what sorts of standards Nietzsche was relativistic about, and what sorts of facts he thought determine the applicability of the standards involved. On the first of these two issues, he is fairly explicit:

> My philosophy aims at an ordering of rank: not at an individualistic morality. The ideas of the herd should rule in the herd – but not reach out beyond it: the leaders of the herd require a fundamentally different valuation for their own actions, as do the independent, the "beasts of prey," etc.
>
> (WM 287)

Nietzsche is relativistic about which morality should "rule" one's actions. By this he presumably means that, for different types of people, different moralities are needed to determine, correctly, what they ought to do. The individualistic sort of morality he usually seems to recommend is actually not applicable to everybody.

What facts are relevant to deciding which morality is applicable in a given case? He says that the creation of a morality is "the erection of the conditions – often erroneous – of existence of a limited group" (WM 260). More exactly, it indicates the group's "consciousness of the conditions for [their] preservation and growth" (WM 258). I think it is fairly clear that Nietzsche thinks that, although this consciousness is often erroneous, when a morality does succeed in creating conditions for the preservation or growth of a given type of person, it is applicable to that type. Consider the fact that the criticisms of anti-natural morality I discussed in the last section only went as far as saying that such moralities are signs of declining life. He did not say, or even suggest, that such a morality should not rule the actions of people who have declined in the relevant way. Elsewhere, he says that it is actually one of "the advantages of the Christian moral hypothesis" that it "prevented man from despising himself as man, from taking sides against life . . . it was a *means of preservation*" (WM 4). This seems to be an important part of the reason why he insists that he makes "war on the anemic Christian ideal . . . not with the aim of destroying it but only of putting an end to its tyranny" (WM 361). Its "tyranny" is its "will to a single morality," which amounts to "a tyranny over other types by that type whom this single morality fits" (WM 315).

The Christian ideal was a means to preservation, but apparently it was not a means to growth. If preservation is one's main problem – if one has trouble maintaining the most basic forms of power and its higher forms are consequently not a real possibility – then one belongs under the rule of a morality like this one, provided that it really is a means to one's preservation. But if this is not one's problem, then a morality that has this lowly aim will not fit one's nature. The emotional and intellectual effects of such a morality will inhibit one from achieving anything higher.

Nietzsche's relativism is what his vitalism yields when it is forced to give answers to a certain important question. If one asks how one determines a person's order of rank, Nietzsche's vitalism, together with the doctrine of power that is supposed to explain what it means, yields an answer which is fairly straightforward. One's rank is a function of the extent to which one has attained power. This principle applies to everyone. In order to apply this idea to cases, we would probably need a good deal of information about the way the human psyche works, and probably an elaborate analysis of the concept of power; but one can hope that the idea could be applied to everyone without the use of any additional evaluative standards.

But if we ask a different question, one that is at least as important – namely: What should a given individual do? – the question is less straightforward in at least one respect. Of course, the principle tells us to do what would conduce to one's preservation or (if possible) one's growth. But "what would conduce to one's preservation or growth" does not describe a readily identifiable class of actions. Consequently, it does not tell one what to do, unless more is said. What must be added before this question is answered for me would be a description of those things which I should do. This would constitute an additional set of evaluative principles. In order to select this additional set, I must know facts about myself that would indicate what conditions would bring about my preservation or growth. Since these conditions differ in different people, these evaluative principles would differ from one person to the next. What I ought to do may not be at all what you ought to do and consequently different moralities may apply to us. Thus Nietzsche must be a relativist about the question of what one ought to do.[17]

Long ago, before the advent of Christianity, people believed that there are many gods. Each culture had its own gods. The gods of others are real, but they are not one's own. Toward the gods of others one owes at most a kind of politeness, but not worship. We owe worship toward our own gods because they make our crops grow and chase the fish into our nets: they help us to flourish. Others have reason to revere the gods with whom they have the same relationship. Universal benevolence would require that we hope that all people have gods of their own, and not that they worship ours. As Zarathustra said: "Precisely this is godlike, that there are gods, but no God" (Z III 12 11; see also WM 1038 and 1039). Nietzsche's ethical relativism amounts to taking a precisely analogous position on standards of right conduct; it is a moral polytheism.

EXPERIMENTALISM AS A PRINCIPLE OF SOCIAL ORDER

The way in which Nietzsche's relativism is connected with his vitalism imposes a certain epistemological problem on those who wish to apply them to their lives: given that the standards which are applicable to each of us may for all we know be different, and given that the correct choice of standards rests on deep facts about ourselves that may at present be unknown, how do we know to which set of values we ought to dedicate our lives? The same constellation of ideas imposes a constraint on the sort of solution that can be given to this problem:

> Virtues are as dangerous as vices in so far as one lets them rule over one as authorities and laws from without and does not first produce them out of oneself, as one should do, as one's most personal self-defense and necessity, as conditions of precisely *our own* existence and growth, which we recognize and acknowledge independently of whether other men grow with us under similar or different conditions.

> (WM 326)

The solution must come from within us, and cannot be imposed from the outside. This important fact, and the reason which lies behind it, indicates something about how we must interpret such comments as this late note:

> From the pressure of plenitude, from the tension of forces that continually increase in us and do not yet know how to discharge themselves, there arises a condition like that preceding a storm: the nature we constitute becomes dark.

This, too, is pessimism. A doctrine that puts an end to such a condition by *commanding* something or other – a revaluation of values by virtue of which the accumulated forces are shown a way, a whither, so they explode into lightning flashes and deeds – certainly does not need to be a doctrine of happiness: by releasing forces that had been compressed and dammed to the point of torment it *brings happiness*.

(WM 1022; see also WM 1007)

If the choice of values cannot be imposed on the virtue-seeking individual, the agent that commands something or other cannot be anyone other than the individual to whom the command is addressed. This is because what we are attempting to discover is, essentially, whether the "whither" that is being commanded can be integrated with certain largely unknown forces within oneself into a more powerful whole. This is something that can only be found out by *trying out* ideals on an individual basis; that is, by individual experimentation. For instance, we may each try devoting ourselves to assimilating as much of the truth as we can. If we find that the experiment vivifies us, we grow into the next experiment; if we note the all-too-familiar symptoms of decline, we retreat from it and try something else. We use vitalism to evaluate our experimental results, each judging for himself or herself.

The language of this late note – in which potentially dangerous psychological forces are said to become benign by receiving direction from an agency with the power to envision and impose purposes – indicates what sort of experiments Nietzsche has in mind. The experimentation he is calling for is simply the process by which, as we saw in Chapter 5, virtue is formed.

By implication, Nietzsche's experimentalist relativism, as it might be called, commits him to a certain view of what a society of people who seek excellence of character would be like. It would resemble a community of scientists who formulate hypotheses, conduct experiments, and learn from one another's results. It would differ from such a community in that, if the experiments are conducted rightly, the members would not all arrive at the same "theory," so to speak. They would not arrive at the same moral code. The society would, if all goes as it should, split into subcultures, each of which is united by the values its members share. Such a society would not be a chaotic one, but the particular order that would be present in it would not be there because someone intended it to be. It would emerge unpredictably from unknown sources within the individual participants. In other words, it would be a form of natural order.

This is important because, as we saw in Chapter 4, natural order was an idea Nietzsche attacked early in his career and toward which he remained suspicious for years afterward. Such a conception of what society would be like would, in fact, be an instance of the liberal conception of order. As such, it would contradict his notion of philosophers as artists who mould and shape humanity according to their own designs. As I pointed out earlier (in Chapter 4, pp. 64–5), one is no artist if one's materials move and form themselves into an orderly whole of their own accord. No doubt, philosophers could play an important role in building such a society. They could, for instance, formulate principles that others could use in evaluating the results of their own experiments. In addition, they could present their evaluations of the results of past experiments, and they could also predict the results of future ones. Finally, and perhaps most importantly, by developing influential theories of moral experimentation, they could help to create the system of shared principles on the basis of which the experimenters relate to one another; such a system would serve as a framework within which new forms of excellence could spontaneously emerge. As important as all these activities would be, they nonetheless cannot be described as ones in which all-powerful artists shape human nature to fit their own designs.

It is not clear to what extent Nietzsche recognized these implications, but he did eventually come to see a conflict between experimentalism and his notion of a world-architect, and what he saw troubled him. In an aphorism added to the 1886 edition of *The Gay Science* he considers the fact that Europe will probably soon make the transition from a traditional society, in which everyone sees their role in life as fixed and given, to the sort of society we find in Periclean Athens and contemporary America, in which the "individual becomes convinced that he . . . *can manage almost any role*, and everybody experiments with himself, improvises, makes new experiments, enjoys his experiments; and all nature ceases and becomes art." As those who experiment with themselves in this way become more plentiful, "another human type is disadvantaged more and more and finally made impossible; above all, the great 'architects.'" Under those conditions, "who would still dare to undertake projects that would require thousands of years for their completion?'' For such projects, one needs as one's materials people who have a certain attitude toward themselves: they must think ''that man has value and meaning only insofar as he is *a stone in a great edifice.*'' Today we find it more or less impossible to see ourselves in this way. This obvious fact yields an inescapable conclusion: ''What will not be built any more henceforth, and *cannot* be built any more, is – a society in the old sense of that word; to build that, everything is lacking, above all the material.'' By ''society in the old sense of that word'' he apparently means a community that is structured by principles like ''classes, guilds, and hereditary trade privileges,'' societies like ''those monsters of social pyramids that distinguish the Middle Ages'' (FW 356).

It is not entirely clear what his attitude toward this great social transition is. One thing, at least, is quite clear: he recognizes that, to the extent that people experiment with their own lives, the work of the artists who fashion new people by issuing values for others cannot be done. To the extent that people are experimenters, their values come from within themselves. He also *seems* to think that experimentalism is now so widespread that this sort of artistry is already impossible, and will remain so.

If this is what he thinks, he only has one alternative, and in one unpublished note he seems, at least momentarily, to be taking it: ''Who creates *the goal* that stands above the individual? Formerly one employed morality for preservation: but nobody wants to preserve any longer, there is nothing to preserve. Therefore an *experimental morality*: to *give* oneself a goal'' (WM 260).[18] If for some reason it is impossible to remake others by issuing goals for them, he is ready to embrace experimentalism as an alternative to it.

Of course, it is quite possible that this is merely a passing mood, and that Nietzsche's more persistent attitude is to hope that the increasingly experimentalist and Americanized masses will eventually become willing once again to accept direction from people they recognize as their superiors. This attitude is at least suggested by the pyramid-shaped utopia he describes in section 57 of *The Antichrist* (see Chapter 6, p. 99 above). The hierarchical structure of such a society might simply consist in the fact that the values that are embraced by the lower orders are handed down to them from above. But where, exactly, would these values come from? One possible answer would be that they are the values which arise from the experiments conducted by the elite. I doubt that this could be the answer that Nietzsche would give, simply because it would be too obviously inconsistent with other things he believes. The idea that the masses can adopt the results of the experiments of the aristocratic few conflicts with his idea that the values of the herd should rule within the herd. If herd-values rule, the values held by aristocratic philosophers do not. What is more important, the idea that anyone can adopt the results of someone else's experiment conflicts with the relativistic basis of his experimentalism. The reason why experiments are needed in the first place is that people are so different that they should not have the same values, and Nietzsche clearly thinks that the elite is very different from the herd. To impose the results of the experiments of the elite on the masses would merely injure the masses and do no one any good.

If we assume that herd-values are to be handed down from above, there seems to be only one other way these values could originate. If they do not emerge from experiments conducted by the aristocrats, they must be consciously invented by them, tailored from whole cloth to fit the vital needs of the lower orders. But this alternative does not seem to be any more congenial to Nietzsche than the other one is. As I have already suggested, he appears to have no objection to the fact that the ideas of Christianity rule the herd. He seems to be willing to accept the verdict of two thousand years' experience, to the effect that Christianity is a means of preservation, and thus suitable to one's needs if what one needs is the wherewithal to survive. Actually, this suggests that Nietzsche does not believe that most people ought to think any differently than they already do.[19]

At this point, a serious difficulty stands in the way of our understanding Nietzsche's final views on the way society should be ordered. Among those who practice the moral experimentalism Nietzsche recommends, shared values would emerge from the interactions among the experimenters themselves. This indicates a desirable sort of social order that can exist, at least, within the aristocracy. But whether Nietzsche's experimentalism can be a principle of order for society as a whole depends on the so far unanswered question of the intended audience for Nietzsche's principle: to whom is he recommending this experimentation? This is where the difficulty arises. If he refuses to extend the experimentalist principle to the lower orders, it seems that the refusal cannot be based on the idea that they should merely accept their values from above.

But he does have other reasons to deny that they should practice the sort of experimentation that is practiced by the aristocracy, reasons which he seems to find conclusive. When he describes the third and lowest caste in *The Antichrist*, "the great majority," he says that the activities they pursue – including "handicraft, trade, agriculture" – are "compatible only with a mediocre amount of ability and ambition." To be "a public utility, a wheel, a function . . . is the only kind of *happiness* of which the great majority are capable" (A 57). To put the matter in language that Nietzsche uses elsewhere, the tasks to which their lives are devoted are mainly directed toward preservation, toward the survival of themselves and the community they serve. The low-level, utilitarian functions they perform are the ones that, as I pointed out earlier (Chapter 6, p. 103), enable the rest of the community to survive. They seem to rule out the growth in excellence of character which is the goal of the aristocrats. Since such growth is precisely the point of the experiments Nietzsche is describing, these experiments can have no interest or value for them.

So far, we are left without a solution to the problem of where the values should come from which order the lives of the vast majority of the human race. As a matter of fact, Nietzsche offers a solution to this problem in the same section of *The Antichrist* from which I have just quoted. He says that the system of rules that orders such a society "originates like every good code of laws: it sums up the experience, prudence, and experimental morality of many centuries; it concludes: it creates nothing further." As a society reaches this stage of its development, "the most circumspect stratum . . . declares the experience according to which one should live – that is, *can* live – to be concluded." They do this because they realize that "what must be prevented above all is further experimentation." It is rather startling to hear Nietzsche say that an ideal society begins when experimentation comes to an end, but one is even more startled when he indicates, a mere page later, that the point of erecting this framework of rules is that it makes possible the "highest caste," which is composed of people who "find their happiness . . . in the labyrinth, in hardness against themselves and others, in experiments" (A 57). Generally, authors who appear to contradict themselves this blatantly are using some word in more than one sense. The experimentation that comes to an end must not be the same as that which is now to be pursued with single-minded intensity by the caste of Nietzschean aristocrats.

One difference between the two sorts of experimentation is more or less obvious. The people who wisely declare that the basic structure of society is finished are putting their stamp on something that has been "*proved* right by a tremendous and rigorously filtered experience," but the experience involved is mostly not theirs. That is, the experiments that lie behind the basic structure were not conducted by them. These experiments seem to be constituted by the experience of whole communities for long periods of time. Here we are concerned with a sort of experimentation in which one clearly *is* expected to adopt the results of experiments conducted by others. Society as a whole is being ordered by the results of experiments conducted by past generations. This fact distinguishes these experiments sharply from the ones Nietzsche associates with the aristocratic caste. This fact is probably connected with the fact that these experiments also have a purpose of their own. They determine, as he says, the laws "according to which one should live – that is, *can* live" (A 57). That is, they make it possible for the group to survive.

Nietzsche is clearly talking about two quite different sorts of experimentation. One of them is only to be practiced by those who, leaving the problems of mere survival behind them, strive for ever greater excellence of character. Because of the nature of the problems they solve, these experiments must necessarily be highly individualistic: their results can only apply directly to the individuals who conduct them. Experiments of the other sort have a more general sort of application, presumably because the more banal problem which they solve remains much the same across generations: How is it possible for us to live together?

The survival-oriented sort of experimentation is the source of all the values by which the vast majority of the human race shall live. Principal among the laws that it determines is the "*order of castes*, the supreme, the dominant law," which "is merely the sanction of a *natural order*, a natural lawfulness of the first rank." As such, it determines the rights and obligations that define the various social classes. Among the elite, this framework is merely the basis upon which they will erect new values which are uniquely their own. For the majority, however, the framework includes all the values they need. Beyond following the basic rules of their class, they are free to pursue their small pleasures and narrowly specialized excellences. "For the mediocre, to be mediocre is their happiness; mastery of one thing, specialization – a natural instinct" (A 57).

Considering its obvious importance, one would like to hear Nietzsche say more about how this sort of experimentation is supposed to work. He does not say any more than this in his later writings. But this may not be necessary, because he has already covered it in detail in his earlier works. The rules he is discussing here seem to represent a form of what, in the writings of the late 1870s and early 1880s, he calls the "morality of custom": the sort of code that represents the accumulated "experiences of men of earlier times as to what they supposed useful and harmful" (M 19); the morality that is "constantly being worked at by everybody" (M 11).

His use of this idea in a description of a utopia written at the end of his career represents a significant shift in this way of thinking, since his earlier discussions of the morality of custom were by no means approving. His disapproval must have been due, at least in part, to the fact that such moralities arise spontaneously as a result of collective experience and are not created by anyone's conscious design. They constitute a form of natural order. This is the sort of order that he had hoped would be replaced by the law-giving moralities designed by philosophers. Now he is embracing the morality of custom as a principle of social order and explicitly acknowledging that the order it establishes is a natural one, "a natural lawfulness of the first rank." This natural order creates a framework *within which* the legislating philosophers fulfill their task. The framework is created by an enactment that merely records and preserves a sorting out of social functions for the members of society which has arisen gradually over generations: it merely "concludes," it "creates nothing further." On the other hand, as I pointed out a few pages ago, the process by which the philosophers' values are formed is characterized by natural order of another sort. Thus Nietzsche's experimentalism eventually leads him to employ, at least implicitly, two sorts of natural order: one of them to guide the elite and the other to govern the lives of the great majority.

WHICH TRAITS ARE VIRTUES?

For Nietzsche, one's virtues belong uniquely to oneself. One discovers which virtues are one's own by discovering the goals toward which one's psychic energies should be directed. These, in fact, are the same thing: according to the theory of virtue offered in *Zarathustra*, virtue is a certain complete integration of the psyche, in which one's passions are directed toward one's highest goals. The question of what the virtues are, in relation to me, is identical to the question of what those goals are toward which I should direct my life. A more radical question, which is apparently also decided by experimentation, is the question of whether I should make a serious attempt to achieve this sort of consecration of goals at all. Most people lack the inner strength and hardness to achieve such full integration. Such people are of a lower rank than those who do have the needed inner resources. It is precisely because of their lower rank that what Nietzsche calls virtue is not for them. Their lives are properly driven by appetites directed toward a miscellaneous set of goals which are sought in no particular order, except that activities which produce things the community needs in order to live will be particularly important. Their appetites will be held in check by a collection of conventional rules, but this of course cannot make them virtuous, in Nietzsche's sense of the word. Mainly, it will make them relatively safe to live with; it will prevent their appetites from posing a threat to the order of society.

Is there anything else one can say about the virtues of those who are capable of virtue? Nietzsche clearly thinks that there are *some* traits that, for such people, are always virtues. The process of acquiring virtue has a certain structure which is the same wherever it occurs, so that there are some traits of character that all virtue-seeking individuals will need. There are, so to speak, second-order virtues, traits that are virtuous because they help one to become more virtuous. This explains why, despite his relativism, Nietzsche speaks of some traits as being virtuous wherever they are found. Some virtues are directed toward goals which, if the agent achieves them, will bring about some necessary condition for the further creation of virtue.

There is one trait that it is particularly obvious Nietzschean experimenters will need. They must know that the experiments they have embarked upon are apt to be very costly in every way, involving as they will many false starts in which valuable resources of every kind will simply be wasted. Yet the experimentation can only be carried out in the right spirit if it is done with the enthusiasm that is appropriate to something that is good in itself. It must be loved as an opportunity to produce and disseminate new value. One can only act in this way if one feels that one possesses the needed resources in overflowing abundance; one must be glad to waste them. This means that one must possess the super-healthy love of the good that Nietzsche calls the "gift-giving virtue" (Chapter 6, pp. 90–4). Further, the experiments will be very difficult and hazardous. The experimenters realize that they are experimenting with their own lives and will inevitably realize that there is always a very real possibility that their adventures will bring ruin upon them in one way or another. Nietzsche apparently believes that they will only be able to do what they must do if this fact only makes their task more interesting to them, which means that they are moved by a positive desire to face danger and in general all things that are difficult to face. This, at any rate, would explain why he regards what he calls *Mut*, or courage, as a virtue wherever it is found.

Nietzsche discusses a second-order virtue of a potentially different sort in a passage in the chapter called "Our Virtues" in *Beyond Good and Evil*. He begins by saying that we are wrong to suppose, because the crudest expressions of cruelty are rather rare in our part of the world, that cruelty itself is rare, that the "savage beast" has at last been "mortified." It is true that the sort of cruelty evinced by the Roman in the arena is rare among us, but we should realize that cruelty is not necessarily something that comes "into being at the sight of the sufferings of *others*." We can realize this if we consider the enthusiasm with which religious ascetics frustrate their strongest desires and violate the integrity of their intellects. Finally, he asks us to "consider that even the seeker after knowledge forces his spirit to recognize things against the inclination of the spirit." After all, "the basic will of the spirit . . . unceasingly strives for the apparent and superficial" and finds our attempts to penetrate appearances and find the truth painful (JGB 229). The way in which things appear to us, being in part a creation of our own wishes, is typically more pleasant than the truth, and is certainly easier to come by.

Nietzsche believes that human beings could not have found as much truth as they have if the search for it were not to some extent driven by a scornful desire to inflict pain on one's own intellectual laziness. It is obvious that he believes that this sort of cruelty is something far higher than the other sorts he mentions in this passage, and the reason clearly lies in the fact that the goal toward which it is turned is far higher in his estimation than the goals sought by the others. Here, one might say, the passion of cruelty is transformed into a virtue of cruelty. Naturally, as he admits later in his discussion of "Our Virtues," "it would sound nicer" if we were to call this trait "extravagant honesty" or perhaps "love of wisdom, sacrifice for knowledge, heroism of the truthful – there is something in [these names] which swells one's pride." But he regards "cruelty" as a more revealing name than the others: "the basic text of *homo natura* must again be recognized" (JGB 230).

The virtue of philosophical cruelty, as one might call it, might not be a trait of character that *all* virtue-seeking individuals need. While his analysis of life enables him to say that the most powerful human lives will be the ones that appropriate and integrate the most truth, his rather extreme views on the dangers and difficulties of knowing the truth at least open the possibility that not *all* individuals who seek virtue need this trait, since not all will have the high ambitions that require it. Nonetheless, he clearly thinks one will need it if one is one of the greatest experimenters. Accordingly, he thinks that this trait is a virtue for all the members of a certain group of people: namely, those who are of the very highest rank.

8

IMMORALISM AGAIN

MORALITY AND MORALITIES

We have seen enough to realize, now, that Nietzsche does advocate a morality – in the lower-case sense of the word – of his own. If this is not entirely obvious, that is due in part to the fact that his code does not tell us, at least not directly, which actions we should do or avoid. It concerns the states of character from which actions arise; it is about virtue. Furthermore, it does not give a list of virtues which it is good for everybody to have. What he manages to show is that something can (conceivably, at any rate) be a morality without doing any of these things. His experimentalism states that one finds one's virtue by creating it, and one creates it by seeking various goals and finding ones which bring about the integration of the self that is required by his vitalism. That is, his code avoids doing these things by making his conception of virtue entirely procedural.[1] By this I mean that it specifies which traits are virtues by indicating a certain process and declaring that any trait that arises from this process is virtuous.[2] It is the fact that a state of character arises in this way that *makes* it virtuous.

Whatever difficulties a morality that is procedural in this way might inevitably bring with it – and I will explore one of them in the next chapter – Nietzsche has voluntarily accepted an additional problem which was not inevitable. Not resting content with defending his own morality, he also attacks Morality in the upper-case sense of the word. This means that, in defending his own views, he is committed to avoiding all the errors he attributes to the target of these attacks. He must avoid using the concept of responsibility and any version of the idea of opposite values. He must avoid making ought-judgements of the sort we have seen him attacking. He must also avoid universalizing his judgements of value (in the sense in which he is opposed to this practice) and he must not require that anyone act disinterestedly. In addition, his own views must be consistent with the various theories he uses to criticize these practices. Does he manage to do all this in the course of developing his own conception of virtue?

RESPONSIBILITY AND "OUGHT"

It is more or less obvious that Nietzsche's own morality makes no use of the idea of "responsibility," in the sense in which his immoralism denies that there is such a thing. That is, it does not assume that one's acts originate in a mental event which is *causa prima*, a cause that is unconditioned by factors outside itself (WM 288). Actions, including mental acts, are evaluated only as expressions of one's character, and this means that they have value insofar as they are *connected* with events other than themselves. Indeed, one's character is virtuous *to the extent that* its parts are connected with one another. Further, the value of one's character as a whole, as a system, does not depend on the extent to which the entire system is independent of factors outside itself. Its value depends only on the extent to which it is characterized by integrated complexity.

Though this may be obvious enough, the situation is less clear if we turn to one of the theories Nietzsche uses in criticizing the idea of responsibility. I have in mind here the idea that he calls the "belief in 'descent.'" In order to show how this idea leads from the "moral" to the "extra-moral" point of view, I have interpreted it as stating that the value of an act or conscious mental event is derived from and identical to the value of its source (Chapter 2, pp. 11–12). At this point, Nietzsche assumes that the source of any given act or conscious mental event is a state of the agent that is unconscious but which nonetheless has the same sort of value that these more derivative goings-on have: they, too, are healthy or unhealthy, noble or base, and so forth. Applied in light of this assumption, the belief in descent yields the result that the antecedents of an act that "can be seen, known, 'conscious'" cannot indicate to us the value of the act, and that "the decisive value of an action lies precisely in what is *unintentional* in it" (JGB 32). The value of what one does is given by an array of unconscious and unintentional occurrences which I have called one's deep character.

146

Applied in this way, the notion of descent is consistent with at least one judgement of value which is crucial to Nietzsche's mature ethical thinking. This is the distinction of rank between those people who are capable of virtue and the great majority who are not. Nietzsche thinks that the acts of these two types of people differ greatly in value, and the reason why they differ in this way does seem to lie in facts about the individual that are unconscious and very deep. They are so deep, in fact, that he suggests that at least in some cases the facts are not psychological but physiological (see Chapter 7, p. 121). Whatever one might think of this notion of differences in rank, it does seem to cohere well with the way he uses the belief in descent in *Beyond Good and Evil* 32.

However, this does not seem to be true of certain other distinctions of value Nietzsche is eager to make: namely, those that are to be made among the members of the higher of the two human types. That is, the way he applies the idea of descent in his critique of Morality does not seem to be consistent with his conception of virtue and, consequently, with the way he thinks virtue differs from one person to another. According to his conception of virtue, one does not find out how virtuous people are by tracing their actions back to their original source in something that cannot be seen, known, or conscious. For the purpose of evaluating a person's way of life, the source of an action (insofar as there is such a thing), is not some single element which lies buried deep within the person; it is the person's character as a whole. One's character is *not* one's deep character. Such deep factors only have whatever ethical significance they have in the context of the purposes around which the entire self is integrated. They are only the materials out of which one's virtue is fabricated. As such, they cannot be decisive in determining the value of one's actions, any more than the value of a marble sculpture can be determined from the value of the stone from which it was cut. What *is* decisive, if any one factor is, is the act by which the self is integrated, the act of dedicating oneself to a code of values. And this is something that, at least in principle, can be conscious and intentional. So it is not true, in all cases, that the value of an action lies precisely in what is unintentional in it.

Nietzsche's theory of virtue is not inconsistent with his denial of responsibility, nor even with the belief in descent to which he appeals in making this denial. It is inconsistent with an assumption which governs the way in which he applies the belief in descent in attacking the idea of responsibility: the assumption that *the* source of an action, as far as its value is concerned, is necessarily something which is unconscious. If we turn from the attack on responsibility to the attack on ought-judgements, there seems at first blush to be an inconsistency which is more straightforward and more obvious. After all, it is undeniable that Nietzsche does make judgements of this sort himself. He says things like: "Life *ought* to inspire confidence" (WM 853; the emphasis is Nietzsche's). More importantly, the point of his theory of virtue consists in the notion that certain people *ought* to take their passions as the materials out of which a more coherent self can be constructed. His relativism, as we saw in the last chapter, can be viewed as a theory of how oughts come to apply to people. This, of course, assumes that oughts do apply to people.

Does the mere fact that Nietzsche makes ought-judgements mean that he is doing the very thing he rejects? Of course not. His rejection of "oughts" does not amount to the bald assertion (which would be incoherent in itself) that one ought never to make ought-judgements. His rejection is less sweeping and more complex than that. However, if we pause momentarily to recall what this rejection really amounts to, we can see that it does involve him in an inconsistency of a certain kind, one which is less straightforward than the one which appears at first blush.

As I presented it on pages 16–18 of Chapter 2, Nietzsche's objection to the Moral "ought" can be read as a dilemma that he presents to the adherents of Morality. It states that there are only two aspects of human life that an "ought" can be meant to change: one's deep character on the one hand, and isolated acts and states of consciousness on the other. The former cannot be changed and, while the latter can be changed, the resulting transformation does not make one a different and better person. But the point of a Moral "ought" is that, through it, one will be changed in a way that will make one a better person. Of course, there is so far nothing wrong with making ought-judgements with the intention of changing some act or state of consciousness, but behind a Moral "ought" there lies the further intention of "improving" someone, an intention which will necessarily be disappointed. Making such judgements is inevitably a pointless activity.

It is at this point, I think, that Nietzsche's critique of "ought" does become inconsistent with his own ethical views. After all, it is difficult to understand the point of Nietzsche's theory of virtue unless it contains ideas of the sort that this argument is meant to rule out of consideration. If this is not obvious, consider the fact that, as far as this argument is concerned, it does not matter whether the idea involved is expressed in terms of the word "ought" (*sollen*) or some close synonym. What matters is that it is motivated by the intention which the argument proscribes. And Nietzsche's theory of virtue does seem to be motivated by the proscribed intention: it seems to be intended to get *some* people to change their lives in such a way that they become better people.

What is more interesting – and certainly more to Nietzsche's credit – is the fact that his theory of virtue suggests a reason why this argument is not a good one. The dichotomy on which the dilemma is based is obviously derived from the psychological assumption in light of which Nietzsche applies the belief in descent: the assumption that the one source of the ethical value of an act or state of consciousness is the agent's deep character. The dichotomy states that there are only two aspects of human life toward which one could possibly direct an ethical imperative: one which is the sole determinant of one's value as a person and cannot be changed, and another which can be changed but has no power to determine what one's value is. Clearly, this dichotomy is based on the assumption that everything has whatever ethical value it has because of some unconscious and uncontrollable state from which it springs. This implies that everything that we can change is ethically significant only as a symptom, while everything that determines value is something we cannot change.

As I have already said, Nietzsche's theory of virtue implies that this assumption is not true. It indicates that the aspect of one's life that gives *all* the other parts – including one's deepest and most intransigent passions – whatever value they have is one's dedication to a code of values. Consequently, it also implies that the dichotomy on which Nietzsche's dilemma is based is a false one: there is a part of life that determines one's value and is *also* subject to being changed by ourselves. After all, the act of dedicating oneself to something can obviously be influenced by one's own ideas. It is an aspect of life toward which ethical imperatives can be directed, and it does not seem to be pointless to do so.

So far in this section, I have claimed that there is a certain conflict between Nietzsche's conception of virtue and the reasoning that lies behind his rejection of responsibility and "ought." Perhaps I should pause for a moment to point out that I am not trying to convict him of having made a stupid mistake. The mistake – if one can call it that – is rather a natural one to make. He developed one system of ideas when he was in what might be called his immoralist mode, and another when he was in his legislating mode. The two groups of ideas are actually similar and closely related. Most importantly, they both include the idea that the source of human action, as far as its merits are concerned, lies in the agent's character. Essentially, this is the idea he calls the "belief in descent." The conflict arises from the fact that two incompatible conceptions of character are involved. In the immoralist version character is interpreted, very narrowly, as something unconscious and peculiarly deep; in the other version, it is not. But these ideas can be stated in such a way that they sound the same. Indeed, this is the way Nietzsche presents these ideas to his readers and, apparently, to himself.

For us, perhaps the question of Nietzsche's intelligence is not a very important one. Certainly more important is the question of whether this conflict among his ideas can be eliminated without sacrificing too many of them. Can one have a Nietzschean critique of responsibility and "ought" – at least the distinctively Moral "ought" – and still accept his theory of virtue? Once again, I think one should realize that the problem involved is rather limited in its scope. The source of the problem lies entirely in the narrow interpretation of character which underlies these immoralist critiques. If one could eliminate this assumption and still formulate usable versions of the critiques, the problem will have been eliminated. There is reason to think that this can be done.

Consider, first, the critique of responsibility. Here, Nietzsche's principal target is the idea that the act of will (or the intention) that immediately precedes an act is the entire history of the act as far as its worth is concerned. I have suggested (Chapter 2, p. 14) that this idea is crucial to the Moral point of view because Morality evaluates individual acts independently of the worth of the agents who do them, in order to base judgements about the worth of the agent on the worth of the individual acts the agent does. This idea is false just in case the value of an act is actually based on factors which come before the act of will – just in case it is based on the character from which the volition arises. This, of course, is what Nietzsche's theory of virtue claims is the case. In other words, one can oppose "responsibility," in this sense of the word, without adopting the narrow interpretation of character. However, some of the remarks I have made in this section suggest that consistency, if it is to be achieved in this way, does have a price. The broader conception of character that Nietzsche uses in his legislating frame of mind cannot be used to show that we necessarily lack responsibility of another sort, one that he also seems to want to deny in his immoralist critique. It cannot be used to show that we are necessarily "irresponsible" in the sense that the value of our actions is *outside our control*. Nietzsche's theory of virtue presents human beings as potentially the architects of their own character. "Responsibility" can mean the metaphysical autonomy one would have if one's act of will were *causa prima*, but it can also mean self-control. Nietzsche's positive ethical views imply that this latter sort of responsibility can exist, and in one of his more affirmative states of mind he is consistent enough to acknowledge this more or less explicitly. In his well-known discussion of the human ability to make and keep promises, he says:

> The proud awareness of the extraordinary privilege of *responsibility*, the consciousness of this rare freedom, this power over oneself and over fate, has in this case penetrated to the profoundest depths and become instinct.

> (GM II 2)

If we combine these ideas with his immoralist critique of responsibility, something will be lost, but it is probably something that he should not want to keep anyway.

Very similar things can be said about the critique of "ought." It is part of the Moral approach to problems of conduct to think that one can express an ethical ideal mainly in terms of which actions one ought to do and which intentions one ought to have. If Nietzsche's theory of virtue is true, such an approach barely touches the surface of those matters which have genuine ethical importance. It implies that if we know, for instance, that I keep my promises because that is the right thing to do, that I do it with the intention of doing the right thing, what we know has little to do with my worth as a person. To know anything important about my worth, we must know why I act that way and why I think such behavior is right. Have I simply absorbed my standards of conduct from others? Am I so punctilious because I have a cowardly fear of being wrong? Am I moved by fear of being blamed and shamed if I do not do what I should? Do I simply lack the imagination needed to conceive of some other way of acting? An ethic that fails to penetrate the immense region behind the agent's intentions must present the agent as a disparate collection of acts and conscious states that, though they may have important economic consequences, will lack ethical meaning and value. This much seems to be implied by Nietzsche's theory of virtue, without assuming the narrow interpretation of what character is. As I have said, however, it does not do away with all oughts whatsoever, But, given his overarching purpose of enhancing human life, it seems best not to get rid of them all anyway.

OPPOSITE VALUES

In defending his own ethical views, Nietzsche must avoid committing himself to some version of "the faith in opposite values." He must avoid using any of those pairs of evaluative concepts – such as right and wrong, good and evil, true and false – one of which is regarded as positive and the other of which is thought of as having the opposite sort of value. So far, my account of Nietzsche's own views has focused on the concept of virtue, a notion that in this sense is entirely positive, and certainly not negative at all. One might suspect, though, that precisely through his use of the concept of virtue he is committed to one pair of opposite values. Traditionally, virtue is paired with vice and (whatever one might mean, exactly, by "opposite" in this context) vice is certainly the opposite of virtue and has the opposite sort of value.

To understand Nietzsche's logical commitments regarding the concept of vice, consider a trait which is normally regarded as vicious: namely, cruelty. Aristotle and his followers would point out that "cruelty," as we ordinarily use the word, actually refers to two different traits, only one of which is properly called a vice. Sometimes it refers to a trait in which one thoughtlessly does hurtful things which one immediately regrets. In that sense, cruelty is a form of *akrasia* (incontinence or moral weakness), a state in which one's conduct conflicts with one's view of how one should behave. I think Nietzsche's conception of virtue could easily be used to formulate a theory of such akratic cruelty and of *akrasia* in general. One could say that the actions of akratically cruel people do not fit into the goals to which they are dedicated, but rather run counter to them. But they do have a motive for acting as they do. Their actions arise from passions of some sort or other. This means that their psyches are not fully integrated: a certain principle of order

152

within the self has failed to impose the character of a function on other elements of the self.[3] On this account, *akrasia* is not so much a trait of character as a way of lacking character. And that, intuitively, is what it seems to be.

However, although Nietzsche's theory of virtue can be used to explain *akrasia*, it does not seem to make room for a concept of vice at all. The reason is that the only way to lack virtue, for Nietzsche, is to lack character in some way or other: it is to have a self which is in some way not fully integrated. Virtue and character, one might say, are the same thing. But vice is not a way of lacking character. It means having a *bad* character, which of course is impossible if character and virtue are the same thing. Traditionally, vicious people are characterized by just the sort of integration that the akratic person lacks, but in such a way that the integration includes bad elements: bad passions or principles or goals. (The viciously cruel person is in some way dedicated to hurting people.) But Nietzsche's theory does not authorize us to think that any of these things can be bad unless they fail to appear in the context of an integrated self. Although he can acknowledge the existence of psychological states that are not good enough to be virtuous, he can regard none as being, so to speak, positively bad in the way that vice is supposed to be. There are only the infinitely varied forms of virtue and the infinitely many ways of lacking it.[4]

DISINTERESTEDNESS AND UNIVERSALITY

Are Nietzsche's own views consistent with his rejection of disinterestedness and universal validity? Once again, certain problems stand in the way of our answering "yes" to this question. While Nietzsche's relativism is an obvious attempt to avoid attributing universal validity to his ideals, another of the theories I discussed in the last chapter seems to do just that. His vitalism seems to claim that there is a single good that is more important than all others and that this claim somehow applies to everyone. This good looks suspiciously like the *summum bonum* of traditional philosophers, a good which is the greatest for everyone. Further, Nietzsche seems to be committed to violating his rejection of disinterestedness merely by setting himself up as a purveyor of new ideals. As we have seen (Chapter 2, p. 21), Nietzsche claims that disinterestedness is not a legitimate part of the ideal because disinterested action does not exist, in the sense that one never acts *just because* one understands that what one is doing is right. The reason we never disinterestedly act on the basis of understanding alone is that understanding itself is highly interested: it is always an expression of one's drives or passions. But if, in telling us that we should change our lives, he is only expressing *his* personal drives and passions, why should his words have any force at all *for us*? Does not the power his words have over us come from our conviction that he has seen some part of the truth, and that he is saying it just because it is right that the truth be said? His own doctrine tells us that no one acts (e.g., speaks) that way. Maybe his position as a prophet of new ideals commits him to abandoning this part of his doctrine.

We can only appreciate the seriousness of these problems if we realize that this part of his doctrine, and his denial of universal validity as well, are embedded in one of his most important and characteristic ideas: his doctrine of perspectivism.[5] This idea contains several distinguishable components. He expresses one small part of it when he tells us that "all evaluation is made from a definite perspective: that of the preservation of the individual, a community, a race, a state, a church, a faith, a culture" (WM 259). Part of what he means by saying that all evaluation is done from a perspective is that it is always done for the sake of some purpose.

He does not limit this claim to evaluations, but extends it to all cognition whatsoever: "there is *only* a perspective seeing, *only* a perspective 'knowing.'" He points out that, in this highly general form, this claim implies that we should reject such "contradictory concepts as 'pure reason,'" or "a 'pure, will-less, painless, timeless knowing subject,'" because "these always demand that we should think of an eye . . . turned in no particular direction, in which the active and interpreting forces, through which alone seeing becomes seeing *something*, are supposed to be lacking" (GM III 12). That is, when he says that evaluation, perception, and knowledge are always made from some perspective, he means that they are always "interpretations," in the somewhat technical sense we encountered in Chapter 5, pp. 73–4: they always involve a more powerful agency of some sort utilizing a less powerful subject-matter for its own ends, imposing a definite character upon it. His remark about pure reason makes one implication of this claim a little more obvious than it would otherwise be: since we would pursue no purposes if it were not for the non-intellectual factors that drive us toward them, our intellects must always be conditioned by such factors – by will and passion. This, of course, means that our understanding is never disinterested. "It is our needs that interpret the world; our drives and their For and Against" (WM 481).

Since it is always possible to bring different drives and purposes to the same subject-matter, it follows that any subject can be interpreted in more than one way. Nietzsche considers this implication important enough to include it as an essential component of perspectivism: "In so far as the word 'knowledge' has any meaning, the world is knowable; but it is *interpretable* otherwise, it has no meaning behind it, but countless meanings. – 'Perspectivism'" (WM 481).

But he does not believe merely that it is always *possible* to interpret things differently. Given Nietzsche's vitalism, he must accept the purposes toward which a given agent strives as relevant to whether that agent should accept any particular interpretation as "true": "Truth is the kind of error without which a certain species of life could not live. The value for *life* is ultimately decisive" (WM 493). We should believe what enables us to flourish. Since the conditions of one's flourishing differ from one living being to the next, he is led to reject a certain habit of the philosophers of the past:

> Are these coming philosophers new friends of "truth"? That is probable enough, for all philosophers so far have loved their truths. But they will certainly not be dogmatists. It must offend their pride, also their taste, if their truth is supposed to be a truth for everyman – which has so far been the secret wish and hidden meaning of all dogmatic aspirations.
>
> (JGB 43)

Dogmatism is, at least in part, the idea that philosophers can produce truths which are for everyone. In denying dogmatism, Nietzsche appears to be rejecting universal validity, not only for ethical ideals, but for philosophy in general.

If we may suppose that this last claim is also an essential component of the doctrine of perspectivism, we can say that this doctrine consists of at least three distinct claims: that all evaluations and all cognitions are interpretations; that any subject-matter can be interpreted in various ways; and that no interpretation put forth by a philosopher should be accepted by everybody. The first claim, when properly spelled out, includes his denial of disinterestedness, and the third includes his denial of universal validity. He cannot abandon either of these denials without more or less demolishing his epistemology, for that is more or less what his perspectivism is. But this is not the only way in which Nietzsche might solve the two problems I have set for him. There is also the possibility that these denials can be interpreted in such a way that they are perfectly consistent with his practice as a prophet of new ideals. In fact, as the reader might already suspect, I think the brief sketch of perspectivism that I have just given suggests plausible interpretations which accomplish precisely this result.

To some extent, the implications my sketch has regarding the denial of universality are obvious. As I have presented it, Nietzsche's perspectivism is based on the same psychological principle upon which his vitalism is based: that all human beings seek power (preservation or growth). Whatever else it means, his perspectivism cannot mean that there are no truths that are true of all human beings. It is too unlikely that he would draw a conclusion which implies the falsity of the premise from which it is drawn. Further, the part of his perspectivism that is immediately concerned with universal validity is based on vitalism itself: it is because of his conception of life, employed as a standard of value and applied to everyone, that he thinks there is no philosophy that everyone should believe. In denying that there is a truth that is ''for'' everyone he must not be denying that there is a truth that is true *of* everyone.

If I am right about what his perspectivism amounts to, he can remain consistent with the denial of universality that it requires by maintaining that there is no ethical standard which everyone should apply to themselves, while reserving for himself and the philosophers of the future the right to apply the same standard to everyone in determining their rank as human beings. This is what I made him out as maintaining in Chapter 7. In fact, the relativism I attributed to him there does seem to imply that not everyone should believe his vitalism (Chapter 7, p. 138). Nietzsche's use of life as his ultimate standard of value is different in one very important way from the traditional philosophers' talk of a *summum bonum*. Traditionally, such talk was an attempt to rank goods according to the value they have in themselves, so that the ranking is one which ought to be applied by everyone in deciding what to do. This is not what Nietzsche's vitalism does.[6]

Given his theory that all thinking is ''interpretation,'' he certainly cannot claim to be speaking disinterestedly as an ethical theorist, nor indeed at any other time. Nonetheless, the psychological basis of his perspectivism suggests why he can think that some people – though not everyone – should find what he says convincing. He can also claim that his words have a *certain* sort of relevance to everyone. At one point, Nietzsche more or less explicitly acknowledges that his vitalism cannot be disinterested. The passage in which he does so deserves a close examination because it suggests something about what he takes this acknowledgement to imply. It occurs in the course of an attack on Socrates and Plato, who, according to him, treated the value of life as an intellectual problem and solved it by taking a "negative attitude to life."

> Judgements, judgements of value, concerning life, for it or against it, can, in the end, never be true: they have value only as symptoms, they are worthy of consideration only as symptoms; in themselves such judgements are stupidities. One must by all means stretch out one's fingers and make the attempt to grasp this amazing finesse, *that the value of life cannot be assessed.* Not by one who is living, for such a one is a party to the dispute, even the disputed object, and not a judge; and not by one who is dead, for a different reason. For a philosopher to see a problem in the value of life is thus an objection to him, a question mark concerning his wisdom, an un-wisdom.
>
> (G II 2)

Nietzsche's recognition of non-disinterestedness here seems at first glance to be very sweeping indeed. In calling judgements of value concerning life "stupidities," he seems to be disallowing *any* valuing of life, including his own vitalism. But I think what he is disallowing is rather more specific than that. He is drawing a distinction between two perspectives: that of a party in a dispute and that of a judge or umpire (*Richter*), who can settle a dispute with the peculiar authority which is only available to non-participants. Only someone in the latter sort of perspective can make what Nietzsche here calls a "judgement." *Urteil*, like the English word, refers to the verdicts and sentences of judges. If the issue is the value of life, this sort of perspective is impossible. This means that the value of life cannot be *abgeschatzt*, a word which I have tried to capture with "assessed." *Schatzen* means to place a value on something, and the prefix *ab* connotes thoroughness and, in this context, objectivity. That something cannot be *abgeschatzt* does not mean that it cannot be *geschatzt* at all. One's valuation of life cannot be given with pretensions of authority based on objectivity. It must be entered as a plea by an interested party. We must understand Nietzsche's own vitalism as a plea of this sort.

At first, this seems to leave us where we started. How can a mere expression of one's interestedness have the main attribute which a *theory* of the value of something should have: the power to convince? Nietzsche's plea can acquire that power if he can show us that in some relevant way we are all interested *in the same way that he is*. Broadly speaking, this is what the conception of life that underlies his perspectivism and his vitalism is supposed to do. We all seek preservation and, if possible, growth. If we have given up on either of these, we have not decided on intellectual grounds that the objective involved is worthless (to claim to have done this is a stupidity), we have merely failed to do what we set out to do. To those of us who are healthy enough to benefit from it, he is offering the advice that we become consistent vitalists. This advice is not offered as a dogmatism in which the preferences of one person are imposed on those who do not already share them: the life which values through him also values through us (see G V 5). Though his vitalism is an expression of his interests, it is not *merely* an expression of his interests. The interests expressed are also those of the audience toward whom his words are aimed.

In addition, though he is not trying to tell them what to do, his vitalism is also relevant in a certain way to those who cannot benefit from his advice. It determines their rank by pronouncing them to be failures. Again, it does not make this determination on the basis of interests that are absolutely alien to theirs: it claims they are failures when judged on their own terms.

NIETZSCHE'S IMMORALISM

Is Nietzsche's procedural conception of virtue compatible with his immoralism? The answer to this question is somewhat complicated, but I think it is fairly close to being "yes." As far as I can see, it is perfectly compatible with his rejection of opposite values, universality, and disinterestedness, and with the arguments he gives against these features of Morality. Where responsibility and "ought" are concerned, the facts are more ambiguous. It does not seem to be compatible with rejecting everything that, at least in a certain frame of mind, he seems to want to reject under the name of "responsibility." Nor does it allow him to jettison all the types of "oughts" that he seems, at least at times, to want to throw out. But it is arguable that it allows him to reject the distinctively Moral *forms* of both these things, and it seems to provide a basis for interesting arguments against them. It could be that, given the purpose and spirit of his philosophical activity, he does not need a stronger immoralism than that.

Of course, none of this means that we should believe his conception of virtue, nor does it mean that it is compatible with everything of importance that he wants to say. I will turn to these two important issues next.

9

CONCLUSION: VIRTUE AND SOCIETY

ASSESSING NIETZSCHE

If we take Nietzsche's ethical and political ideas seriously – and I
have assumed throughout this book that we should – the most
important problem facing us is to determine where we should agree
with them and where we should not. In this chapter I would like
to say something about the implications which the preceding eight
chapters have for the solution of this problem. It would be foolish
of me to attempt a summary view of "what is living and what is
dead" in the philosophy of Nietzsche: the issues he raises are too
complex and difficult to be settled in one brief chapter. What I
would like to do, though, is to begin by posing a problem that
appears when we try to put together some Nietzschean themes into
a coherent position on the basis of which human beings might do
well to live. I think it is a problem that anyone who is inclined to
accept Nietzsche's ideas must try to resolve somehow.

CHARACTER AND THE GOOD SOCIETY

The problem I have in mind has to do with the relations between
several different parts of Nietzsche's ethical and political theory.
The nature of the problem permits it to be discussed, to some
extent, in very concrete terms. That is what I will do, at least by
way of setting it up. I will discuss the broad theoretical aspects after
I have given some idea of the sort or problem I have in mind.

Among the more provocative of Nietzsche's many comments on
historical personalities are his several references – all of them
extremely laudatory – to the Hohenstaufen Frederick II, Emperor
of Sicily and Lower Italy in the thirteenth century. He calls him
"that *first* European after my taste," one of "those magical,

incomprehensible, and unfathomable ones . . ., those enigmatic men predestined for victory and seduction" (JGB 200). Elsewhere, he calls him "an atheist and enemy of the church *comme il faut*, one of those most closely related to me," and promises to build a monument in his memory some day (EH III Z 4). In another place, he has this to say about him:

"War to the knife against Rome! Peace and friendship with Islam" – thus felt, thus *acted*, that great free spirit, the genius among German emperors, Frederick II. How? Must a German first be a genius, a free spirit, to have *decent* feelings?

(A 60)

Who was Frederick II? If we turn for enlightenment to Jacob Burckhardt's description of his policies, a description with which Nietzsche must have been familiar, the results are at least as mystifying as they are enlightening, at least if we are looking for insight into Nietzsche's own views. Burckhardt claims that Frederick was "the first ruler of the modern type who sat upon a throne."[1] His policies were

aimed at the complete destruction of the feudal state, at the transformation of the people into a multitude destitute of will and of the means of resistance, but profitable in the utmost degree to the exchequer. He centralized, in a manner hitherto to unknown in the West, the whole judicial and political administration. . . . Here, in short, we find, not a people, but simply a disciplined multitude of subjects.

He prohibited his subjects from studying abroad and became the first ruler to restrict the freedom of study in a university. He organized an efficient system of taxation and an effective and widely feared internal police force, and restricted the economic activities of his subjects in various ways, transforming the production of many commodities into state monopolies. Finally, he "crowned his system of government by a religious inquisition, which will seem the more reprehensible when we remember that in the persons of the heretics he was persecuting the representatives of a free municipal life."

If we place this description of Frederick II in the context of Burckhardt's understanding of political history, we can see at least part of the reason why he regarded this remarkable emperor as a "modern" phenomenon: Burckhardt sees the state Frederick created as an early instance of what he later called the "centralized modern state, dominating and determining culture, worshipped as a god and ruling like a sultan" (see Chapter 3, p. 27). Of course, this is also the main reason he disapproves of Frederick's policies. Frederick increased the power of the state at the expense of the powers of individual human beings, including the powers that enable them to develop and act on ideas of their own. Burckhardt valued the capacities that Frederick tore down more highly than the ones he built up.

What is mystifying, when we turn to Nietzsche's views, is the fact that he always speaks of Frederick with unqualified approval, despite the fact that, as I tried to show in Chapter 3, he agrees with the valuation that stands behind Burckhardt's disapproval. The state that Frederick founded, in Burckhardt's account, sounds very much like the one Nietzsche attacks in "On the New Idol." Further, he gives no evidence of disagreeing with Burckhardt on the facts concerning Frederick's policies. He merely talks about other facts. In the comments I have quoted, he seems to be praising him for purely personal characteristics he thinks he possessed, including attitudes and convictions evinced in his quarrel with the Pope and his sympathy with "the rare and refined luxuries of Moorish life" (A 60). In one of them, he takes him as a paradigm of the type of person in whom "powerful and irreconcilable drives" exist alongside "mastery and subtlety in waging war against oneself," including mastery of the arts of "self-control" and "self-outwitting" (JGB 200; see also WM 871). It sounds very much as if Nietzsche is attributing virtue, as he understands it, to Frederick. More generally, in all his comments about him, he is praising him for his character alone. This means that, at any rate, these comments are not evidence that Nietzsche is wavering in his political views or retreating from his critique of the state. He is not, for instance, praising Frederick as an artist–tyrant who uses the state to mould human beings according to his will. He is not talking about his domestic policies at all.

Yet an unsettling possibility lurks behind the fact that Nietzsche is able to separate these two subjects, character and policy, so easily and so completely. He is commenting on someone who he had reason to believe was pursuing policies which were inimical to the existence of the sort of society he himself admired. If Burckhardt had the facts right, Frederick's policies would tend to prevent the formation of an elite of bold ethical experimenters. There would tend to be no room in such a state for any experiment but his own. Yet Nietzsche's comments suggest that he does not see in this any reason to regard Frederick as anything less than a heroically admirable person.[2] This raises the possibility that Nietzsche's ethical ideal – his conception of virtue – does not necessarily lead to behavior which is compatible with the existence of what, in Nietzschean terms, must be regarded as a good society. Of course, this at present is only a possibility, since he might merely think – though I doubt he does – that Burckhardt had the facts wrong. In the next two sections of this chapter I will argue that, if we look at Nietzsche's ethical and political philosophy as I have presented it here, we can see that this possibility is indeed the case.

Perhaps I should pause, first, to point out, in case it is not sufficiently obvious, that this possibility does present a problem for Nietzsche's position. First of all, anyone who promulgates an ideal of individual conduct that, when people act on it, undermines the conditions for the existence of the sort of society they admire is doing something which they want to avoid doing if they can. Though what they are doing may not be logically inconsistent, it does involve having two objectives, one of which tends to defeat the other. I will be better off in my own terms if I have some assurance that this will not happen. Most of the working moralities that actually govern people's lives do provide assurances of this sort. For instance, whenever people deliberately do things that violate the principles on which a liberal society is based, liberals are able to make disapproving judgements about their character. Depending on the nature of the violation involved, they can say that such people are, for example, intolerant or unfair or irrational. It is impossible to live up to the liberal notion of good character while deliberately doing things that violate the liberal conception of a desirable social order. To the extent that this is true two important parts of the liberal program are mutually compatible.

Anyone who has a conception of what a good society is needs some assurance that whatever ethical ideals they defend will not interfere with the existence of such a society. In Nietzsche's case, this need is particularly acute, since the entire point of the society he envisions is that it permits the formation of virtue in those who are able to achieve it, and his procedural conception of virtue *is* his ethical ideal. In other words, his conception of the good society is identical to his conception of the social conditions for the achievement of the ideal. If he lacks the needed assurances, then the very act of setting forth his own ethic may, for all he knows, be self-defeating. It may be an act that destroys the conditions for its own success.

I can only find two ways in which Nietzsche might conceivably provide assurances of this sort. In the next two sections of this chapter I will try to show that Nietzsche cannot use either method without revising his views in some drastic way or other.

VIRTUE AND GOALS

Like his critique of the state (Chapter 3, pp. 37–8), Nietzsche's conception of a healthy society is entirely teleological: what is good about a good society is that it promotes a certain goal, just as what is bad about the state is that it interferes with the achievement of the same goal. This goal, of course, is the formation of virtue in those who are capable of it. The teleological character of his conception of the good society suggests one method he might conceivably use to integrate his theory of virtue with his social and political views in the needed way. He could claim that the goal of the good society is one which is always pursued by people who, according to his way of thinking, are virtuous. Perhaps the most immediately obvious way to make this claim would be to say that it is a virtue – it is one of the things that make a person a good person – to actively promote the conditions of virtue in others. Perhaps this could give him some assurance that those who fully practice his ideal will not do things which he is committed to hoping they will not do.

Oddly enough, I do not think Nietzsche ever explicitly held that promoting this goal is a virtue. One might hope that this trait is in some way very closely connected with what Zarathustra calls the "gift-giving virtue," but in fact they are not relevantly related at all. I have argued (Chapter 6, pp. 91–3) that the sort of activity Zarathustra is praising is not a response to the needs of the people who are affected by it and that it, as matter of fact, is not altruistically motivated at all. It resembles generosity in that it is not a response to moral necessity but, unlike generosity, its beneficial effects on others are not – or at least not necessarily – intended. The virtue we are contemplating here does involve doing things for the sake of others. Further, it involves benefiting others in a specific way: it would involve seeing certain needs of others as requiring a certain response from oneself. This makes it quite different from the gift-giving that Zarathustra is talking about.

Actually, Nietzsche's theory of virtue *prevents* him from saying that it is generally virtuous to promote a goal like the one we are now considering. To see why, we need only rehearse and bring together some of the things I have said about the way in which goals are related to his theory as it stands.

I have said that his conception of virtue is entirely procedural (Chapter 8, p. 45). The very same thing can be said concerning the identity of the goals that, according to him, are capable of making one a virtuous person. Goals can acquire this status by being selected in the course of a successful experiment. In that case, the reason why they make the agent a better human being is precisely the fact that they are selected in this way. Of course, part of the importance experimentation has for Nietzsche lies in his conviction that the identity of the goals that are made good in this way cannot be predicted in advance of the experiments in which they are selected. To the extent, then, that goals are specified in this way, it is an entirely open question whether any particular experimenter needs to promote the conditions of virtue in others in order to be a good person: the method requires that we wait to see if the pursuit of this goal brings about the required integration of the self.

However, I have indicated (Chapter 7, p. 142) that Nietzsche does think that he can say, independently of the results of any *particular* experiment, that certain traits are virtues because of features that all successful experiments (or the most successful ones) have in common. He believes that there are "second-order virtues," as I have called them. This means that he also must think he can say, before any experimental results are in, that certain goals are good for experimenters (at least the best ones): namely, the ends toward which these second-order virtues are directed.

One can wonder, then, whether promoting the conditions of virtue for others might be the goal of one of these traits. I believe that we have encountered no evidence that Nietzsche thinks that it is. We have seen three second-order virtues that Nietzsche recognizes. In two of them, the fact that one is pursuing the relevant goal is simply that fact that one is experimenting in a certain *way*: the goal is the experiment itself. In the gift-giving virtue, one pursues one's experiments enthusiastically, as things which are good in themselves. In Nietzschean courage one pursues them because they are dangerous or difficult. Such goals are quite neutral as to which substantive goals (as they might be called) one pursues within the experimental projects involved. Promoting a community in which virtue can thrive is obviously a substantive goal in this sense. The third second-order virtue we have looked at – the virtue of philosophical cruelty – *is* directed toward a substantive end. But here the goal involved is truth and this, once again, is obviously distinct from the goal which is our present concern. Nietzsche is able to declare truth to be a valuable goal, independently of the results of particular experiments, because of the peculiar relationship between the value of truth and his conception of life (Chapter 7, p. 130). Because of this relationship, he is able to recognize successfully incorporating the truth as a uniquely great exercise of power. It may well be the only substantive goal that he can recommend as the object of a virtue on the basis of his mature views on the subject.

There is one other way in which he might conceivably be able to integrate the promotion of the conditions of virtue into his theory of virtue. Instead of saying that it is a goal that is internal to virtue – instead, that is, of saying that seeking it is one of the things that make one a good person – he might be able to show that it is nonetheless something that good human beings inevitably do seek: perhaps it is an epiphenomenon of virtue. That some goals, at any rate, are related to virtue in this way is suggested by his comment that noble human beings help the unfortunate because they are "prompted . . . by an urge begotten by an excess of power" (JGB 260; see Chapter 6, pp. 97–8). Helping others is not a goal that makes them powerful (it does not create the relevant integration of their character) but it is very natural that people with power will do such things.

Much the same idea seems to lie behind some surprising remarks he makes in *Beyond Good and Evil* about the value of pity. There he reveals that, contrary to what he suggests elsewhere (A 7), he is not opposed to pity as such. Addressing his remarks to those who believe "hedonism or pessimism, utilitarianism or eudaemonism," he says that he feels pity for them, and explains: "Pity for *you* – that, of course, is not pity in your sense: it is not pity with social 'distress,' with 'society' and its sick and unfortunate members." He rejects this sort of pity because of the goal that he believes makes this distress an object of concern. "You want, if possible . . . *to abolish suffering*." This, he claims, is not a worthy goal because suffering is not as such undesirable. "The discipline of suffering . . . has created all enhancements of man so far." He calls his own pity "a higher and more farsighted pity," and the distant object that it farsightedly sees is, as in the other sort of pity, a goal to which one is committed. To explain the difference between the two goals, he briefly recapitulates the idea of overcoming from Zarathustra. "In man, *creature* and *creator* are united: in man there is material, fragment, . . . nonsense, chaos; but in man there is also creator, form-giver, hammer hardness. . . . And *your* pity is for the 'creature in man'" (JGB 225; see also WM 367).

The distress which is the object of hedonistic pity (as it might be called) is injury to the feelings that we already possess, and is motivated by a desire to preserve this side of our nature from various assaults that life inevitably commits against it. Of course, this side of human nature should not be preserved at all, but transformed – in some cases pitilessly – in order to make better human beings of us. Consequently hedonistic pity is not a valuable trait. On the other hand, he obviously thinks that the sort of pity he claims to feel, which is directed toward the creative side of human nature, *is* a worthwhile trait. What is interesting for our purposes is the possibility that, while he does not actually say so, he thinks that people who pursue a life of experimentation will tend to feel it too, that they too will be distressed by injuries suffered by the part of us that enables us to create virtue. Perhaps he thinks that a commitment to achieving excellence in one's own life naturally leads to this sort of concern for the conditions of excellence in others – at least one will be distressed by the fact that they believe ideas (such as hedonism) which stand in the way of their own enhancement. It is at least conceivable that his theory could be amended in such a way that it would explain why this would happen.

This, however, would not quite give us what we are looking for, since feeling distress when the creation of virtue is thwarted is not the same thing as actively promoting the conditions of such creativity. Still, it seems natural that people who feel this way will do something to bring about or maintain the social conditions in which virtue can arise. Suppose that Nietzsche is prepared to maintain that this is true: would this give him the assurance he needs that those who pursue his ideal of ethical experimentation will not interfere with the social conditions that make such experimentation possible?

I do not think it would. It would only mean that promoting the relevant social conditions would be *one* of the goals that the members of Nietzsche's elite would pursue. The mere fact that one is committed to a certain goal indicates nothing about its importance in relation to one's other goals (see Chapter 5, pp. 85–9). What guarantee does he have that they would not simply drop this goal when some interesting experiment of their own seems to require it? Their pursuit of this end could only provide such a guarantee if it were to override all their other ends. As we have seen (Chapter 5, p. 89), however, ranking goals at all – let alone asserting that one should override all the others – seems to be ruled out by Nietzsche's desire to keep reason as far as possible out of his theory of virtue. Further, to rank them in this way seems to be incompatible with what I have called his relativism. It would require him to say, in advance of any experimental results, what one's highest goal should be. This, of course, is just the sort of thing that the experiments are supposed to decide.

JUSTICE AGAIN

It appears that Nietzsche is not set up to provide himself with the assurances he needs by claiming that there is a certain goal that everyone who is virtuous will pursue. There is, however, another way in which he might try to achieve the same result. This method is particularly promising because at least some of the views it requires him to hold are ones that he does explicitly embrace.

We have seen (Chapter 6, pp. 98–100) that he conceives of a "healthy society" as a system of three castes which are articulated by a system of "unequal" rights. The rights each individual has are those that enable one to carry out one's functions. Though he does not give examples of the rights involved, one can easily imagine what the rights of people in the lowest caste, which includes all workers and professionals, would have to be like. Depending on the nature of the individual's function, they would have to include rights more or less like these: the right to possess the tools of one's trade; rights to acquire and exchange professional knowledge; the right to refuse to divulge professional secrets; perhaps the right to confidentiality in relations with one's clients. The effective functioning of their caste and of the society as a whole require that no one do things to them which violate rights of this general sort. This means that members of the elite must see the rights of lowest members of society as constraints on the means they employ in the pursuit of their own individual goals, whatever they may be. The rights of the various groups constitute the framework within which it is possible for the elite to pursue their experimental projects. This is especially true of the rights of the members of the elite – whatever those rights might be – which enable them to "find their happiness . . . in the labyrinth, in hardness against themselves and others, in experiments" (A 57).

This suggests what seems to be an easy and obvious way to integrate Nietzsche's theory of virtue with his social theory. To observe rights is, according to the view of the matter Nietzsche holds at the end of his career, what justice is (Chapter 6, pp. 98–100). He clearly thinks that justice is a virtue (Chapter 6, pp. 95–6) and, consequently, would think that people who live up to his ethical ideal would be just. Since rights are what makes the good society possible, it seems that he would be able to say that his ethical ideal would necessarily lead to behavior which is compatible with his conception of a good society. Virtue would tend to support its own social conditions. Does this not mean that he already possesses the solution to the problem I have posed to him?

I think the answer to this question is "no." This solution requires him to say that justice is a virtue, that being just is something that makes a person a good person, and I do not think his theory of virtue enables him to say this. The reasons for this have to do both with the nature of justice and with the nature of his theory.

Whatever one's conception of the moral virtue of justice might be, there are general limits on the grounds to which one can appeal in calling an act just. If justice is observng the rights of others, then which acts can be just depends crucially on what those rights are. If workers have a right to possess the tools of their trades, then stealing their tools is unjust because they do have that right. For the same reason, refraining from stealing from them is the sort of act that can be just. More generally, the justice of an act depends in part on facts about the person to whom the act (which, in this context, may be an omission) is done. This is true whether one thinks that justice is observing rights, giving people what they desire, or giving them what they need – indeed, no matter what one's conception of justice is. Of course, whether an act is just *also* depends on the reason for which it is done: it must be done *because* it is someone's right or what they deserve, and so forth, and not for some other reason. But the justice of an act cannot depend entirely on the spirit in which it is done. Any theory that claimed that an act can be virtuous independently of the actual characteristics of the person to whom it is done would not be a theory of justice, but of some other virtue.

Given this, it is perhaps obvious why Nietzsche's theory of virtue makes it impossible for him to say, coherently, that justice is a virtue. Insofar as his theory can characterize an act – as opposed to a whole way of life – as virtuous, this characterization will depend entirely on the act's position in a great ensemble of facts which are *about the agent*. To put the matter in the most general possible terms, one's act will be virtuous to the extent that it indicates success in one's efforts to "become master of the chaos one is; to compel one's chaos to become form" (WM 842). An act is virtuous to the extent that it arises from this essentially psychological process. Its actual relations to anything outside the agent, including other people, are irrelevant.

This means that, as far as we can know, Nietzschean experimenters living in what Nietzsche regards as a healthy society might have reason to think that they can promote their own virtue by doing things that are unjust. This is because the facts that make something virtuous, in Nietzsche's terms, and the facts that make something just are completely different sorts of facts. Nietzschean experimenters might think that a life that includes great crimes would integrate their characters better than anything else. Further, if they do think this, they will have no reason at all to avoid committing crimes and violating rights, since cultivating their Nietzschean virtue is their only purpose in life. Of course, if they are good Nietzscheans, they would think that such behavior is undermining the only sort of society which can make the formation of virtue anything more than a fortuitous occurrence. But this thought, by itself, can carry no weight with them unless they rank the conditions of virtue for all who are capable of it above the creation of their own virtue, and Nietzsche's theory offers them no reason to do this. A society which manages to foster Nietzschean virtue might systematically breed its own worst enemies.

Years ago, most people who thought they knew something about Nietzsche believed that he advocates great crimes and acts of violent predation. Since Walter Kaufmann argued against this idea,[3] it has gradually gone out of fashion. I hope it is obvious that I am not going back to this primitive misreading of Nietzsche. He did not advocate such things. What I am saying is that, if his positive ethical theory were put into practice without some radical revision, it might well have the same effect as if he did. The reason lies in the logic of his theory and not in his intentions.

The reason is that Nietzsche holds what might be called a "pure ethics of virtue": a theory which holds that whatever ethical merit an act possesses depends entirely on the virtuousness of the states of character from which the act arises.[4] He does have grounds for thinking that people should treat one another in certain ways: namely, a certain conception of human rights. But these grounds and his theory of virtue are mutually irrelevant. Earlier in this chapter, I pointed out that in his remarks on Frederick II Nietzsche is praising someone's character despite the fact that his policies at least seem to violate Nietzsche's own preferences about how people should treat one another. If what I have said in this section is true, we can see that, regardless of what he thought regarding the historical facts of Frederick's career, this is just the *sort* of thing that Nietzsche's view prepares him to do.

A PLAUSIBLE ETHICS OF VIRTUE

I would like to conclude my discussion of Nietzsche's ethical and political views by experimentally suggesting a possible solution to the problem I have presented for him in this chapter. Actually, I must admit that my suggestion will only be a proposal for an experiment rather than the execution of the experiment itself. If I am right in what I have said in this chapter, any solution to this problem would have to include reworking some important element or other of Nietzsche's philosophy, and this would obviously require a project much longer than the one I am about to carry out here. I should also admit that there are probably other possible solutions, quite different from my suggested one. My reason for offering this one rather than some other is that it uses ideas which may be more or less within Nietzsche's reach, and that I find it a congenial one. Others might want to try a different solution.

The problem I have presented, once again, is this: How could one overcome the mutual irrelevance of Nietzsche's conception of justice and his conception of virtue? More exactly, it is: How could one show, in more or less Nietzschean terms, that a fact about the circumstances in which a act is done (that is, actual characteristics of the person to whom it is done) can be part of what makes the act virtuous? This problem can be made more specific by finding solutions to two other problems, related to this one but distinct from it. The first is: Why is it a good thing that actions of this sort be done in such circumstances? The second is: What reasons do the members of Nietzsche's elite have for acting in this way?

Nietzsche already has an answer to one of these problems. It is a good thing that just acts be done because they, or the rights which they observe, are the framework which provides the indispensable environment within which virtue can emerge. This is why it would be disastrous, from a Nietzschean point of view, if such acts were not done. As I have pointed out, this idea does not by itself give us a solution to the second of these two problems. It does not provide Nietzsche's elite with a reason for acting justly, at least if it is not supplemented by some other idea.

Actually, I have already suggested an idea that could conceivably play this supplementary role (Chapter 6, pp. 103–4). I suggested that the social framework that makes virtue possible might be founded upon an agreement reached between the elite and their subordinates. Perhaps the fact, if it were a fact, that the aristocrats have agreed to observe the rights of others could constitute a reason for observing them.

I have also already suggested that this idea brings new problems with it. We have seen plenty of evidence in Chapter 6 that Nietzsche's views on the relations between the most powerful and the least powerful members of society undergoes a deep transformation between his earliest and latest writings on the subject. In his earliest comments on the subject, the aristocrats are distinguished by their possession of an overwhelming capacity for brute force, which they use to dominate their inferiors and thus promote their own interests. By the time he describes the ideal society in *The Antichrist* 57, however, the aristocracy exercises a rather different sort of power. Their only interest seems to be the exploration of the self and the creation of virtue. They are kept alive by those who, unlike themselves, are economically productive, but they do not seem to otherwise meddle in the affairs of others. They apparently do not even create ideas which would be useful or interesting to the masses: for instance, they do not invent rules by which others should live. As different as these two relationships between the more and less powerful are, they are similar in that both are exploitative, in the sense that both involve unilateral transfers of value, in which one side gains something and the other merely loses. Relationships which are exploitative in this sense are not self-maintaining, as trade relations are (see Chapter 6, pp. 100–1).

They cannot be created and preserved simply by making an agreement, because the losing side has no reason to enter such an agreement. Some additional factor must be present – such as political power, private terrorism, or superstitious fear – which gives them a reason to enter the relationship. The elite caste in Nietzsche's later view differs from that of the earlier one in that it does not seem to have such resources at its disposal. More importantly, if its members do have and make use of such sources of influence, they have no reason to enter into an agreement, since they can impose the desired order on the rest of society without committing themselves to any obligations in return. But if they do not accept any commitments themselves, they have (so far) no reason to follow the rules which constitute the social framework.

As a matter of fact, we have seen (Chapter 7, pp. 139–41) that Nietzsche does tell us, in *The Antichrist* 57, why the lower orders of this utopia accept their relationship with the aristocracy. Not surprisingly, he does not say that their reason for accepting the special position of Nietzsche's artist–philosophers rests on an agreement. Instead, he says that the aristocracy rests its position on an already existing traditional code of values, one which merely "sums up the . . . experimental morality of many centuries," and which the lower orders already accept. That is, their position rests simply on an appeal to tradition. In certain ways such an appeal is quite different from resting one's case on some sort of social contract, which would presumably involve some rational insight, on the part of both parties to the agreement, into the conditions of their own well-being. Faith in tradition seems to involve just the sort of irrationality which might enable the aristocrats to gain the help and support of people to whom they contribute nothing.

Nonetheless, I think it is extremely unlikely that such an appeal would be available to them, for much the same reason that their position could not be created and preserved by a social agreement. I think one can see this if one merely asks and tries to answer the following question: Why would such traditions have evolved in the first place? That I accept something on the basis of tradition simply means that I accept it because people have accepted it in the past. In the world as we know it, it is of course true that the authority of aristocracies has often been based on tradition. But these traditions have evolved in the context of factors that would play no role in Nietzsche's utopia. People have at times accepted the position of the aristocrats because, for generations, they have believed that the aristocrats are gods, or the descendants of gods, or at least were granted their present privileges by the gods. Alternatively, they may have accepted it because the aristocrats are warriors who have frightened them into submission or granted them protection against other gangs of warriors. In short, the people of the past must have had some reason for accepting the present arrangement, just as one must have some reason for entering an agreement. But what reason would people have had in the past for accepting Nietzsche's arrangement? Presumably, Nietzsche's artist–philosophers would make no appeals to the gods, nor would they work as soldiers or as anything else. They would also not contribute to the community by managing public affairs, as the aristocrats of history have always done. The people of the past, it seems, could have had no reason for accepting their position in the world and, if this is true, there could be no tradition of accepting it.[5]

In that case, what sort of framework could provide an environment within which Nietzschean virtue could emerge? I have claimed that the particular system Nietzsche describes cannot be supported by a mere agreement because this system is essentially an exploitative one. Obviously, this claim leaves open the possibility that an agreement could support a system which is not exploitative but which does nonetheless make possible the formation of what Nietzsche calls virtue. Is such a thing really possible?

Clearly, Nietzsche believed that it is not possible – why else would he have made his utopia of virtue an exploitative system? But what reasons did he have for believing this? Perhaps it is a belief that should be discarded.

The exploitative character of Nietzsche's system consists in the fact that the people who seek virtue are economically unproductive and are supported by the great majority who do produce. Those who seek virtue do not work and those who work do not seek virtue. It is a safe bet that Nietzsche thought these are two ineluctable facts of nature which his system merely acknowledges and does not create. His reasons for thinking this, whatever they might be, would also be his reasons for believing that a utopia of virtue would have to be an exploitative hierarchy.

Surprisingly, Nietzsche's writings contain almost nothing in the way of reasons for believing these things. There is only one group of passages which seem at all relevant: namely, the ones in which he explains why some people accept the confusing and stultifying ideas of the ascetics (see Chapter 7, pp. 116–20). There he says that such ideas are ways of counteracting chronic feelings of displeasure, which themselves are caused by physiological factors of some sort. The idea that the causes are ultimately purely physical is probably helpful in establishing what Nietzsche needs to establish. The causes would have to be something relatively profound and intransigent in order to support the hardness of the distinction between types of people that his system requires. For instance, if the cause of chronic malaise were something relatively superficial and meliorable, such as frustrated desire, it would not justify sequestering those who suffer from it in a separate caste. If we are justified in institutionally shutting people out from the quest for virtue, they must be marked by some flaw that will not change. Yet, as far as I know, Nietzsche never gives nor suggests an argument for the notion that these feelings of displeasure must have purely physical causes. This seems to be pure speculation on his part.

Further, ascetic ideas are only one reason why someone would be unsuited to the quest for virtue: certainly not everyone who is economically productive is devoted to asceticism. Some more general argument is needed to justify the hard distinction embedded in Nietzsche's system. What is needed is either a reason why seeking virtue and work are in themselves mutually incompatible activities, or a reason why people who are suited for one of them are somehow unsuited for the other. As I have suggested, though, Nietzsche does not give any such reasons that I am aware of.[6]

As a matter of fact, it seems to me that no such reasons – at least, no good ones – can be given, because no such incompatibilities exist. On the contrary, it is arguable that productive work, or something relevantly like it, is actually necessary for the formation of virtue. What is it to do what is virtuous – to do what is courageous, generous, honest, courteous, and so forth? Of course, many profound and conflicting answers can be given to this question, but there is one part of the answer which is not especially profound and should not be controversial: to do such things is to do something, and to do it courageously, generously, honestly, courteously, and so forth. That is, to do a virtuous act is to do some other act – fighting for a cause, giving something away, saying something, requesting something – and do it in a certain way. Virtue presupposes activities and interests other than virtue itself. This means that there could not exist a group of people who really have nothing to do but to be virtuous. Further, since one becomes virtuous by acting and especially by doing virtuous things, there can be no caste that literally has no function other than to create virtue. Nietzsche's aristocrats must have some other, more fundamental, activities and interests upon which their new virtues will supervene. They need something to do.

What indeed would these people be doing? They would be freed from the necessity of doing anything whatsoever in order to stay alive, and would not have any managerial or religious functions. The activities which would be monopolized by the lower orders of society would include not only manufacturing, trade, and agriculture, but also *"science,* the greatest part of art, the whole quintessence of *professional* activity" (A 57). There seems to be precious little for the elite to do. To that extent, their task resembles the impossible one of developing virtue without doing anything else.

The problem they face is not quite that bad, however, because the system does not exclude them from doing absolutely anything. But the only activities that they are not excluded from seem to be philosophy and certain forms of art. This, however, leaves them with what amounts to the same problem in a diluted form. Being excluded from almost all human activities and interests is only marginally better than being excluded from all of them. Just as to do a virtuous act requires that one also do some other act, so exemplary virtue would seem to require that one have opportunities to pursue a relatively rich variety of activities. The various aspects of human excellence supervene upon different human pursuits. No human activity, if done in isolation from all other activities, could come very close to embodying most of the virtue that is within the reach of human beings. This is at least as true of philosophy and the creation of esoteric art as it is of other human activities.

There are of course reasons why creativity in these fields can generate and express virtue, but many of these reasons would not apply to a caste of people who are guaranteed, by the work of others, that they have no need at all to do anything else. If it is true that innovation tends to be virtuous, it is true in large part because innovation is difficult and dangerous. Much of the difficulty and danger is due to the fact that innovators tend to offend people whose cooperation they need and cannot extract by force. They need the help of others in order to consummate their projects, even in order to survive, and this simple but profound fact throws many obstacles in their way, which cost them many virtues to overcome. The members of Nietzsche's elite would live in a frictionless world in which their projects could encounter no resistance and their innovations would cost them nothing. Perhaps it is true that living in such an environment would make it more likely that they would be more productive in their chosen fields (though one certainly could doubt even that), but it seems much less likely that it would encourage the formation of excellence of character.

Given their interest in creating virtue, the candidates for Nietzsche's elite have no reason to want the unique economic position he would offer them and they even have reason to avoid it. If they do not accept these privileges, or others that are relevantly like them, they will not comprise a caste which would exploit the rest of society. In that case, if they could still enter into a social agreement which would serve the end of protecting their pursuit of virtue, it would no longer face the impossible task of upholding an exploitative system. What sort of agreement could serve this end?

Once the requirement of erecting a hierarchy of castes has been thrown aside, it becomes relatively easy to determine roughly what such an agreement would have to be like. The quest for virtue, as Nietzsche understands it, would require an unlimited freedom to carry out vital experiments and the will to use that freedom. There are many things societies and states can do to violate this sort of liberty or discourage its use. A Nietzschean utopia could only arise within the framework of a set of shared principles which prohibit and prevent such things from being done.

The participants must forswear all laws and social norms that would impose a way of life upon those who do not choose it for themselves, with the exception of whatever laws and norms are needed to assure that those who wish to may work out their own experiments in living, free from interference and intimidation. Further, since the all-too-human tendency to loathe the experiments of others simply because they are different from one's own discourages experimentation, they may also have to agree – so far as this is humanly possible – to the principle that diversity in ways of life is as such a good thing, since it is a sign that one's society is indeed the sort in which the best ways of life are possible.[7] Finally, since their agreement would not attempt to divide their social world into castes, it would not require them to presume that they know in advance who would be pursuing virtue and who would not. Indeed, they have no reason to make such a presumption. As Hesiod suggests in "The Works and Days," the poem Nietzsche cites as corroborative testimony in "Homer's Contest," human excellence is something that can be realized in every sort of work and play (Chapter 4, pp. 60–1). There is no reason to think that philosophers and avant-garde artists can seek and achieve excellence while potters, farmers, singers, tycoons, scientists, and spotwelders cannot. The participants in Nietzsche's utopia might as well agree to grant freedom of experimentation, simply, to whomever wishes to use it. They might as well grant the same rights to everyone.

If Nietzschean experimenters were to enter into such an agreement, the fact that they have done so would seem to constitute a reason for observing the rights of all others. But what sort of weight could such a reason carry with them? Since the cultivation of virtue is their one ultimate goal, they cannot be relied upon to be moved by this reason unless they think that acting for this reason engenders virtue in themselves. But how, from a more or less Nietzschean point of view, would they be able to think this? To this important question I can only suggest the following highly speculative answer.

We have seen that Nietzsche sees the process of achieving virtue as essentially individual and psychological: one integrates the self, becoming master of the chaos that one is. But we have also seen some evidence that one should also see one's attainment of virtue as a social process as well, at least if one lives in Nietzsche's experimentalist utopia. In "Homer's Contest", Nietzsche and Hesiod describe a system in which each individual who pursues and achieves virtue does so partly because the system itself supports this pursuit. Because of the shared principles that constitute the system, the individuals in it strive to equal and outdo one another in excellence and, by virtue of this fact, the system itself spontaneously generates character (see Chapter 4, pp. 62–3). To the extent that Nietzschean experimenters live in a system like this one, they should not see what they do as a solitary enterprise, but as essentially social. Further, as I have already suggested (Chapter 7, pp. 135–6), Nietzsche's conception of the origin of virtue commits him to the view that a community of people who seek excellence of character would resemble a community of scientists in that the individual participant would learn from the experiments of others and from the critical reactions of others to one's own experiment. People who live in such a system should realize that they could not have achieved what they did – may even have fallen far short of it – had they lacked the good fortune to live in that particular system with those profoundly useful friends and enemies. To the extent that Nietzschean experimenters live in the sort of environment in which virtue can emerge, they should see interaction with others in the community as a crucial source of their own excellence. It could be argued that, for this reason, observing the principles which form the indispensable framework for peaceful interaction between people is not merely a matter of refraining from destroying opportunities for those who are less developed than oneself, it is necessary if one's own virtue is to survive and increase. If the connection between one's virtue and one's involvement with other people is sufficiently strong and deep, there might be good reason for revising Nietzsche's conception of virtue, so that it is not merely a certain integration of the self but, in addition, a certain integration of the self into the community around one. More precisely, the trait by which one observes the rights of others – that is, justice – would in that case be a virtue: it would be one of the second-order traits which are virtues because they help us to become more virtuous (see Chapter 7, pp. 142–4).

The suggestions I have made in this section are, to say it once more, highly speculative, a proposal for an experiment and not the experiment itself. If these suggestions could actually be followed out – if the needed explanations and arguments could be given – the result would obviously represent no small change in Nietzsche's ethical and political philosophy. The resulting system would probably be a very interesting one. For instance, it is clear from what I have said in the last few pages that it would include a version of what I earlier called "liberalism with teeth" (Chapter 4, p. 65). It would include a justification of a certain set of free institutions on the grounds that they spontaneously create character. As such, it might provide a powerful argument, free from some of the shortcomings of more traditional liberal theories, for an idea for which Nietzsche himself showed no sympathy: the idea that everyone should be free.[8]

NOTES

PREFACE AND ACKNOWLEDGEMENTS

1 Several years later, this paper appeared in print, in somewhat abbreviated form, as "Generosity," *American Philosophical Quarterly*, 12, 3 (July, 1975), pp. 235–44.

2 See David B. Allison, ed., *The New Nietzsche: Contemporary Styles of Interpretation* (New York: Dell, 1977); and Alexander Nehamas, *Nietzsche: Life as Literature* (Cambridge, Mass.: Harvard University Press, 1985).

3 Richard Schacht limits the scope of his impressive book on Nietzsche in this way on the grounds that Nietzsche's earlier works were inferior to what he wrote later on: "Prior to *The Gay Science* he was only on the way to becoming the important philosopher he came to be" (*Nietzsche* (Boston: Routledge & Kegan Paul, 1983), p. xiii). Whether one thinks this is true depends, of course, on the standards one is employing. The ideas in Nietzsche's early works are generally less clear and less brilliantly stated than those in the later ones, but I think that they are sometimes also closer to the truth, and truth is certainly one of the things that make an idea important and interesting.

4 George A. Morgan, *What Nietzsche Means* (Cambridge, Mass.: Harvard University Press, 1941). Morgan's book is a marvel of integration and condensed exposition. Despite its title, though, it does not tell us much about what Nietzsche means: it is really about what Nietzsche says. In an introduction this is probably a virtue.

5 Three important books on Nietzsche did not become available – to me, at least – until I had already been at work on this project for several years and had become rather set in my ways as far as my conception of Nietzsche is concerned. I doubt if any of them influenced this conception in a fundamental way, but this has much more to do with my inflexibility than with their merits. The books I am referring to are those by Nehamas and Schacht cited in notes 2 and 3 above, and Gilles Deleuze, trans. Hugh Tomlinson, *Nietzsche and Philosophy* (New York: Columbia University Press, 1983). Deleuze's book is less clear than the texts it comments upon, and that is a considerable vice in a commentary, but he has a sympathetic understanding of Nietzsche's view of life that I find almost uncanny.

1 INTRODUCTION: READING NIETZSCHE

1 This is from a discarded draft of *Ecce Homo*, translated by Walter Kaufmann in *The Basic Writings of Nietzsche* (New York: Modern Library, 1968), p. 796.

2 Nietzsche probably wants us to compare this injunction with Jesus' prediction that Peter will deny him three times before the cock crows twice, and Peter's guilt when the prediction turns out to be true (*Mark* 14: 30 and 72). The comparison underscores the novelty of Nietzsche's conception of the relationship between teacher and pupil. For Jesus, and for most of us, denial is incompatible with loyalty to one's teacher; for Nietzsche, it is implied by it.

3 Perhaps I should mention that, despite what I have said here, it is still true that if I attribute an argument to Nietzsche that I find convincing there is an obvious sense in which I may feel that I am compelled to believe its conclusion. Further, if I *correctly* attribute an argument to Nietzsche which I find compelling, then in a way he will have exerted his power over my mind after all. But this will have been the outcome of a process in which I was a full contributor and collaborator, vividly *aware* that that is what I am. This awareness diminishes my tendency to think of myself as the mere receptacle of his wisdom. My point here is really a psychological one. It would be interesting to attempt to go further than this and consider the essentially logical question of whether the arguments that can be correctly attributed to Nietzsche typically are coercive ones. Robert Nozick has denied that philosophical arguments really need to be of this sort in *Philosophical Explanations* (Cambridge, Mass.: Harvard University Press, 1981), pp. 1–24. I will not explore this issue explicitly here, but I think the evidence that will emerge in the chapters that follow will suggest that his arguments are typically not like this at all. The sort of argument that seems to me to be most typical of his way of thinking consists in offering some conclusion of his as the best available explanation of certain phenomena, which are assumed to exist. This is the nature of his critique of ascetic morality, as I hope to show in Chapter 7, pp. 115–20. Such arguments are, at least as Nietzsche uses them, radically incomplete. His readers only have a right to accept his conclusion on the basis of this sort of evidence if they make an honest and competent effort to try to devise a better explanation. Only then can they have good reason to think his explanation is the best. A *logically* essential part of the argument is not given in the text at all, and requires the creative participation of the reader.

4 For something like a variation on this theme, see Philippa Foot, "Nietzsche: The Revaluation of all Values," in Robert C. Solomon, ed., *Nietzsche: A Collection of Critical Essays* (New York: Doubleday, 1973), pp. 156–68. Professor Foot explains what she takes Nietzsche's ideas to be, and makes it plain enough that she disapproves of them, but she does not, as far as I can see, tell us why she believes they are wrong.

2 IMMORALISM

1 Later in the same section he ridicules the idea that "all should become 'good human beings,' herd animals, blue-eyed, benevolent, 'beautiful souls' – or as Mr. Herbert Spencer would have it, altruistic."

2 Walter Kaufmann, *Nietzsche: Philosopher, Psychologist, Antichrist* (New York: Meridian, 1956), p. 353. Writers who seem to deny that we should take seriously any of the *positive* things Nietzsche says about moralities include the following: Maudmarie Clark, "Nietzsche's Attack on Morality," unpublished Ph.D. dissertation, University of Wisconsin, 1977. Gilles Deleuze, *Nietzsche and Philosophy*, trans. Hugh Tomlinson, (New York: Columbia University Press, 1983), pp. 97–9. Alexander Nehamas, *Nietzsche: Life as Literature* (Cambridge, Mass.: Harvard University Press, 1985), Ch. 7.

3 In this respect, the extreme form of morality is the idea of sin, which is the concept of a *single act* that spoils the worth of the agent, until it is erased somehow (by repentance, for instance). Here the worth of the act is prior to the worth of the agent, with a vengeance.

4 Very briefly, the roots of this idea lie in the basic tenets of his doctrine of the will to power. As he eventually developed it, this doctrine included the notion that all of the "properties of a thing are effects [it has] on other 'things'" (WM 557), that in fact they are its effects on *all* other things (WM 556). In itself, apart from its foreign relations, it has no definite nature at all: it is a mere *"pathos"* (WM 635), an "I know not what" (WM 602). Thus if one fact were removed from the universe, everything else would perforce be changed. (See also WM 634.)

5 The distinctive character of the judgements Nietzsche has in mind here can perhaps be made more vivid by contrasting them with the ones that, in English, are often expressed by saying "should." If I say "You should have parked in lot 10" I need not be saying that there is anything bad about the place where you parked; I may only be saying that lot 10 would have been better. In such should-judgements, states of affairs are being ranked, but nothing negative is necessarily being said about any of them. Actually, this is the way in which "ought" is often used in non-Moral contexts, but that is not the sort of judgement Nietzsche is discussing here.

6 There may be another way in which this rejection of his is rooted in ideas that lie outside his ethics. He claims that apparently opposite properties in nature "actually express only variations in degree that from a certain perspective appear to be opposites" (WM 552c). He has in mind here something like the theory which reduces the apparent opposites, heat and cold, to differences in degree in a single property – namely, a certain sort of motion – with their oppositeness inhering merely in the way we perceive these differences. He may have thought that this reductionist theory of his implies that schemes of opposite values cannot legitimately be applied to the world. In that case, he would be assuming that opposite values cannot legitimately be applied to situations in which the facts differ in degree only. But this assumption would not be very plausible. There is no apparent illegitimacy in saying that if

Cleopatra's nose had been three times its actual size (a difference of degree) she would have not been beautiful but the opposite – ugly. As we shall see in later chapters, Nietzsche has other arguments for rejecting opposite values in ethics which are more interesting and more plausible than this one.

7 Note that I am not saying that it is a correct interpretation of Kant's notion.

8 Perhaps I should also point out that it is typical for attacks on Kant to take the form of asserting either that Kant was wrong about what "morality" is or that he did not give the best defense of it. This is not what Nietzsche is doing. In effect, he treats Kant as a good anthropologist, someone who has provided us with superb ethnographic documents revealing what Morality has come to be at certain points in European history. He attacks the object which Kant reveals.

9 On the other hand, it may be that these characteristics cannot be found in some of the oldest philosophical systems because their authors are too close to the pre-moral period of human development to think that way. It could easily be argued that this is true of Plato's ethics, for instance. The same sort of case could be made for Aristotle, though with greater difficulty, since he does have words for "that which one ought to do" (*to deon, ta deonta*) and he relies heavily on them. But Elizabeth Anscombe has claimed that these words do not have at all the same meaning that the roughly equivalent words have when they are used by contemporary moral philosophers: see her *Intention* (Ithaca: Cornell University Press, 1976), p. 35. Such interpretations of Plato and Aristotle could undermine the novelty of what Nietzsche is saying. Still, he could argue that consciously making war on Morality, as he does, is quite a different position from simply being innocent of it.

10 Note that, at this point, I am only defending Nietzsche on the question of his consistency. The fact that I have said that he accepts a morality of some sort should not make his way of thinking sound comfortingly similar to one's own. The same thing can be said, using the same sense of the word "morality," of crooked speculators, Oscar Wilde, and the senior Doolittle, as I pointed out on pages 9–10 of this Chapter.

3 POLITICS AND ANTI-POLITICS

1 Kurt Rudolf Fischer, "Nazism as a Nietzschean 'Experiment,'" *Nietzsche Studien*, 6 (1977), pp 116–22. W.H. Sokel, "Political Uses and Abuses of Nietzsche in Walter Kaufmann's Image of Nietzsche," *Nietzsche Studien*, 12 (1983), pp. 436–42. Tracy Strong, *Friedrich Nietzsche and the Politics of Transfiguration* (Berkeley: University of California Press, 1976), pp. 215–16. Ofelia Schutte argues that Nietzsche justifies "highly authoritarian systems of government" in her *Beyond Nihilism: Nietzsche Without Masks* (Chicago: University of Chicago Press, 1984), Ch. 7. See also Bruce Detwiler, *Nietzsche and the Politics of Aristocratic Radicalism* (Chicago: University of Chicago Press, 1990).

2 H.L. Mencken, *The Philosophy of Friedrich Nietzsche* (Port Washington, N.Y.: Kenikat, 1964), p. 192. The anarchism Nietzsche considers in the

passage I have just quoted is clearly an instance of the individualist anarchism Robert Nozick discusses in *Anarchy, State, and Utopia* (New York: Basic Books, 1974), pp. 10–119, and not the collectivist anarchism of the political left.

3 Walter Kaufmann, *Nietzsche: Philosopher, Psychologist, Antichrist* (New York: Meridian, 1956), pp. 135 and 357.

4 In the third *Untimely Meditation*, which is nominally about Schopenhauer, nearly the only Schopenhaurean idea he actually states is the following familiar axiom of classical liberalism: "Concerning the state he held, as is well known, that its sole purpose is to give protection – externally, internally, and against protectors as well – and were one to impute other purposes besides protection to it, one could easily endanger its true purpose" (U III 7). When this statement is read in the context of Nietzsche's hero-worshipping essay, it is impossible to escape the impression that he strongly sympathizes with the idea it states.

5 These lectures were published in the twentieth century as *Weltgeschichtliche Bertrachtungen* (Leipzig: Alfred Kroner, n.d.). I will quote from the English translation: James Hastings Nichols, ed., *Force and Freedom: An Interpretation of History* (New York: Meridian, 1955). The page numbers cited in my text refer to this edition. Kaufmann states that Nietzsche attended some of Burckhardt's lectures during his years at Basel (*Nietzsche*, p. 35). He adds (pp. 35–6) that the contact they had during these years did not result in Nietzsche's being influenced by Burckhardt – a claim that I hope to convince the reader is surely not true.

6 He continues, in the next paragraph, with a remark which probably cannot be understood without relating it to the passage I have just quoted from *Schopenhauer as Educator*: "'German' has become an argument, *Deutschland, Deutschland über alles* a principle." Elsewhere he tells us that this principle "was the end of German philosophy" (G VIII 1; see also FW 357). He has already indicated in the meditation on Schopenhauer that the proper pursuit of the aims of culture, and especially philosophy, requires that one place something above the state; to place one's country, on the contrary, above all else (which, of course, is what this principle means) would then represent the opposite of what the aims of culture require.

7 The idea that the great powers of the modern state result in part from a desire to make the world safe for business can also be found in Burckhardt. See *Force and Freedom*, p. 200.

8 I do not mean to suggest that he meant anything particularly horrible by this – after all, he thought that people that work in factories for wages are slaves (M 206).

9 It would probably lead, ultimately, into what might be called Nietzsche's ontology, since this psychological principle appears to be an application of two principles of the theory of power to be found in the *Nachlass* of the 1880s: that the quantity of power in the universe is fixed and that any constellation of power quanta can only expand by diminishing others.

10 Of course "perfection," here, cannot refer to a single state of affairs

toward which all human life is expected to aim. What perfects one person would only spoil another. I will discuss Nietzsche's conception of perfection in Chapter 7, pp. 122–30.

11 Sokel, "Political Uses," p. 440.
12 Strong, *Friedrich Nietzsche*, p. 205.
13 This is how Strong translates it: *Friedrich Nietzsche*, p. 212.
14 Kaufmann translates this statement: "the time is coming when politics will have a different meaning."

4 CHAOS AND ORDER

1 This attitude toward marriage has been extinct for so long that some readers may well need examples of it in order to have some idea of what Nietzsche is talking about. The clearest cases in our own tradition are probably the pioneers who came to the West a century and more ago to beget families and carve out a place in the world for those families to grow in for generations to come. Their attitude is powerfully described by Willa Cather, especially in the closing chapters of *My Ántonia*, when Jim Burden describes Ántonia after she has begun to raise a family of her own.

> She had only to stand in the orchard, to put her hand on a little crab tree and look up at the apples, to make you feel the goodness of planting and harvesting at last. . . . It was no wonder that her sons stood tall and straight. She was a rich mine of life, like the founders of early races.
>
> (Willa Cather, *My Ántonia*
> (Boston: Houghton Mifflin, 1918), p. 353)

2 In recent philosophy, the classic discussion of spontaneous order is, of course, Robert Nozick, *Anarchy, State, and Utopia* (New York: Basic Books, 1974), pp. 18–22. For a more detailed and systematic discussion, see Edna Ullmann-Margalit's "Invisible-hand Explanations," *Synthese*, 30 (1978), pp. 263–91.

3 It is interesting that, in a very late note, Nietzsche makes this same point as an objection to utilitarianism: "But does one know [an action's] consequences? For five steps ahead, perhaps. Who can say what an action will stimulate, excite, provoke? As a stimulus? Perhaps as a spark to touch off an explosion? – The Utilitarians are naive" (WM 291). I will suggest later on, in Chapter 7, pp. 134–41, that around the time he wrote this note (1888) he was beginning to change his mind about the issues I am discussing here.

4 The quotations in this paragraph are from "Nominalist and Realist," in Brooks Atkinson, ed., *Essays: Second Series. The Selected Writings of Ralph Waldo Emerson* (New York: Modern Library, 1940), pp. 436 and 443.

5 Very probably, this is just what Nietzsche would say. Consider, for instance, one of his comments on members of political parties: "Now this wishing-*not*-to-see what one does see . . . is almost the first condition for all who are *party* in any sense: of necessity, the party man becomes a liar" (A 55).

6 *Selected Writings*, p. 436.

7 In fact, when he eventually discusses the idea in print, he uses *Wettstreit*, with its more strongly economic associations, instead of *Wettkampf*. M 38.

8 The translations from Hesiod that follow are from Richmond Lattimore, trans., *Hesiod: The Works and Days, Theogony, The Shield of Herakles* (Ann Arbor: University of Michigan Press, 1959), pp. 19–20. In several places, I have had to alter Lattimore's translation to bring it closer to Nietzsche's German renderings. Nietzsche's quotations from Hesiod are omitted from the abridged version presented by Walter Kaufmann in *The Portable Nietzsche* (New York: Viking Press, 1954), pp. 32–9.

9 He says that the "original meaning" of the "curious institution" of ostracism was that of a means of preventing such results by preventing anyone from winning the contest and thus ending it. It did so by banishing conspicuously eminent individuals from the community. He cites, as evidence, the declaration made by the Ephesians when they banished Hermodorus: "Among us, no one shall be the best; but if someone is, then let him be elsewhere and among others" (H). Nietzsche's explanation of ostracism is interestingly different from the one given by Aristotle. Aristotle also says it originated from a need to eliminate men who are "superlatively excellent" from the community, and adds that this is needed because "there is no law that can govern these exceptional men." "They are themselves law and anyone who tried to legislate for them would be snubbed for their pains" (T.A. Sinclair, trans., *The Politics* (Baltimore: Penguin Books, 1962), p. 132.) Aristotle's point seems to be that ostracism was originally supposed to protect the public peace by ejecting from the community people we cannot hope to control. Nietzsche's view is that it was a way of protecting not peace so much as conflict of a certain sort. The good sort of conflict tended to prevent the bad sort from happening. It was an impersonal system which on its own exercised a measure of control over otherwise dangerous individuals.

10 This is a system one can perhaps only admire if one admires greatness more than happiness or satisfaction, since it encourages greatness and also produces frustration.

11 As we shall see in Chapter 5, he did eventually develop such a theory.

12 As in *Daybreak*, Nietzsche is beginning to build an account of the way in which contentiousness can result in actions that are good in themselves. Note that basing the value of a drive on the aim toward which it strives is not the same thing as basing it on the consequences it actually achieves. We will see in Chapter 5 that the account he gives here resembles, in a more obvious way than the account suggested in *Daybreak*, the ethical theory he eventually develops.

13 Incidentally, there may be a conceptual problem involved in the way he formulates this idea. It sounds like he is saying that the Greek ideal is to act selfishly, but only in order to promote the public good. But this would be incoherent, since anything that is done with the sole ultimate purpose of serving the public good is not selfish at all.

5 VIRTUE

1 Nietzsche sometimes expresses the same idea, more dramatically than I have here, as the "doctrine of the derivation of all good impulses from wicked ones." This way of putting it emphasizes the fact that – as Zarathustra's examples of the choleric, the voluptuous, the fanatic, and the vengeful suggest – the passions generally are wicked before they are reinterpreted as virtues. It also enables him to formulate a startling idea that he believes is an implication of his theory of virtue: that as human beings become more virtuous they also become more "wicked," that "the effects of hatred, envy, covetousness, and the lust to rule" must actually be "further enhanced if life is to be further enhanced" (JGB 23; see also JGB 201). Apparently, he is assuming that one possesses more of a given virtue as one acquires more of the passion out of which it was formed.

2 On the idea of intellectual virtue, see Aristotle, *Nicomachean Ethics*; VII, i.

3 *Nicomachean Ethics*, 1106b36–1107a1.

4 The two relevant passages are: "*The good four*. – *Honest* towards ourselves and whoever *else* is a friend to us; *courageous* toward the enemy; *generous* toward the defeated; *polite* – always; this is what the four cardinal virtues want us to be" (M 556). "To live with tremendous and proud composure; always beyond. . . . And to remain master of one's four virtues: of courage, insight, sympathy, and solitude" (JGB 284). Both lists are obviously very interesting for the purpose of understanding the values Nietzsche recommends, but the clear reference to the Platonic and Thomistic catalogue (both his lists contain four members and he calls one of them "cardinal virtues") might lead us to expect more than this. We might expect them to play the same crucial role in his theory of virtue that Thomas' list plays in his. Actually, they seem to be almost causally tossed off. Not only are the two lists different, but the second is not accompanied by any reference to the first and neither is referred to or repeated in any of his other works.

5 For an interesting discussion of conflicts between certain sorts of virtues, see Susan Wolf, "Moral Saints," *The Philosophical Review*, 79, 8 (August, 1982), pp. 420–7. I think several of the conflicts she discusses can be fully explained on the grounds that all of the virtues involved consist largely in the fact that the agent is seeking some goal, the goal of each virtue being different.

6 *Nicomachean Ethics*, VI, 13.

7 Kant's position is similar to Aristotle's but more extreme. He holds that the virtues are the result, not merely of a single intellectual ability, but of a single *principle* – the categorical imperative (*Groundwork of the Metaphysic of Morals* (New York: Harper Torchbooks, 1964), p. 54). Since he also holds that virtue is one's readiness to act on principle, he concludes that (in a way) there is really only one virtue. It seems to be a form of conscientiousness (*Groundwork*, pp. 53–4, 70, and 111).

8 The fact that Nietzsche believes in the enmity of the virtues has been pointed out by Philippa Foot in a passage quoted with approval by

Nehamas: *Nietzsche: Life as Literature* (Cambridge, Mass.: Harvard University Press, 1985), p. 210. Foot describes this belief of Nietzsche's as "the thought that so far from forming a unity in the sense that Aristotle and Aquinas believed they did, the virtues actually conflict with each other: which is to say that if someone has one of them he inevitably fails to have some other." So far, her description of this idea is fairly close to the one I have given, but she gives a very different account of the reason why Nietzsche believed it. She says it is based on his idea that one "can only become good in one way by being bad in another," which means, more specifically, that "hatred, envy, covetousness, and the lust to rule must be present in the 'general economy of life,' and must be 'further enhanced if life is to be enhanced'" ("Moral Realism and Moral Dilemma," *The Journal of Philosophy*, 80, 7 (July, 1983), pp. 396–7). Here she is referring to an idea that I have presented as Nietzsche's definition of virtue: hatred, envy, and the like are passions out of which virtue is constructed (see n. 1 in this chapter). By explaining the enmity of the virtues in this way, she seems to be making two assumptions: first, that Nietzsche thinks that passions like hatred and envy are bad; and, second, that he thinks that possession of any bad trait (including these affects) makes it impossible for one to possess some virtue. I have tried to show that the first assumption is not true: that, as Zarathustra says, the formation of virtues out of such passions is the transformation of "devils" into "angels." The idea that these supposedly bad traits exclude one from having some virtue or other seems to be close to the opposite of what he is saying: he is saying that these are passions *required by* virtue. So far, what he is saying does not imply that one cannot have all the virtues at once: what it does imply is that if one could have all the virtues, one would also have to have many traits that are thought to be bad (and which he denies are bad). Nietzsche has several reasons for thinking that one cannot have all the virtues, but I do not think this is one of them.

9 Interestingly, Aristotle thought that courage *resembles* anger (*thumos*). See *Nicomachean Ethics*, 1116b24–30. As is well known, Plato thought that courage is the virtue of the angry part of the soul (*Republic*, 442b and c). That is, Nietzsche is contrasting courage with something with which it is traditionally associated in a positive way.

10 This idea is no doubt closely related to his conviction that "the secret for harvesting from existence the greatest fruitfulness and the greatest enjoyment is – to *live dangerously*!" (FW 283).

11 Nietzschean courage sets no limit to the extent to which dangerous and difficult situations should be sought and faced. It is clearly absurd to think that such things would be sought out without point or limit, as Nietzsche would no doubt agree. His theory only allows one way in which one's virtue could set such a limit. This would occur in the event that one's courage were overcome by some other virtue; for instance, one's love of truth might become the sole criterion concerning which dangers or difficulties should be accepted and which should not. Courage would then serve some purpose other than its own. Aside from the fact that this would leave open the question of how far this further

purpose should be pursued, Nietzsche's theory would imply that it would represent the extinction of courage as a virtue. If the theory were modified so as to allow that one virtue can be the slave of another and yet remain a virtue, it would then lose the implication that the virtues are in a state of mutual enmity. Courage would not be in competition with a trait that determines which ends it ultimately seeks.

12 I do not mean to deny that there are valuable insights tangled up with the main point of *The Gay Science* 340. It can probably be adapted into a powerful argument in favor of the importance of positive virtues in general and, with the same force, against moralities that place excessive emphasis on negative virtues.

6 JUSTICE AND THE GIFT-GIVING VIRTUE

1 Nietzsche's views on mercy are most powerfully evident in his many criticisms on punishment. See especially GM II 10.

2 Note that here, and throughout the rest of this chapter, the sort of justice I am discussing is a moral virtue: it essentially includes doing something. The justice I was concerned with in Chapter 5, pp. 74–7, on the other hand, is an intellectual virtue.

3 Immanuel Kant, *Groundwork of the Metaphysic of Morals*, trans. H.J. Paton (New York: Harper, 1956), p. 80.

4 In recent years, many moral philosophers have come to recognize that there are actions which it would be good to do but not wrong to omit. Such actions are nowadays called "supererogatory." A rather large literature seems to be rapidly growing up around the subject of supererogation. Two early contributions to this literature are: J.O. Urmson, "Saints and Heroes," in A.I. Melden, ed., *Essays in Moral Philosophy* (Seattle: University of Washington Press, 1958), pp. 198–216; Joel Feinberg, "Supererogation and Rules," *Ethics*, 71 (1961), pp. 276–88. The general point of this literature is to acknowledge the existence of supererogatory acts and understand their implications. Nietzsche clearly places more importance on supererogation than these authors do though, based on what he makes Zarathustra say, it is not easy to tell how much heavier his emphasis is. It is obvious, at any rate, that he is saying that it not only exists but is deeply typical of what virtue is, and *not* merely in the platitudinous sense that the most virtuous actions involve doing "more than duty requires." The gift-giving virtue includes an indifference to duty as such, and to necessity in general.

5 For an extended discussion of this and related points, see Lester H. Hunt, "Generosity," *American Philosophical Quarterly*, 12, 3 (July, 1975), pp. 235–44.

6 That is, Zarathustra seems to be saying that all other-regarding virtuous actions are supererogatory (see n. 4 in this chapter).

7 Whatever status Nietzsche is prepared to grant human beings, he seems to be unwilling to give it anything like a Kantian explanation. Today, the fashionable way of putting the Kantian explanation is to say that all human beings are persons and all persons have this status (including

non-human persons, if there are any). Richard Schacht has pointed out (citing WM 319 and WM 886) that Nietzsche explicitly denies that most human beings are persons at all. See his *Nietzsche* (Boston: Routledge & Kegan Paul, 1983), pp. 386–8. Schacht adds that Nietzsche holds the few who are persons to be valuable, not because they are persons, but for another reason.

8 These books were written in 1884–6.

9 Incidentally, the similarity between this system and the one in Plato's *Republic* can hardly escape notice.

10 Since in this system each person evidently prefers his or her own rights to those of the other castes, it is somewhat misleading of Nietzsche to call these rights "unequal." What he finds offensive about "the doctrine of 'equal rights for all'" is the fact that it means that every person "has equal rank with everyone else" (A 43). What is unequal, in his doctrine, is the *rank* that the rights define, not the value that the rights have *to the individual* who possesses them.

7 WHICH TRAITS ARE VIRTUES?

1 This passage contrasts in an interesting way with his earliest statement of the same idea. There he says that eventually theories drawn from sciences like physiology, medicine, and sociology will be the "foundation-stones of new ideals." But during the moral *"inter-regnum"* between the old morality and the new, "the best we can do . . . is to be as far as possible our own *reges* and found little *experimental states*. We are experiments: let us also want to be them!" (M 453). Here, making experiments of our lives is seen as a second-best makeshift, inferior to the method of – apparently – constructing theories out of finished results drawn from the sciences. In the later statement it is apparently not seen as second-best at all. Evidently, the ideal of moral experiment became more important to him after his first thoughts about it.

2 Gilbert Harman, *The Nature of Morality* (New York: Oxford University Press, 1977), pp. 3–9. The examples I use in this paragraph are drawn, somewhat modified, from Harman.

3 Harman, *The Nature of Morality*, p. 6.

4 A word Nietzsche often uses in these contexts, *Versuch*, means both "experiment" and "attempt." See JGB 210.

5 In view of the fact that, at FW 110, he says that the search for truth is "the experiment," one wonders whether this is the only experiment he has in mind. In a much later note (WM 1041), the idea of experimentation is once more closely associated with the ability to endure truth. But in at least one place in his published works (JGB 210) he calls for "experiments," in the plural. He probably only meant that this one is the most important one. Since one would only turn one's life into an experiment if one is willing to risk something for the truth, he may have thought of this experiment as a sort of "universal" experiment, of which all others are instances. Whatever else experimenters are doing, they are *always* testing their ability to assimilate the truth.

6 This is particularly obvious in the case of his aesthetic theory. See, for instance, G IX 24, where he opposes *l'art pour l'art* with his own conception of art as "the great stimulus to life."

7 In the 1886 preface to *The Birth of Tragedy* he suggests that it can be found already in his first book. He says that "the task which this audacious book dared to tackle for the first time" was "*to look at science in the perspective of the artist, but at art in that of life*" (GT P 2; emphasis in the original).

8 It is possible, however, that Nietzsche does make this assumption. Note that Nietzsche's theory of virtue makes heavy use of the relationship between means and ends and does not show any awareness of any other way in which values can be ranked. The assumption may even be implicit in the doctrine of the will to power. The most obvious way to apply the doctrine to the problem of how values are ordered would be to see them as objects of two drives, one of which has dominated the other. Considering what I have already said in Chapter 5, pp. 72–4, this would seem to mean that the one has come to impose on the other the character of a function, directing it toward its own end. This would seem to mean that the object of the weaker drive is then sought only as a means to the object of the stronger one.

9 He takes poverty, humility, and chastity to be the paradigm ascetic ideals (GM III 8).

10 He contrasts this sort of asceticism with certain apparently self-sacrificial practices one observes in intellectuals, athletes, and parents, in which one natural need is frustrated in order to achieve the ends of another one (GM III 8).

11 Remember that "the" ethical experiment is the one that determines how much truth one can assimilate. I will return to this point later.

12 I probably should point out that, in an ethic as strongly character-based as Nietzsche's, *ad hominem* attacks are not necessarily fallacious, at least in the ethical realm. People sometimes speak of "talking about the issues" instead of "discussing personalities." For Nietzsche, the ethical issues *are* personalities. More exactly, to assess an ethical judgment is, to a large extent, to assess the value of the way of life of which it is a part. His many personal remarks about particular people cannot be separated from his philosophy. They are part of the argument.

13 The emphasis is in the original.

14 As I have said, Nietzsche needs to say the exercise of the will to power has a fairly strong tendency to support one's survival. He seems to be saying it does at JGB 13 and WM 656. Unfortunately, though, he is not very consistent about this. For instance, he says: "the higher type represents an incomparably greater complexity – a greater sum of co-ordinated elements: so its disintegration is also incomparably more likely. The 'genius' is the sublimest machine there is – consequently the most fragile" (WM 684; see also G IX 44). Since the highest types have that status because of the extent to which they have achieved power, this would mean that the will to power undercuts one's prospects for survival, and that the ability to survive is evidence of relative weakness. This is very close to saying that the strong seek power instead of

survival, and the weak seek survival instead of power. There are times when he seems to be saying precisely that (e.g. G IX 14 and WM 684 *passim*). But this would mean that living beings seek two fundamentally different ends, which would demolish his argument for vitalism. Furthermore, his suggestion that the highest types tend to disintegrate directly conflicts with his conception of perfection as the *successful* integration of coordinated elements. Perhaps what we have here is Nietzsche in two moods: a classicizing one which stresses the fact that power brings about order, and a romanticizing one which emphasizes (or overemphasizes) the fact that it welcomes danger (see the next paragraph of this chapter). (I suspect that his idea that the genius is fragile is an overgeneralization from his own case. Actually, if we read the biographies of geniuses we encounter rather few fragile creatures with a tendency to spontaneous disintegration. For every van Gogh or Schubert there seems to be a dozen Wagners, Beethovens, and Goethes – people who if anything are all too good at the arts of survival.)

15 We will also see that, if he did hold such a position, he would have to abandon an important part of his ethical theory.

16 On this point my definition of ethical relativism is different from the most familiar ones. They generally define it in such a way that it maintains that things are only right or wrong, good or bad, if someone believes they are. See as an example Richard Brandt, "Ethical Relativism," in Paul Edwards, ed., *The Encyclopedia of Philosophy* (New York: Macmillan, 1967), vol. III, p. 76. For another definition that is inconsistent with mine, though in a somewhat different way, see Michael Slote, "Relative Virtues," in his *Goods and Virtues* (New York: Oxford University Press, 1983), p. 59. I would say that someone is clearly espousing ethical relativism if they say, for instance, that there is no such thing as wrongness *simpliciter*, but that things are always wrong for a certain person or in a certain community (wrong-for-me, wrong-for-you, wrong-in-Madison, wrong-in-Bali). (See, for example, Harman, *The Nature of Morality*, p. 45.) One can say that this is so without also claiming that it is so merely because different people believe different things. One can claim that these profound differences exist because of other, "objective," differences between people exist, differences which may be psychological, social, genetic, economic, or climatic. There should be a name for claims such as these, and "relativism" seems to be a perfectly natural choice, since they all amount to saying that the applicability of some standards is, so to speak, "relative to" one thing or another.

17 Perhaps I should point out that Nietzsche, in a way, is justifying moral codes on the basis of their consequences. This may seem to be inconsistent with Nietzsche's expressions of contempt for consequentialist ethics; for instance: "Slave morality is essentially a morality of utility" (JGB 260). He does seem to reject certain sorts of consequentialism. I think he rejects it as an account of what makes actions or individuals admirable. Individuals and their acts are admirable because of what precedes their acts, not because of what follows from them. Actions are admirable because of the psychological causes from which they spring.

He is not a consequentialist about the question of rank; at most, he is a consequentialist about the ought-question. Actually, the consequence by which the highest moralities are justified is the fact that, when planted in the right sort of psyche, they yield the sort of character that is good in itself. In this context, it is rather misleading to say that Nietzsche is a consequentialist, since usually the point of consequentialism is to justify ethical practices in general by showing that they lead to some non-ethical good (such as pleasure). Here the good that does the justifying is itself ethical.

18 It would be useful to know when this note was written, but unfortunately the date given by the editors of *The Will to Power* is simply 1883–8.

19 H.L. Mencken stated the matter – and probably overstated it – with startling bluntness: "The fact is that Nietzsche had no interest whatever in the delusions of the plain people – that is, intrinsically. It seemed to him of small moment *what* they believed, so long as it was safely imbecile" (Friedrich Nietzsche, *The Antichrist*, trans. and ed. by H.L. Mencken (New York: Knopf, 1923), p. 18).

8 IMMORALISM AGAIN

1 I am putting it this way because the idea involved is perfectly analogous with what Rawls calls "pure procedural justice." "Pure procedural justice obtains when there is no independent criterion for the right result: instead there is a correct or fair procedure such that the outcome is likewise correct or fair, whatever it is, provided that the procedure has been properly followed" (*A Theory of Justice* (Cambridge, Mass.: Harvard University Press, 1971), p. 86).

2 Incidentally, this means that Alexander Nehamas is expressing a half-truth – simultaneously illuminating and misleading – when he says that "Nietzsche cannot . . . have a general view of conduct that can apply to everyone and also be specific and interesting" (*Nietzsche: Life as Literature* (Cambridge, Mass.: Harvard University Press, 1985), p. 229). Nietzsche's general view of conduct, in the sense that Nehamas means this phrase, is his conception of virtue. If it is considered simply as a description of what virtue is, it is utterly uninformative about how anyone should live. But it is equivalent to a description of a process, together with the claim that anything which arises when the process is successfully carried out by a specific individual is virtuous. As such, Nietzsche thinks that it can tell us a good deal that is specific and interesting. In this way, his pure procedural virtue is analogous to the pure procedural justice which – on one interpretation, anyway – one can find in Rousseau's *The Social Contract*. Rousseau's theory of the General Will is, as it sits on the pages of Rousseau's book, uninformative about what any state should do. But this theory is an account of the process by which polities construct their principles of justice and it also includes Rousseau's assurance that whatever result it obtains is *made just* by having arisen in that way. Both Nietzsche and Rousseau think that what is best to do varies from one specific circumstance to

another, and both are very careful to avoid laying down general formulae that predict, independently of circumstances, what it will be best to do. The advantage that procedural theories have in ethics and politics is that they enable one to formulate a standard that is general and at the same time *very* specific.

3 See G V 2 and Chapter 7, pp. 125–8, above.

4 Perhaps I should point out that the ought-judgements which, as I claimed in the previous section of this chapter, Nietzsche is committed to allowing need not violate his stricture against opposite values. They need not imply that there is something bad about not obeying them. As I pointed out in Chapter 2, n. 5, in non-Moral contexts, ought-judgements often fail to have this implication. If I say that you ought to dust before you vacuum, I may not be saying that vacuuming before you dust is *bad*. I may only mean that it fails to be the best you could do. Such oughts do not bring about the "necessitation" of the will that I discussed in Chapter 6, p. 94. One could say that this means they are not Moral oughts.

5 My discussion of Nietzsche's perspectivism will necessarily be rather brief. This is a bit awkward, given that many others have written on it at considerable length. My apparent curtness on this subject is not as great as it might seem, however, because, as the reader may soon realize, I have already discussed all the elements of perspectivism elsewhere in this book, though I have so far only treated them as they apply to Nietzsche's ethics. For more elaborate discussions, see the following works: Arthur C. Danto, *Nietzsche as Philosopher* (New York: Macmillan, 1965), Ch. 3; Ruediger H. Grimm, *Nietzsche's Theory of Knowledge* (New York: Walter de Gruyter, 1977), Ch. 4, sections 1 and 2; Alexander Nehamas, *Nietzsche*, Ch. 2. My account of Nietzsche's perspectivism will differ in some substantial ways from all of these.

6 Because Nietzsche does believe that, in a certain way, there is an ultimate value, it sometimes takes a special effort to distinguish his way of speaking from traditional talk of a *summum bonum*. Nietzsche himself, in a late note, describes the traditional point of view in a way that makes it sound startlingly similar to his own:

> What, then, is regressive in the philosopher? – That he teaches that *his* qualities are the necessary and sole qualities for the attainment of the "highest good" (e.g., dialectic, as with Plato). That he orders men of all kinds *gradatim* up to *his* type as the highest. That he despises what is generally esteemed – that he opens up a gulf between priestly values and worldly values. That he *knows* what is true, what God is, what the goal is, what the way is – The typical philosopher is here an absolute dogmatist. (WM 446)

Nehamas (*Nietzsche*, p. 68) takes this note as showing that Nietzsche refuses to "grade people and views along a single scale." I think this clearly is what he does. It is even more obvious that, to use the words Nietzsche uses in this note, he "despises what is generally esteemed." The difference between his despising and that of the typical philosopher is that he does not take his attitude as a prescription addressed to all human beings such that, if they disobey it, they are simply wrong. Similarly, the principle by which he grades people is not such that, if others do not use it in their lives, their lives are simply no good. He is against the "priestly" way in which philosophers have typically done these things (see WM 447).

9 CONCLUSION: VIRTUE AND SOCIETY

1 All the quotations that follow are from *The Civilization of the Renaissance in Italy*, trans. S.C.C. Middlemore (New York: The Modern Library, 1954), pp. 5–6.

2 Nietzsche's remarks about Bismarck provide an interesting contrast here. They are all unfavorable in one degree or another, and they all seem to be about Bismarck's policies. Nietzsche does not seem to care what sort of person Bismarck is. One wonders why he does not treat Bismarck's bold and cunning statism as evidence that he, too, was a "genius," just as Frederick was (though perhaps not in the same degree). Surely, such a case could be made. Perhaps, if he had only talked about Frederick's policies and Bismarck's character, the facts would have forced him to reverse the tone of his remarks about these two politicians, speaking only ill of Frederick and only good of Bismarck. There seems to be a double standard at work here. If there is, it may be due to the fact that Nietzsche had to *live* with the policies of the Iron Chancellor, while Frederick had been safely dead for centuries.

3 I am referring, of course, to his *Nietzsche: Philosopher, Psychologist, Antichrist* (New York: Meridian, 1956).

4 I take this term from Gregory W. Trianosky, "What is Virtue Ethics All About? Recent Work on the Virtues," forthcoming in *American Philosophical Quarterly* (1990). I have altered his definition of it somewhat.

5 I can think of one alternative scenario that could be imagined to lead to the result that Nietzsche wants. The relevant traditions might evolve in a context in which the needed factors are present: for instance, the aristocrats are simply a caste of warriors. Over time, one might imagine, the warriors are replaced somehow by Nietzschean philosophers. Meanwhile, the structure of differential rights that holds the highest caste in place survives. One should wonder, though, why the traditional privileges would continue to exist when the context that gives the lower orders a reason for accepting them has disintegrated. While it is conceivable (just barely) that it could survive, the aristocracy would be foolish to bet its way of life on the proposition that it would in fact do so.

6 There is one possible exception to the claim I have just made. In Chapter 7, p. 139, I have quoted some remarks from A 57 that can be taken as a prediction that the people who do the sort of work that is done in the lowest and largest caste would not be interested in the quest for virtue. If this is what he means, he gives no reason to think this prediction is true.

7 I am not entirely certain of this point because, as I indicated earlier, a certain tension between innovators and the rest of society seems to be one of the reasons why innovation is virtuous. It is nonetheless true,

though, that this part of the agreement would be perfectly compatible with a critical attitude toward the innovations of others – especially if these people realize that new ideas and practices very often are mistakes and should be received with skepticism.

8 See Chapter 4, p. 54. The social agreement I have suggested as a basis for a Nietzschean utopia could be worked out in a way that strikingly resembles the "framework for utopia" with which Robert Nozick concludes his *Anarchy, State, and Utopia* (New York: Basic Books, 1974), Ch. 10. There would be one notable difference, however: Nozick, in the manner that is typical of traditional liberalism conceives of utopia as a place where everyone is as happy as they can be; the corresponding neo-Nietzschean utopia would be one in which everyone is as *good* as they can be.

INDEX